THE GREATEST MOUNTAIN MEN
STORIES EVER TOLD

Also edited by Lamar Underwood
Into the Backing: Tales of Fly-fishing Action
Bowhunting Tactics of the Pros: Strategies for Deer and Big Game
Whitetail Hunting Tactics of the Pros: Expert Advice to Help You be a Successful Hunter
Greatest Fishing Stories Ever Told: Twenty-Eight Unforgettable Fishing Tales
Tales of the Mountain Men: Seventeen Stories of Survival, Exploration, and Outdoor Craft
Greatest Hunting Stories Ever Told: Twenty-Nine Unforgettable Tales
Greatest Flying Stories Ever Told: Nineteen Amazing Tales from the Sky
Greatest Adventure Stories Ever Told: Gripping Tales of Wild Places
Greatest Survival Stories Ever Told: When Things Go Wrong Outdoors
Maneaters: True Tales of Humans as Prey
Theodore Roosevelt on Hunting
Survive: Tales of Man versus Weather, Wilderness, and Wild Animals
Great American Survival Stories: Lyons Press Classics
War Stories: 37 Epic Tales of Courage, Duty, and Valor

Also authored by Lamar Underwood
The Quotable Soldier
The Quotable Warrior
The Quotable Writer
On Dangerous Ground: A Novel

THE GREATEST MOUNTAIN MEN STORIES EVER TOLD

EDITED BY LAMAR UNDERWOOD

Guilford, Connecticut

An imprint of The Rowman & Littlefield Publishing Group, Inc.,
4501 Forbes Blvd., Lanham MD 20706

Distributed by NATIONAL BOOK NETWORK

British Library Cataloguing in Publication Information Available

Library of Congress Cataloging-in-Publication Data

ISBN 978-1-4930-3287-7 (paperback)
ISBN 978-1-4930-3288-4 (e-book)

♾™ The paper used in this publication meets the minimum requirements of American National
Standard for Information Sciences—Permanence of Paper for Printed Library Materials, ANSI/
NISO Z39.48-1992.

Contents

CONTENTS

Behind the Ranges

By Lamar Underwood

LET'S SAY IT'S AN EARLY-FALL DAY WITH THE SUN WARM ON YOUR shoulders and the light breeze tangy with autumn scents coming on strong. You're standing on the crest of a rocky ridge dotted with stunted jack-pines and overlooking a valley where creek courses are marked by lines of timber curving into view. They disappear into a vastness splashed with the deep yellows of aspen groves. The horizon is a jagged line of soaring peaks, snow-capped summits bright in the sun, with deeply-shadowed valleys between the ridges. The sight holds you hard, and you linger for a while, clutching the reins of your horse, soaking in the vision that has been like a dream during weeks of overland travel.

The sound of packs scraping brush interrupts your reverie, and you turn to see your pack mule rooting for grass among the jack pines and rocks on the scrubby hillside. Down the long hill you have just climbed, you see the open prairie stretching toward humped blue ridges of lesser mountains. You think of the countless campfires you have sat beside down there, of the vastness of buffalo herds, and the easy way elk, deer, antelope, turkey and waterfowl have fallen to your Hawken. You have eaten well during your journey, for this is country unspoiled by other hunters and travelers.

You turn back to gaze once again on the valley and mountain country before you. Now you have arrived. The best country on earth lies before you. Your footprints here may be the first a white man has ever made. Among those tiny creeks and water courses you will find beaver, filling your traps with pelts that come Spring you can sell at Rendezvous and resupply your whole outfit for another year in the wild—another year of freedom to live the outdoor life a man treasures and lives to the hilt.

Suddenly a voice stirs your imagination like a clap of thunder. "Wagh, pilgrim! You're looking to go under. Get rubbed out. That's Blackfeet country down there."

"Plenty of plews, though," your voice answers.

"Furs won't do a dead man any good," the voice replies.

This little scenario played out in the Rocky Mountain is one that you actually could have lived—had you been born 250 years ago, coming into manhood in the early 1800's. Your dreams of roaming unspoiled wilderness, trapping beaver and other valuable pelts, shooting and eating the game you needed, wandering free as a bird, taking orders from no man, would have been a siren call leading to an early end to your ventures. Going it alone would almost certainly lead to "going under."

"All right, I'll take a companion then."

"Wagh," the voice answers back. "You'd better take 30 or 40, like we did back in the day."

The vision of a strong and independent mountain man like Jerimiah Johnson—a "free trapper" as they were called—is hard to forget. We envy that life: lifting beaver traps in quiet waters below peaks of staggering beauty; feeling the warmth of a campfire, the aroma of meat roasting, the night sounds of coyotes and owls beginning to stir. No alarm clocks, no commitments except our self-chosen chores, no orders from bosses looking over our shoulders.

It's a pity, really, that such romantic visions do not match the reality most mountain men experienced. Instead of the solitary life in the wilderness as depicted in the movie *Jerimiah Johnson*, and the book *Mountain Man* by Vardis Fisher, the mountain man working alone faced dangers in every moment that would leave him facing death—alone, his skeleton to become lost and unseen in the vastness. Like it or not (it's hard to put aside our romantic notions) most mountain men who "valued their hair" were forced to travel, camp and trap in large groups, called "brigades" like military units. For quick and correct images of these groups, to stir your imagination, see the movie *Across the Wide Missouri*, a superb MGM film starring Clark Gable and adapted from Bernard De Voto's non-fiction masterpiece of the same title.

One of our major contributors in this collection, A. C. Laut, in his book *The Story of the Trapper*, first published in 1902, paints a vivid picture of the real world of the mountain men in an excerpt I have chosen here to complete the reader's introduction to this book. The trappers' world and situations described here by Mr. Laut are like a movie-trailer, previews of what you can expect in the pages ahead.

It was two thousand miles by trappers' trail from the reach of law. It was too remote from the fur posts for trappers to go down annually for supplies. Supplies were sent up by the fur companies to a mountain rendezvous, to Pierre's Hole under the Tetons, or Jackson's Hole farther east, or Ogden's Hole at Salt Lake, sheltered valleys with plenty of water for men and horses when hunters and traders and Indians met at the annual camp.

Elsewhere the hunter had only to follow the windings of a river to be carried to his hunting-ground. Here, streams were too turbulent for canoes; and boats were abandoned for horses; and mountain cañons with sides sheer as a wall drove the trapper back from the river-bed to interminable forests, where windfall and underbrush and rockslide obstructed every foot of progress. The valley might be shut in by a blind wall which cooped the hunter up where was neither game nor food. Out of this valley, then, he must find a way for himself and his horses, noting every peak so that he might know this region again, noting especially the peaks with the black rock walls; for where the rock is black snow has not clung, and the mountain face will not change; and where snow cannot stick, a man cannot climb; and the peak is a good one for the trapper to shun.

One, two, three seasons have often slipped away before the mountaineers found good hunting-ground. Ten years is a short enough time to learn the lie of the land in even a small section of mountains. It was twenty years from the time Lewis and Clark first crossed the mountains before the traders of St. Louis could be sure that the trappers sent into the Rockies would find their way out. Seventy lives were lost in the first two years of mountain trapping, some at the hands of the hostile Blackfeet guarding the entrance to the mountains at the head waters of the Missouri, some at the hands of the Snakes on the Upper Columbia, others between the Platte and Salt Lake. Time and money and life it cost to learn the hunting-grounds of the Rockies; and the mountaineers would not see knowledge won at such a cost wrested away by a spying rival.

Then, too, the mountains had bred a new type of trapper, a new style of trapping.

Only the most daring hunters would sign contracts for the "Up-Country," or Pays d'en Haut as the French called it. The French trappers, for the most part, kept to the river valleys and plains; and if one went to the mountains for a term of years, when he came out he was no longer the smug, indolent, laughing, chattering voyageur. The great silences of a life hard as the iron age had worked a change. To begin with, the man had become a horseman, a climber, a scout, a fighter of Indians and elements, lank and thin and lithe, silent and dogged and relentless.

In other regions hunters could go out safely in pairs or even alone, carrying supplies enough for the season in a canoe, and drifting down-stream with a canoe-load of pelts to the fur post. But the mountains were so distant and inaccessible, great quantities of supplies had to be taken. That meant long cavalcades of pack-horses, which Blackfeet were ever on the alert to stampede. Armed guards had to accompany the pack-train. Out of a party of a hundred trappers sent to the mountains by the Rock Mountain Company, thirty were always crack rifle-shots for the protection of the company's property. One such party, properly officered and kept from crossing the animal's tracks, might not drive game from a valley. Two such bands of rival traders keen to pilfer each other's traps would result in ruin to both.

That is the way the clash came in the early thirties of the last century.

All winter bands of Rocky Mountain trappers under Fitzpatrick and Bridger and Sublette had been sweeping, two hundred strong, like foraging bandits, from the head waters of the Missouri, where was one mountain pass to the head waters of the Platte, where was a second pass much used by the mountaineers. Summer came with the heat that wakens all the mountain silences to a roar of rampant life. Summer came with the fresh-loosened rocks clattering down the mountain slopes in a landslide,

and the avalanches booming over the precipices in a Niagara of snow, and
the swollen torrents shouting to each other in a thousand voices till
the valleys vibrated to that grandest of all music—the voice of many
waters. Summer came with the heat that drives the game up to the cool
heights of the wind-swept peaks; and the hunters of the game began
retracing their way from valley to valley, gathering the furs cached
during the winter hunt.

Then the cavalcade set out for the rendezvous: grizzled men in
tattered buckskins, with long hair and unkempt beards and bronzed skin,
men who rode as if they were part of the saddle, easy and careless but
always with eyes alert and one hand near the thing in their holsters;
long lines of pack-horses laden with furs climbing the mountains in a
zigzag trail like a spiral stair, crawling along the face of cliffs
barely wide enough to give a horse footing, skirting the sky-line
between lofty peaks in order to avoid the detour round the broadened
bases, frequently swimming raging torrents whose force carried them half
a mile off their trail; always following the long slopes, for the long
slopes were most easily climbed; seldom following a water-course, for
mountain torrents take short cuts over precipices; packers scattering to
right and left at the fording-places, to be rounded back by the
collie-dog and the shouting drivers, and the old bell-mare darting after
the bolters with her ears laid flat.

Not a sign by the way escaped the mountaineer's eye. Here the tumbling
torrent is clear and sparkling and cold as champagne. He knows that
stream comes from snow. A glacial stream would be milky blue or milky
green from glacial silts; and while game seeks the cool heights in
summer, the animals prefer the snow-line and avoid the chill of the iced
masses in a glacier. There will be game coming down from the source of
that stream when he passes back this way in the fall. Ah! What is that
little indurated line running up the side of the cliff—just a
displacement of the rock chips here, a hardening of the earth that
winds in and out among the devil's-club and painter's-brush and
mountain laurel and rock crop and heather?

"Something has been going up and down here to a drinking-place," says
the mountaineer. . .

The trapper's experienced eye is reading "sign," a piece of the puzzle that becomes great drama out in the wilds. He knows the ending of the drama can be tragic. But he will go on, drawn by the elusive lure so eloquently described by Rudyard Kipling in his poem, "The Explorer":

> *"Something hidden. Go and find it.*
> *Go and look behind the Ranges—*
> *Something lost behind the Ranges.*
> *Lost and waiting for you. Go!"*

—LAMAR UNDERWOOD

Editor's Note:
Preserving Authenticity

In the interest of story-telling authenticity, the stories presented in this book have not been corrected for spelling, punctuation, or with fact-checking. They are presented as originally published, excerpted from the works mentioned in the introductions and in the "Sources" list at the end of the book. The prose is sometimes awkward, the spelling almost child-like in the manner of those days. Often the sentences ramble in a romantic, overly-detailed descriptions. Then again, many of these works are remarkably clear and lucid. These explorers knew how to write, and they had much to write about.

—Lamar Underwood

CHAPTER 1

Bold Men, Shining Mountains

By Jim Merritt

To anchor the stories in this book with a sense of time and place—a "fix," if you will, in our readers' minds—we begin with a sweeping look at how mountain men became an American icon. This is from Jim Merritt's book The Last Buffalo Hunt and Other Stories, *published in 2012. The story was originally titled "The Right Stuff: Mountain Men & Voyageurs" and is reprinted here by permission of the author.*

ON A PARCHED AFTERNOON IN MAY 1834, FOUR MEN STOOD ON THE Nebraska prairie around the carcass of a buffalo they'd just shot. Members of a fur-trade brigade bound for the Rocky Mountains, they had left the main group early that morning to hunt and had been without water for hours. The hot wind and dust and the work of butchering the buffalo under the blazing sun—propping it up, stripping back the hide, and flensing the choice meat from its hump—added to their thirst.

One of the men, a greenhorn named Townsend, suggested a dash to the Platte River for water. But the Platte was many miles away. Richardson, a seasoned mountain man and the brigade's chief hunter, knew of another source of liquid closer at hand. As Townsend related the incident later, after they rolled the buffalo over on its side, the hunter sliced into its belly, exposing the "still crawling and twisting entrails." While the greenhorn gaped in astonishment "and no little loathing," Richardson plunged his knife "into the distended paunch, from which gushed the green and gelatinous juices."

With a tin pan he strained off the water from the animal's innards, then tossed back his head and drank to the dregs this prairie elixir, "smacking his lips, and drawing a long breath after it, with the satisfaction of a man taking his wine after dinner."

Doubtless the mountain man was grandstanding some for the greenhorn's benefit. But water is where you find it, and finding it in a buffalo's guts showed the kind of resourcefulness that meant the difference between life and death on the plains.

For the mountain men of the American fur trade and for their spiritual kin, the voyageurs who plied the water routes of Canada in the employ of French and British fur companies, survival depended on resourcefulness, physical stamina, and wilderness skills acquired in the relentless pursuit of beaver.

From the Algonquian tribes along the St. Lawrence, the voyageurs adopted the birch-bark canoe as their means of penetrating into the heart of the vast continent. From the 1680s until well into the 1800s, flotillas of canoes from eastern Canada and Hudson Bay supplied a network of trading posts that eventually stretched from the Great Lakes to the Columbia and Yukon Rivers.

A fur company typically signed up a voyageur for two or three years of backbreaking work. Portages, in which canoes and goods were carried overland to bypass falls and rapids, were divided into brief rest stops a third of a mile apart. A voyageur carried his load in 90-pound packs secured to his back by a leather harness that included a forehead strap to help distribute the weight. A standard load was two packs (180 pounds), but sturdier voyageurs doubled that; bragging rights began in earnest at five packs (450 pounds), and a few Paul Bunyan types reputedly carried eight—720 pounds. Bruised feet and sprained ankles went with the job, and more serious injuries like slipped disks and hernias could lead to paralysis or death.

Winter tested the mettle of voyageurs. Those who lived through the cold months in the wilderness boasted of their status as *hivernants* ("winterers") and looked down on the *mangeurs du lard* ("pork-eaters") who returned to the settlements in the fall. On hunting excursions or when ferrying supplies and furs between posts, voyageurs traveled by dogsled and on snowshoes. Camping at night, they made a hearth of green logs, cut long—up to twenty feet—and laid on the snow. They cut balsam branches for their beds and slept huddled together under skins and blankets, feet to the fire. Burning through the night, a fire could melt a ten-foot-deep pit in the snow, and voyageurs took care not to roll into it.

Staggering under loads that would flatten a mule, paddling at forty strokes a minute for twelve to fifteen hours a day, or slogging on snowshoes through the frozen landscape, a voyageur burned more calories than a marathon runner. He lived off the land to the extent possible: depending on where he found himself, his daily ration might be measured in geese, rabbits, moose or buffalo meat, whitefish, or salmon. If game was scarce or the press of a journey left no time for hunting and fishing, he turned to staples such as dried corn and peas. If staples ran out and no fish or game could be had, the food of last resort was a variety of lichen known as *tripe de roches* ("rock tripe," so-called because it resembled chopped intestines). Boiled, it turned into a vile, viscid, foul-smelling gruel, "black and clammie & easily to be swallowed," as the trader-explorer Pierre Radisson described it. The Indians dubbed this starvation food *windigo wakon*, after a woods spirit that out of hunger devoured its own lips.

West of Lake Winnipeg, where the forests gave way to buffalo plains, the voyageur's chief staple was pemmican. Packed with carbohydrates and protein, pemmican was the ultimate trail food. To make it, the voyageur started with strips of dried buffalo meat, called *charqui* (jerky). He removed any gristle or sinew, pounded the meat to break it down, added dried berries and melted fat, and packed the whole into a buffalo-skin bag. (According to one observer, "hair, sticks, spruce leaves, stones, sand, etc." often found their way into the mix, too.) Sewing the bag shut made an air-tight receptacle. Thus sealed, pemmican could keep for years. Voyageurs ate it raw or cooked. A favourite meal was *rababou*—pemmican sliced and boiled with flour. After a long day of paddling and portaging, voyageurs sometimes couldn't wait for it to cool in a bowl. Instead, as one amazed witness recorded, they poured this hearty stew over a rock and licked it up like dogs.

Voyageurs were hired hands, working under contract for giant firms like the Hudson's Bay Company that acquired furs by trading with Indians at posts scattered throughout the Canadian West. American fur companies didn't depend on Indians to do the trapping. At first they employed their own trappers, but the system that ultimately took hold in the Rockies relied on "free trappers." These were the mountain men of legend, men like Joe Walker, Jim Bridger, and Kit Carson—independent operators who worked alone or in small groups and sold their pelts to traders at an annual trappers' rendezvous.

Rollicking bacchanals of drinking and gambling, rendezvous drew both whites and Indians and were held each summer between 1825 and 1840 along the continental divide, in what is now west-central Wyoming. John Kirk Townsend, the greenhorn who weeks earlier had witnessed the hunter Richardson drink from the guts of a dead bison, attended the rendezvous of 1834. He was laid up with a fever for much of the time. "There is a great variety of personages amongst us," he wrote in his journal,

> *most of them calling themselves white men, French-Canadians, half-breeds, &c., their colour nearly as dark, and their manners wholly as wild, as the Indians with whom they constantly associate. These people, with their obstreperous mirth, their whooping, and howling, and quarrelling, added to the mounted Indians, who are constantly dashing into, and through our camp, yelling like fiends, the barking and baying of savage wolf-dogs, and the incessant cracking of rifles and carbines, render our camp a perfect bedlam. A more unpleasant situation for an invalid could scarcely be conceived. I am confined closely to the tent with illness, and am compelled all day to listen to the hiccoughing jargon of drunken traders, the* sacré *and* foutre *of Frenchmen run wild, and the swearing and screaming of our own men, who are scarcely less savage than the rest, being heated by the detestable liquor which circulates freely among them.*

George Frederick Ruxton, an Englishman who ventured into the southern Rockies in the 1840s, never attended a rendezvous but reconstructed this scene from accounts related to him by trappers he knew:

Seated, Indian fashion, round the fires, with a blanket spread before them, groups are seen with their "decks" of cards, playing euker, poker, and seven-up, the regular mountain games. The stakes are "beaver," which here is current coin; and when the fur is gone, their breeches are staked. Daring gamblers make the rounds of the camp, challenging each other to play for the trapper's highest stakes—his horse, his squaw (if he have one), and, as once happened, his scalp. "There goes hos and beaver!" is the mountain expression when any great loss is sustained; and sooner or later, "hos and beaver" invariably find their way into the insatiable pockets of the traders.

Ruxton also left us an account—one so graphic an editor refused to include it in the published version of his journal—of gastronomic sport between two trappers on the upper Arkansas River. On slaughtering a buffalo cow, Ruxton wrote, "the hunter carefully lays by, as a tidbit for himself, the 'boudins' and medullary intestine," which he prepared by partially cleaning and lightly charring over a fire.

I once saw two Canadians commence at either end of such a coil of grease, the mess lying between them on a dirty apishamore like the coil of a huge snake. As yard after yard glided glibly down their throats, and the serpent on the saddlecloth was dwindling from an anaconda to a moderate-sized rattlesnake, it became a great point with each of the feasters to hurry his operation, so as to gain a march upon his neighbour, and improve the opportunity by swallowing more than his just proportion; each, at the same time, exhorting the other, whatever he did, to feed fair, and every now and then, overcome by the unblushing attempts of his partner to bolt a vigorous mouthful would suddenly jerk back his head, drawing out at the same moment, by the retreating motion, several yards of boudin from his neighbour's mouth and stomach— for the greasy viand required no mastication, and was bolted whole—and, snapping up himself the ravished portions, greedily swallowed them; to be in turn again withdrawn and subjected to a similar process by the other.

Because he could trade at the rendezvous for the few manufactured items required for survival, the free trapper had little need to visit civilization.

Jim Bridger spent seventeen straight years in the mountains. In all that time, Old Gabe claimed, he never once tasted bread.

Anyway, who needs bread when buffalo—40 million meals on the hoof—are there for the taking? Bridger really may have believed, as he said, that a man who ate only buffalo meat would never die. It was the mountain man's staff of life. The most tender cuts came from the hump of a young cow. Tongue was also a favorite, along with kidney fat eaten raw on the spot, sliced and dried for later consumption, or boiled down into tallow and packed in skins for a high-fat protein trail snack. A particular delicacy was *Boudin blanc*, a sausage made from hump meat and kidney fat stuffed in a piece of lower intestine, then boiled and fried in bear grease.

The sweet, tender meat of beaver—especially the tail—was another delicacy (as it was for Lewis and Clark), and beaver livers made a rich repast. The mountain man varied his carnivorous diet with the fruit of wild plants (berries, grapes, plumbs, hazelnuts), lambs-quarters (a green collected along river banks), and potato-like camas roots. Both plants and animals were sources for pharmaceuticals. Powdered cornflower root mixed with water made a poultice guaranteed to cure snakebite. An all-purpose salve—good for wounds and sores and joints that ached from too many hours setting traps in frigid streams—was concocted from bear's oil and beeswax mixed with gunpowder.

In a country so bountiful the mountain man was seldom wanting, and with his basic kit—a sturdy plains rifle, tomahawk, Green River knife, and "possibles" bag filled with items of varying degree of practicality, from castoreum or "medicine" (beaver musk) for baiting traps to small bones and pebbles and similar talismans—he made the Rockies his own.

His shelter was a simple lean-to or a tipi, his usual bedding a blanket roll. His clothes were of buckskin, but he also wore (and preferred) cotton or wool if he'd traded recently at a fort or a rendezvous. He carried a sewing kit, of course, to repair his clothes and make moccasins, and it also came in handy for emergency medical treatment: one of the most harrowing descriptions in the literature of the fur trade is Jim Clyman's account of the impromptu plastic surgery he performed on Jedediah Smith after a grizzly mauling that ripped his scalp and nearly severed an ear. In 1823, near the Black Hills, Smith was leading a party of trappers when a grizzly surprised them. As Clyman wrote in his journal, before Smith could raise his rifle the bear took him in its "capcious mouth." The grizzly threw him to the ground, breaking several ribs and nearly tearing off his scalp.

Clyman and others chased off the bear and did what they could for their leader. Blood pulsed from a gaping slash wound that had bared his skull, and one ear was almost severed. On Smith's orders, Clyman produced a needle and thread and began putting his boss back together, stitching "through and through and over and over laying the lacerated parts together as nice as I could." Smith pulled through and before too long was up and about. As Clyman noted, the experience "gave us a lisson on the charcter of the grissly Barre which we did not forget."

The mountain man could make a fire any number of ways, using a bow drill like the Indians if he had to, but more likely by striking a fire-steel against a flint, sending sparks into a pile of "punk," or crumbled deadwood from a pine tree. In wet weather he might add a pinch of black powder. Once lit, he folded the smouldering punk into a bed of dry grass, then blew on the grass or waved it in the air until it ignited. Many mountain men continued to use flintlock rifles long after the introduction of percussion weapons, in part because they could double as fire starters.

The knives carried by both the mountain men and voyageurs varied in style, although most were simple trade knives manufactured in England and the eastern United States. The typical "scalper" had a six-inch blade and wooden handle. Fur companies ordered them by the hundreds of dozens at wholesale prices of less than 10 cents per knife, then sold them to trappers at trading posts or rendezvous at a 1,000-percent markup. Many English knives were stamped with the initials "G.R.," for Georgius Rex, in deference to the British monarch. Some mountain men wrongly assumed the initials stood for the Green River in Wyoming, in whose valley their rendezvous were held. The confusion was understandable, for other knives they carried bore the name "Green River" on their blades. These, however, were made by the American firm of J. Russell at a factory on the Green River in Massachusetts. The mountain man's expression "up to Green River" was probably first applied in a literal sense to mean burying a knife "to the hilt" in an adversary's ribs. Metaphorically, it became a term of praise for any job done thoroughly.

The trade knife was an all-purpose tool whose uses were hardly limited to skinning, butchering, and self-defence. On many occasions it did yeoman service as a surgical instrument. A trade knife saved the life of trapper Tom Smith in a particularly grisly episode in 1827. During an Indian attack on his party, a bullet hit Smith just above an ankle, shattering the bone. In agony he cried out for someone to amputate his mangled leg. According to a contemporary account, after his companions balked at the gruesome task, Smith asked one of them for a knife, and with it "he severed the muscles at the fracture with his own hand." Another man then "took the knife . . . and completed the operation by severing the tendon achilles," then bound up the wound "with an old dirty shirt."

Smith lost an extremity but gained a moniker ("Peg-Leg"), and the mountains gained another legend.

—◆—

Today, any hunter venturing into the wilderness would include among his gear a map and compass and probably a GPS. Yet the mountain man and voyageur managed quite well with none of these aids. Of course, there were no maps to speak of other than the ones engraved on gray matter: it's been said that Jim Bridger, who could neither read nor write, carried in his head a map of a third of the continent. After the fur trade ended in the 1840s, Bridger and other ex-trappers like Joseph Walker guided the army cartographers who produced the first detailed maps of the West. Walker's photographic memory of terrain dumbfounded the soldiers he led on an expedition in 1859. The old frontiersman took them up a part of the Colorado River he had gone down just once, more than twenty years before. Every morning prior to starting out, he drew an unfailingly accurate map of the country they expected to cover that day, showing where the valley widened and narrowed, where tributaries entered, and where they could find good grazing for their horses.

In *Across the Wide Missouri*, his magisterial tribute to the mountain man, Bernard DeVoto ponders the wilderness skills and exquisitely honed senses that enabled him to survive:

Why do you follow the ridges into or out of unfamiliar country? What do you do for a companion who has collapsed from want of water while crossing a desert? How do you get meat when you find yourself without gunpowder in a country barren of game? What tribe of Indians made this trail, how many were in the band, what errand were they on, were they going to or coming back from it, how far from home were they, were their horses laden, how many horses did they have and why, how many squaws accompanied them, what mood were they in? Also, how old is the trail, where are those Indians now, and what does the product of these answers require of you? Prodigies of such sign-reading are recorded by impressed greenhorns, travelers, and army men, and the exercise of critical reference and deduction which they exhibit would seem prodigious if it were not routine.

At the next level of insight is "the interpretation of observed circumstances too minute to be called sign":

A branch floats down a stream—is this natural, or the work of animals, or of Indians or trappers? Another branch or a bush or even a pebble is out of place—why? On the limits of the plain, blurred by heat mirage, or against the gloom of distant cottonwoods, or across an angle of sky between branches or where hill and mountain meet, there is a tenth of a second of what may have been movement—did men or animals make it, and, if animals, why? Buffalo are moving downwind, an elk is in an unlikely place or posture, too many magpies are hollering, a wolf's howl is off key—what does it mean?

"The mountain man" observed DeVoto, "had mastered his conditions—how well is apparent as soon as soldiers, goldseekers, or emigrants come into his country and suffer where he has lived comfortably and die where he has been in no danger."

───◆───

Finally—as the ordeal of Peg-Leg Smith makes plain—a mountain man's survival depended on sheer grit and the will to live. To last in a country where bears, Indians, or a simple miscalculation could kill him, he needed "the right stuff" (including luck) as surely as any astronaut.

Bridger and Walker had it in spades. So too did Hugh Glass and Jim Clyman.

After a severe mauling by a grizzly while hunting in present-day South Dakota, Glass was tended by two companions for several days. When the trapper appeared near death, they left him to his fate. But Glass recovered enough to begin a hike back to Fort Kiowa on the Missouri River, 350 miles away. He had been stripped of his rifle and was so weak he covered most of the distance on his hands and knees. At one point in his journey he subsisted for ten days by a spring, eating cherries and buffalo berries, and later devoured raw the flesh of a buffalo calf after chasing off the wolves that had killed it.

Like most mountain men, Glass was known to embellish a tale, and a few historians dismiss his story as so much campfire talk. But none doubts the truthfulness of Clyman's account of his 600-mile walk across much of present-day Wyoming and Nebraska. Clyman (the "surgeon" who repaired Jed Smith's lacerated head) had become separated from his party near South Pass. Indians had stolen his horse, and he started on his way back to civilization with only eleven balls for his rifle. Whenever he could after shooting a buffalo, he dug the spent bullet from its flesh and rounded it back into shape with his teeth. He killed three in a row this way, all with the same ball. Near the end of his journey game became scarce, but he happened upon two badgers fighting. When his rifle misfired, he, grabbed a bone off the ground and clubbed them both to death. After gathering grass and willow bark, he sparked a fire using the flint from his rifle (Indians having also stolen his fire steel), then roasted the badgers and made moccasins from their hides.

That proved to be Clyman's last meal for a while. Weakened by hunger, and wet and cold from three days of unseasonable rain, he staggered on. After eighty days on the trail, he topped a rise and saw below him the winding Missouri and an army post with the stars and stripes waving over it. He literally fainted with joy. Ten days later, the three other trappers in his party arrived at the fort "in a more pitible state if possible than myself," as Clyman later described the scene. His companions, he learned, had lost all their bullets when crossing a river. No matter: they made new ones by stripping the brass mounting from one of their guns and pounding the metal into balls. The buffalo they killed with this makeshift ammo kept them going until they reached the fort. Like the hunter drinking from a buffalo's gut and the voyageur gagging down boiled lichen, they did what it took to survive.

Chapter 2

The Explorer

By Rudyard Kipling

Granted that this is a rather unusual and surprising chapter for an anthology promising stories. But before you have a chance to skim over it, perhaps remembering how many pieces of verse have bored you in the past, your editor urges you to not miss this memorable tribute to the men who first set foot in the mighty mountains. It's from the pen of world-renowned author Rudyard Kipling.

*"There's no sense in going further—it's the edge of cultivation,"
So they said, and I believed it—broke my land and sowed my crop—
Built my barns and strung my fences in the little border station
Tucked away below the foot hills where the trails run out and stop.*

*Till a voice, as bad as Conscience, rang interminable changes
On one everlasting Whisper day and night repeated—so:
"Something hidden. Go and find it. Go and look behind the Ranges—
"Something lost behind the Ranges. Lost and waiting for you. Go!"*

*So I went, worn out of patience; never told my nearest neighbours—
Stole away with pack and ponies—left 'em drinking in the town;
And the faith that moveth mountains didn't seem to help my labours
As I faced the sheer main-ranges, whipping up and leading down.*

*March by march I puzzled through 'em, turning flanks and dodging shoulders,
Hurried on in hope of water, headed back for lack of grass;
Till I camped above the tree-line—drifted snow and naked boulders—*

Felt free air astir to windward—knew I'd stumbled on the Pass.
'Thought to name it for the finder: but that night the Norther found me—
Froze and killed the plains-bred ponies; so I called the camp Despair
(It's the Railway Camp to-day, though). Then my Whisper waked to hound me:—
"Something lost behind the Ranges. Over yonder! Go you there!"

Then I knew, the while I doubted—knew His Hand was certain o'er me.
Still—it might be self-delusion—scores of better men had died—
I could reach the township living, but. . . He knows what terrors tore me.
But I didn't. . . but I didn't. I went down the other side.

Till the snow ran out in flowers, and the flowers turned to aloes,
And the aloes sprung to thickets and a brimming stream ran by;
But the thickets dwindled to thorn-scrub, and the water drained to shallows,
And I dropped again on desert—blasted earth, and blasting sky. . . .

I remember lighting fires; I remember sitting by them;
I remember seeing faces, hearing voices through the smoke;
I remember they were fancy—for I threw a stone to try 'em.
"Something lost behind the Ranges" was the only word they spoke.

I remember going crazy. I remember that I knew it
When I heard myself hallooing to the funny folk I saw.
Very full of dreams that desert: but my two legs took me through it. . .
And I used to watch 'em moving with the toes all black and raw.

But at last the country altered—White Man's country past disputing—
Rolling grass and open timber, with a hint of hills behind—
There I found me food and water, and I lay a week recruiting,
Got my strength and lost my nightmares. Then I entered on my find.

Thence I ran my first rough survey—chose my trees and blazed and ringed 'em—
Week by week I pried and sampled—week by week my findings grew.
Saul he went to look for donkeys, and by God he found a kingdom!
But by God, who sent His Whisper, I had struck the worth of two!

Up along the hostile mountains, where the hair-poised snowslide shivers—
Down and through the big fat marshes that the virgin ore-bed stains,
Till I heard the mile-wide mutterings of unimagined rivers,
And beyond the nameless timber saw illimitable plains!

Plotted sites of future cities, traced the easy grades between 'em;
Watched unharnessed rapids wasting fifty thousand head an hour;
Counted leagues of water-frontage through the axe-ripe woods that screen 'em—
Saw the plant to feed a people—up and waiting for the power!

Well I know who'll take the credit—all the clever chaps that followed—
Came, a dozen men together—never knew my desert fears;
Tracked me by the camps I'd quitted, used the water-holes I'd hollowed.
They'll go back and do the talking. They'll be called the Pioneers!

They will find my sites of townships—not the cities that I set there.
They will rediscover rivers—not my rivers heard at night.
By my own old marks and bearings they will show me how to get there,

By the lonely cairns I builded they will guide my feet aright.
Have I named one single river? Have I claimed one single acre?
Have I kept one single nugget—(barring samples)? No, not I!
Because my price was paid me ten times over by my Maker.
But you wouldn't understand it. You go up and occupy.

Ores you'll find there; wood and cattle; water-transit sure and steady
(That should keep the railway rates down), coal and iron at your doors.
God took care to hide the country till He judged His people ready,
Then He chose me for His Whisper, and I've found it, and it's yours!

Yes, your "Never-never country"—yes, your edge of cultivation
And "no sense in going further"—till I crossed the range to see.
God forgive me! No, I didn't. It's God's present to our nation.
Anybody might have found it but—His Whisper came to me!

CHAPTER 3

For Love of the Wild Places

By George Laycock

The mountain man depicted on the cover jacket of this book was the first to clap eyes on the splendours of what we call Yellowstone Park today. He saw the great geysers spewing steam, rivers flowing clear and strong through untouched wilderness. His name was John Colter, and he was there because Meriwether Lewis and William Clark had released him from duty. Their epic journey to the Pacific was in its final stages, the return home, when their party met a group of trappers, headed for the upper Missouri. Colter joined the new explorers, headed back to the mountains, leaving civilization behind. George Laycock's story follows John Colter through adventures so gripping men sometimes thought Colter was a liar, a teller of tall tales. He wasn't. It all really happened.

THROUGH THE SOFT DAYS OF EARLY OCTOBER, THE EASTERNER MOVED swiftly along the woodland trails, always headed west, up and over the mountains. His trip turned out to be an adventure as wild as any North American outdoorsman has ever known.

The mountainsides around him and the forest giants forming their canopy over his trail were splashed with fiery autumn colours. He must have watched the gray squirrels gathering nuts for the winter, the wild turkeys walking in the forest, the deer and the black bear hurrying out of sight. But he was in a hurry too. Word was out that Captain Meriwether Lewis was signing on hunters and boatmen for a grand journey into the distant Rocky Mountains, to places new to the white man.

The traveller's immediate destination was Limestone, Kentucky, a settlement on the south bank of the Ohio River, fifty miles or so upstream from Cincinnati. The little riverside village was already famous as a landing for flatboats and keelboats bringing people down the Ohio to the western frontier.

In Limestone, which we now call Maysville, the woodsman soon spotted a big keelboat tied to the bank. He introduced himself to the captain and outlined his qualifications. He had been a hunter, trapper, and horseman since he was a boy on the farm in Virginia. Captain Lewis sized him up. The applicant stood five feet ten inches tall, looked strong, and seemed to be quiet and reserved but quick-witted and decisive in his manner. The captain noticed that this stranger was not the loudmouthed braggart often found along the rivers. He was instead somewhat inclined to weigh his words. When the keelboat eased into the current to head on down the Ohio toward Louisville, a new member was aboard. Captain Lewis had signed on John Colter, and apparently neither of them ever regretted the decision.

The deeper Lewis and Clark travelled into the wilderness with their little band of explorers, the more they came to rely on the skills of Private John Colter. They frequently relieved him of his other duties and sent him with Drouillard to roam the countryside on foot or horseback and supply the company with meat. Colter was a specialist in travelling alone in the wilderness, sometimes for days or weeks at a time, always finding his way back.

As Lewis and Clark were returning to St. Louis near the end of their two-year-long journey, Colter seemed in no rush to return to civilization. The Lewis and Clark party was within six weeks of reaching St. Louis when it tied up beside a little two-man camp on the banks of the Missouri.

The two strangers explained that they had come into the mountains from their homes in Illinois in 1804, to trap beaver. They found beaver aplenty in the mountains, but Indians had robbed them so often that they had little to show for the time and work. They still nurtured their dreams of growing rich trapping furs in the western mountains.

Colter was especially interested when the two trappers, Forrest Hancock and Joe Dixon, said they were headed back toward the wilderness, up the Yellowstone River, where the beaver lived. Furthermore, they needed a partner who knew the Yellowstone country. There was then probably no white person anywhere who knew it better than John Colter did.

Colter took the idea to Captain Lewis and Captain Clark. Would they perhaps discharge him here on the Missouri instead of back in St. Louis? Lewis and Clark considered the long months of faithful service Colter had rendered. Why not? They took the matter up with the rest of their crew. They would release Colter, providing no others in the party would make similar requests before reaching St. Louis. The chances are good that no other man in the group gave serious thought anyhow to turning back into the mountains with St. Louis so close at hand.

The Lewis and Clark party moved off downstream and was soon out of sight. The three trappers, Hancock, Dixon, and Colter, turned upstream toward the distant peaks and ridges. They spent that winter of 1806–1807 in the upper Yellowstone where, it is believed, they built a shelter and waited out the worst of the weather.

None of these three pioneering mountain men was strong on writing. Little can be known for sure of what they saw. But their association was not especially profitable and did not last long. By the following spring, Colter had carved himself a dugout canoe from a cottonwood log and was soon headed downstream alone, once more St. Louis bound.

By this time, however, Manuel Lisa, the crusty fur trader who guided the fortunes of his Missouri Fur Company, was moving toward the Rocky Mountains in pursuit of beaver plews. In due time Lisa's party had wrestled his keelboats up the Missouri River as far as the mouth of the Platte, and were tied up there when John Colter's little canoe slid into view around the bend.

Colter, the mountain man, once more turned his back on St. Louis and headed for the mountains, this time working for Manuel Lisa.

Lisa moved his party up the Missouri as far as the Yellowstone, then turned up that tributary and followed it to where the Bighorn River fed into it sixty miles or so downstream from where Billings, Montana, stands today. Here Lisa's men began felling timbers and constructing an unimpressive shelter that became the first fur trading post in the upper Missouri country. It was probably close to where Colter, Dixon, and Hancock had wintered the year before.

Although Lisa intended to send his own trappers out on the beaver waters, he also expected to barter for furs with the Indians of surrounding tribes. He had, with Colter's guidance, selected a good location. People of the Crow nation wintered in this region, and so did large numbers of wild game animals that would provide food for the trappers.

But unless someone went out among the Indians to spread the word about Lisa's arrival, and his new commercial enterprise, there would be few furs. This may have been the hazardous assignment Lisa had in mind for Colter from the first. Nowhere could he have found a better qualified person.

Colter said he would travel alone. He liked being alone in the mountains, depending on his own survival skills, making his own decisions, going where he pleased. He would seek out the Indians in their wintering camps, and he would spread the word-there was now a trading post at the mouth of the Bighorn. He put together the essentials-powder, lead, flint and steel, sharpening stone, jerky, some lightweight trade goods, a blanket or robe, in a pack weighing thirty pounds-picked up his rifle, and set out on a five-hundred-mile winter hike through the mountain stronghold of the Crows.

About where Cody, Wyoming, stands today he came upon an Indian village of perhaps a thousand people. They talked with the lightly equipped trapper and allowed him to go on. This camp was on the Shoshone River, which was then called the "Stinking Water." It was near here that Colter witnessed springs bubbling from the ground and filling the air with their sulphurous odour. When he later described the scene to his fellow trappers, they laughed and slapped their buckskin leggings, declaring, "That's some, that is! This child's heard it all now. Old Colter's found his hell, sure enough 'em I wouldn't say so." In due time, the springs of Colter's Hell subsided.

Colter crossed the mountains over Shoshone Pass and down into the Wind River Range, then turned northwest toward Yellowstone. Among the mysteries surrounding Colter's life are the details of the route he followed on the remainder of this journey. But there is agreement that he crossed the area that later became Yellowstone National Park. He skirted Yellowstone Lake. Then traveling north, he went down the Yellowstone River and finally turned east again to cross the mountains and come down into the headwaters of Clark's Fork of the Yellowstone. He was now making his way back toward Cody.

There are no records telling us how long Colter needed for this winter hike of more than five hundred miles. He may not have considered the time important and surely did not anticipate that researchers would one day scour old records, hoping to uncover bits and pieces of information revealing the details of his life and travels. To the mountain man, his trip on foot, while living off the land, was a job, and he did it.

Spring was probably at hand by the time Colter returned to Lisa's fort. But soon, he was sent off again on another journey as ambassador to the Indians. He was going about his business visiting with the Crows, when the Crows' traditional enemies, the Blackfeet, attacked. An attack by the Blackfeet was always a serious matter. On that spring day in 1808, Colter had little choice: he joined his hosts in their efforts to repel the Blackfeet.

Some historians believe that the Blackfeet held a grudge from that moment on against not only Colter but all white men. At any rate, this marked the beginning for John Colter of a series of almost unbelievable close encounters.

Coming from Joe Meek, Jim Beckwourth, or some other trapper famed for his storytelling skills, the account of Colter's amazing escape might have been questioned. But the quiet Colter was known for his honesty. He later told the story to Thomas James, and James wrote it down. He also vouched for Colter. "His veracity was never questioned among us," wrote James, "and his character was that of a true American back woodsman . . . of the Daniel Boone stamp. Nature had formed him, like Boone, for hardy endurance of fatigue, privations, and perils. He had gone with a companion named Potts to the Jefferson river which is the most western of the three forks, and runs near the base of the mountains."

Colter and Potts, each in his own canoe, were working their way slowly upstream, running their beaver sets, and Colter was edgy because they were deep into Blackfoot territory. He had good reason for his uneasiness. Suddenly several hundred Indians materialized on the east shore of the river and there was little hope that the white trappers could escape.

When the chiefs ordered the trappers to come ashore, Colter obeyed, figuring that he would thereby add, at least briefly, to his life span.

Killing him where he sat in his canoe would be easy enough for this many warriors. He no sooner touched shore than the squaws began ripping the clothes off his body and soon he stood before the yelling warlike Indians, stripped of all clothing and weapons.

The chiefs again demanded that Colter tell Potts to come on in. Colter relayed the message. He also advised Potts to do as he was told. Potts said something akin to, "Wagh. Them red devils will kill this child, sure enough, same's they're fixin' to do you and from here I can leastways take one of 'em with me." With this, one of the Indians put a ball in Pott's shoulder.

Potts did what he said he would do; he recovered enough to lift his gun and kill the Indian who shot him. In the next minute Potts was, in Colter's words, "made a riddle of."

The screaming Indians now dragged Potts's body from the river while others turned their fury on Colter. He fully expected to black out, permanently, from the quick blow of one of the tomahawks being lifted against him, but the chiefs managed to push back the young warriors. Meanwhile, some of the Indians were hacking off chunks of Potts. One of the squaws walked up close to Colter and threw Potts's penis and testicles in his face. They continued pelting him with various bloody parts of his partner's body, using for the purpose, as Tom James wrote, "the entrails, heart, lungs, etc."

Then came a squabble about what to do with their white captive. Colter figured maybe Potts had taken the best way out after all. But his wits were still with him, and given the slightest opportunity, he was keyed up for escape.

One of the chiefs walked up to Colter. Was he a good runner?

Not very, Colter lied. The satisfied chief, surrounded by powerful young men eager to prove how fast they could run, gave Colter his instructions. He led the naked trapper out behind the main group of warriors onto the open plain, and told Colter to start running.

Colter noticed, in a glance, that the warriors were stripping themselves of all clothing and extra weight and now he fully understood the odds against him. He dashed off across the flatlands toward the river six miles away.

Perhaps no runner ever had greater motivation than John Colter did in that hour. Ignoring the thorns of the prickly pear cactus through which his bare feet raced, Colter, toughened by his years in the mountains, ran at his fastest speed. Glancing over his shoulder, he saw the band of runners racing along silently, each intent on being first to come within spear-throwing range of the white man.

Colter got his second wind. He did not slow his pace. Blood began flowing from his nose. It spattered against his sweating chest, dropping onto his bare legs. He raced on beneath the brilliant sun, oblivious to everything but maintaining his grueling pace.

One by one, the exhausted Indians fell far behind. One of them, however, was an exceptionally strong runner and Colter knew that the warrior was closing the distance between them.

When it became obvious that he could not outrun the Indian, Colter took a bold chance. He jerked to a halt, and wheeled to meet the Indian, calling to him to stop and talk the matter over. The Indian kept coming and, as he drew near, he raised his spear over his head and lunged at the trapper. Colter side-stepped, grabbed the spear, and put enough pressure on it to throw the off-balance Indian to the ground. The tumbling Indian was no sooner rolling on the ground than Colter ran him through with the spear point, pinning him to mother earth.

He grabbed the Indian's blanket and, once more, began running. He was now well ahead of the nearest warrior. At last he came to the river and, for the first time, began to think that he might have a good chance of escaping. He swam to the end of a small island where he dove under a pile of tangled driftwood that had washed up against the land.

Within minutes, dozens of Indians were running up and down the riverbank. They probed each hiding place with their spears, and searched around the roots of the cottonwoods. They even swam out to search the island. They climbed onto the pile of logs beneath which Colter clung in the darkness with his head barely above water. He waited for them to drive their spears through the brush pile, or set it afire.

The search continued throughout much of the day. Darkness settled over the river. At last the Indians withdrew, and Colter slipped from beneath his shelter and swam the river. Instead of crossing the mountain pass, which was the easiest way out of the valley, but probably guarded by the frustrated Indians, he climbed the nearly vertical slope to the distant ridge. For the next eleven days he stopped only to sleep or to gather the roots and plants that sustained him. When he reached Lisa's Fort, the other trappers scarcely recognized him.

Colter told the story of his escape in detail to Tom James and others on a later trip as they travelled through the area where he had made his unforgettable run for freedom. He pointed out the mountain he had scaled. As Colter quietly related the details of that day, his companions grew silent. One of the trappers listening to the story, fully aware that they were in hostile country said, "I never felt fear before, but now I feel it." His fear should have been a warning. A few days later this trapper was caught by the Blackfeet and killed.

Those traps Colter had quietly dropped overboard when the large band of Blackfeet discovered him and Potts were very much on his mind. Traps were hard to come by in the mountains and there was no substitute for them if a man was to take plews. The possibility of recovering the traps lured Colter back to the scene. He had stopped to cook supper and rest, and as he settled down he heard the sound of rustling leaves in the darkness.

The mountain man, like the hunted animal lived with all senses alert. Every sign was weighed for what it might mean in terms of survival. Now, he heard a noise the meaning of which was known to him instantly; beyond his campfire guns were being cocked.

He leaped over the fire and raced off through the brush as shots rattled around him. Once more he scaled the mountain to avoid the pass, and once more John Colter escaped. But he was beginning to get the message. He came back to the fort this time saying that he had made a promise to his Maker; providing he could survive, he would leave the country.

He still had one test ahead of him. He was finally on his way downriver with a companion headed for the distant sights and sounds of St. Louis when the Blackfeet attacked. This time Colter and his companion hid in the bushes, and the Indians, who had high respect for the trappers' rifles, did not come after them.

John Colter never counted coup. He was no braggart and no bully. Perhaps in all his years in the mountains he killed only one Indian, and that time to save his own life. For all this, he had little to show. He came down from the mountains without much more than memories. He moved to a farm near where Dundee, Missouri, is today. He married, and all we know of his wife is that he called her Sally.

Colter, the pioneering trapper and explorer, who specialized in traveling alone, had spent six years in the mountains. He had played his role in the historic adventures of Lewis and Clark, traveled where no white man had gone before, discovered on his own the wonders of Yellowstone, and set an example for hundreds of fur trappers who would soon follow him to the mountains. John Colter, the soft-spoken mountain man, became a legend in his own day. He died in bed in November 1813, of jaundice.

CHAPTER 4

The Free Trapper: Life at Its Most Dangerous

By A. C. Laut

On his own in the wilderness, free to trap and hunt and travel as he saw fit, the life of the mountain man sounds too appealing to be real. It was real all right, but you might not call a lifestyle "appealing" death is only a tomahawk swing away.

LONG BEFORE SUNRISE HUNTERS WERE ASTIR IN THE MOUNTAINS.

The Crows were robbers, the Blackfeet murderers; and scouts of both tribes haunted every mountain defile where a white hunter might pass with provisions and peltries which these rascals could plunder.

The trappers circumvented their foes by setting the traps after nightfall and lifting the game before daybreak.

Night in the mountains was full of a mystery that the imagination of the Indians peopled with terrors enough to frighten them away. The sudden stilling of mountain torrent and noisy leaping cataract at sundown when the thaw of the upper snows ceased, the smothered roar of rivers under ice, the rush of whirlpools through the blackness of some far canyon, the crashing of rocks thrown down by unknown forces, the shivering echo that multiplied itself a thousandfold and ran "rocketing" from peak to peak startling the silences—these things filled the Indian with superstitious fears.

The gnomes, called in trapper's vernacular "hoodoos"—great pillars of sandstone higher than a house, left standing in valleys by prehistoric floods—were to the Crows and Blackfeet petrified giants that only awakened at night to hurl down rocks on intruding mortals. And often the quiver of a shadow in the night wind gave reality to the Indian's fears. The purr of streams over rocky bed was whispering, the queer quaking echoes of falling rocks were giants at war, and the mists rising from swaying waterfalls, spirit-forms portending death.

Morning came more ghostly among the peaks.

Thick white clouds banked the mountains from peak to base, blotting out every scar and tor as a sponge might wash a slate. Valleys lay blanketed in smoking mist. As the sun came gradually up to the horizon far away east behind the mountains, scarp and pinnacle butted through the fog, stood out bodily from the mist, seemed to move like living giants from the cloud banks. "How could they do that if they were not alive?" asked the Indian. Elsewhere, shadows came from sun, moon, starlight, or camp-fire. But in these valleys were pencilled shadows of peaks upside down, shadows all the colours of the rainbow pointing to the bottom of the green Alpine lakes, hours and hours before any sun had risen to cause the shadows. All this meant "bad medicine" to the Indian, or, in white man's language, mystery.

Unless they were foraging in large bands, Crows and Blackfeet shunned the mountains after nightfall. That gave the white man a chance to trap in safety.

Early one morning two white men slipped out of their sequestered cabin built in hiding of the hills at the head waters of the Missouri. Under cover of brushwood lay a long odd-shaped canoe, sharp enough at the prow to cleave the narrowest waters between rocks, so sharp that French voyageurs gave this queer craft the name "canot à bec d'esturgeon"— that is, a canoe like the nose of a sturgeon. This American adaptation of the Frenchman's craft was not of birch-bark. That would be too frail to essay the rock-ribbed cañons of the mountain streams. It was usually a common dugout, hollowed from a cottonwood or other light timber, with such an angular narrow prow that it could take the sheerest dip and mount the steepest wave-crest where a rounder boat would fill and swamp. Dragging this from cover, the two white men pushed out on the Jefferson Fork, dipping now on this side, now on that, using the reversible double-bladed paddles which only an amphibious boatman can manage. The two men shot out in mid-stream, where the mists would hide them from each shore; a moment later the white fog had enfolded them, and there was no trace of human presence but the trail of dimpling ripples in the wake of the canoe.

No talking, no whistling, not a sound to betray them. And there were good reasons why these men did not wish their presence known. One was Potts, the other John Colter. Both had been with the Lewis and Clark exploring party of 1804–'05, when a Blackfoot brave had been slain for horse-thieving by the first white men to cross the Upper Missouri. Besides, the year before coming to the Jefferson, Colter had been with the Missouri Company's fur brigade under Manuel Lisa, and had gone to the Crows as an emissary from the fur company. While with the Crows, a battle had taken place against the Blackfeet, in which they suffered heavy loss owing to Colter's prowess. That made the Blackfeet sworn enemies to Colter.

Turning off the Jefferson, the trappers headed their canoe up a side stream, probably one of those marshy reaches where beavers have formed a swamp by damming up the current of a sluggish stream. Such quiet waters are favourite resorts for beaver and mink and marten and pekan. Setting their traps only after nightfall, the two men could not possibly have put out more than forty or fifty. Thirty traps are a heavy day's work for one man. Six prizes out of thirty are considered a wonderful run of luck; but the empty traps must be examined as carefully as the successful ones. Many that have been mauled, "scented" by a beaver scout and left, must be replaced. Others must have fresh bait; others, again, carried to better grounds where there are more game signs.

Either this was a very lucky morning and the men were detained taking fresh pelts, or it was a very unlucky morning and the men had decided to trap farther up-stream; for when the mists began to rise, the hunters were still in their canoe. Leaving the beaver meadow, they continued paddling up-stream away from the Jefferson. A more hidden water-course they could hardly have found. The swampy beaver-runs narrowed, the shores rose higher and higher into rampart walls, and the dark-shadowed waters came leaping down in the lumpy, uneven runnels of a small canyon. You can always tell whether the waters of a canyon are compressed or not, whether they come from broad, swampy meadows or clear snow streams smaller than the canyon. The marsh waters roll down swift and black and turbid, raging against the crowding walls; the snow streams leap clear and foaming as champagne, and are in too great a hurry to stop and quarrel with the rocks. It is altogether likely these men recognized swampy water, and were ascending the canyons in search of a fresh beaver-marsh; or they would not have continued paddling six miles above the Jefferson with daylight growing plainer at every mile. First the mist rose like a smoky exhalation from the river; then it flaunted across the rampart walls in banners; then the far mountain peaks took form against the sky, islands in a sea of fog; then the cloud banks were floating in mid-heaven blindingly white from a sun that painted each canyon wall in the depths of the water.

How much farther would the canyon lead? Should they go higher up or not? Was it wooded or clear plain above the walls? The man paused. What was that noise?

—◦—

The free trappers formed a class by themselves.

Other trappers either hunted on a salary of $200, $300, $400 a year, or on shares, like fishermen of the Grand Banks outfitted by "planters," or like western prospectors outfitted by companies that supply provisions, boats, and horses, expecting in return the major share of profits. The free trappers fitted themselves out, owed allegiance to no man, hunted where and how they chose, and refused to carry their furs to any fort but the one that paid the highest prices. For the mangeurs de lard, as they called the fur company raftsmen, they had a supreme contempt. For the methods of the fur companies, putting rivals to sleep with laudanum or bullet and ever stirring the savages up to warfare, the free trappers had a rough and emphatically expressed loathing.

The crime of corrupting natives can never be laid to the free trapper. He carried neither poison, nor what was worse than poison to the Indian—whisky—among the native tribes. The free trapper lived on good terms with the Indian, because his safety depended on the Indian. Renegades like Bird, the deserter from the Hudson's Bay Company, or Rose, who abandoned the Astorians, or Beckwourth of apocryphal fame, might cast off civilization and become Indian chiefs; but, after all, these men were not guilty of half so hideous crimes as the great fur companies of boasted respectability. Wyeth of Boston, and Captain Bonneville of the army, whose underlings caused such murderous slaughter among the Root Diggers, were not free trappers in the true sense of the term. Wyeth was an enthusiast who caught the fever of the wilds; and Captain Bonneville, a gay adventurer, whose men shot down more Indians in one trip than all the free trappers of America shot in a century. As for the desperado Harvey, whom Larpenteur reports shooting Indians like dogs, his crimes were committed under the walls of the American Fur Company's fort. MacLellan and Crooks and John Day—before they joined the Astorians—and Boone and Carson and Colter, are names that stand for the true type of free trapper.

The free trapper went among the Indians with no defence but good behaviour and the keenness of his wit. Whatever crimes the free trapper might be guilty of towards white men, he was guilty of few towards the Indians. Consequently, free trappers were all through Minnesota and the region westward of the Mississippi forty years before the fur companies dared to venture among the Sioux. Fisher and Fraser and Woods knew the Upper Missouri before 1806; and Brugiere had been on the Columbia many years before the Astorians came in 1811.

One crime the free trappers may be charged with—a reckless waste of precious furs. The great companies always encouraged the Indians not to hunt more game than they needed for the season's support. And no Indian hunter, uncorrupted by white men, would molest game while the mothers were with their young. Famine had taught them the punishment that follows reckless hunting. But the free trappers were here to-day and away to-morrow, like a Chinaman, to take all they could get regardless of results; and the results were the rapid extinction of fur-bearing game.

Always there were more free trappers in the United States than in Canada. Before the union of Hudson's Bay and Nor' Wester in Canada, all classes of trappers were absorbed by one of the two great companies. After the union, when the monopoly enjoyed by the Hudson's Bay did not permit it literally to drive a free trapper out, it could always "freeze" him out by withholding supplies in its great white northern wildernesses, or by refusing to give him transport. When the monopoly passed away in 1871, free trappers pressed north from the Missouri, where their methods had exterminated game, and carried on the same ruthless warfare on the Saskatchewan. North of the Saskatchewan, where very remoteness barred strangers out, the Hudson's Bay Company still held undisputed sway; and Lord Strathcona, the governor of the company, was able to say only two years ago, "the fur trade is quite as large as ever it was."

Among free hunters, Canada had only one commanding figure— John Johnston of the Soo, who settled at La Pointe on Lake Superior in 1792, formed league with Wabogish, "the White Fisher," and became the most famous trader of the Lakes. His life, too, was almost as eventful as Colter's. A member of the Irish nobility, some secret which he never chose to reveal drove him to the wilds. Wabogish, the "White Fisher," had a daughter who refused the wooings of all her tribe's warriors. In vain Johnston sued for her hand. Old Wabogish bade the white man go sell his Irish estates and prove his devotion by buying as vast estates in America. Johnston took the old chief at his word, and married the haughty princess of the Lake. When the War of 1812 set all the tribes by the ears, Johnston and his wife had as thrilling adventures as ever Colter knew among the Blackfeet.

Many a free trapper, and partner of the fur companies as well, secured his own safety by marrying the daughter of a chief, as Johnston had. These were not the lightly-come, lightly-go affairs of the vagrant adventurer. If the husband had not cast off civilization like a garment, the wife had to put it on like a garment; and not an ill-fitting garment either, when one considers that the convents of the quiet nuns dotted the wilderness like oases in a desert almost contemporaneous with the fur trade. If the trapper had not sunk to the level of the savages, the little daughter of the chief was educated by the nuns for her new position. I recall several cases where the child was sent across the Atlantic to an English governess so that the equality would be literal and not a sentimental fiction. And yet, on no subject has the western fur trader received more persistent and unjust condemnation. The heroism that culminated in the union of Pocahontas with a noted Virginian won applause, and almost similar circumstances dictated the union of fur traders with the daughters of Indian chiefs; but because the fur trader has not posed as a sentimentalist, he has become more or less of a target for the index finger of the Pharisee.

North of the boundary the free trapper had small chance against the Hudson's Bay Company. As long as the slow-going Mackinaw Company, itself chiefly recruited from free trappers, ruled at the junction of the Lakes, the free trappers held the hunting-grounds of the Mississippi; but after the Mackinaw was absorbed by the aggressive American Fur Company, the free hunters were pushed westward. On the Lower Missouri competition raged from 1810, so that circumstances drove the free trapper westward to the mountains, where he is hunting in the twentieth century as his prototype hunted two hundred years ago.

In Canada—of course after 1870—he entered the mountains chiefly by three passes: (1) Yellow Head Pass southward of the Athabasca; (2) the narrow gap where the Bow emerges to the plains—that is, the river where the Indians found the best wood for the making of bows; (3) north of the boundary, through that narrow defile over-towered by the lonely flat-crowned peak called Crows Nest Mountain—that is, where the fugitive Crows took refuge from the pursuing Blackfeet.

In the United States, the free hunters also approached the mountains by three main routes: (1) Up the Platte; (2) westward from the Missouri across the plains; (3) by the Three Forks of the Missouri. For instance, it was coming down the Platte that poor Scott's canoe was overturned, his powder lost, and his rifles rendered useless. Game had retreated to the mountains with spring's advance. Berries were not ripe by the time trappers were descending with their winter's hunt. Scott and his famishing men could not find edible roots. Each day Scott weakened. There was no food. Finally, Scott had strength to go no farther. His men had found tracks of some other hunting party far to the fore. They thought that, in any case, he could not live. What ought they to do? Hang back and starve with him, or hasten forward while they had strength, to the party whose track they had espied? On pretence of seeking roots, they deserted the helpless man. Perhaps they did not come up with the advance party till they were sure that Scott must have died; for they did not go back to his aid. The next spring when these same hunters went up the Platte, they found the skeleton of poor Scott sixty miles from the place where they had left him.

The terror that spurred the emaciated man to drag himself all this weary distance can barely be conceived; but such were the fearful odds taken by every free trapper who went up the Platte, across the parched plains, or to the head waters of the Missouri.

The time for the free trappers to go out was, in Indian language, "when the leaves began to fall." If a mighty hunter like Colter, the trapper was to the savage "big Indian me"; if only an ordinary vagrant of woods and streams, the white man was "big knife you," in distinction to the red man carrying only primitive weapons. Very often the free trapper slipped away from the fur post secretly, or at night; for there were questions of licenses which he disregarded, knowing well that the buyer of his furs would not inform for fear of losing the pelts. Also and more important in counselling caution, the powerful fur companies had spies on the watch to dog the free trapper to his hunting-grounds; and rival hunters would not hesitate to bribe the natives with a keg of rum for all the peltries which the free trapper had already bought by advancing provisions to Indian hunters. Indeed, rival hunters have not hesitated to bribe the savages to pillage and murder the free trapper; for there was no law in the fur trading country, and no one to ask what became of the free hunter who went alone into the wilderness and never returned.

Going out alone, or with only one partner, the free hunter encumbered himself with few provisions. Two dollars worth of tobacco would buy a thousand pounds of "jerked" buffalo meat, and a few gaudy trinkets for a squaw all the pemmican white men could use.

Going by the river routes, four days out from St. Louis brought the trapper into regions of danger. Indian scouts hung on the watch among the sedge of the river bank. One thin line of upcurling smoke, or a piece of string—babiche((leather cord, called by the Indians assapapish)—fluttering from a shrub, or little sticks casually dropped on the river bank pointing one way, all were signs that told of marauding bands. Some birch tree was notched with an Indian cipher—a hunter had passed that way and claimed the bark for his next year's canoe. Or the mark might be on a cottonwood—some man wanted this tree for a dugout. Perhaps a stake stood with a mark at the entrance to a beaver-marsh—some hunter had found this ground first and warned all other trappers off by the code of wilderness honour. Notched tree-trunks told of some runner gone across country, blazing a trail by which he could return. Had a piece of fungus been torn from a hemlock log? There were Indians near, and the squaw had taken the thing to whiten leather. If a sudden puff of black smoke spread out in a cone above some distant tree, it was an ominous sign to the trapper. The Indians had set fire to the inside of a punky trunk and the shooting flames were a rallying call.

In the most perilous regions the trapper travelled only after nightfall with muffled paddles—that is, muffled where the handle might strike the gunwale. Camp-fires warned him which side of the river to avoid; and often a trapper slipping past under the shadow of one bank saw hobgoblin figures dancing round the flames of the other bank—Indians celebrating their scalp dance. In these places the white hunter ate cold meals to avoid lighting a fire; or if he lighted a fire, after cooking his meal he withdrew at once and slept at a distance from the light that might betray him.

The greatest risk of travelling after dark during the spring floods arose from what the voyageurs called embarras—trees torn from the banks sticking in the soft bottom like derelicts with branches to entangle the trapper's craft; but the embarras often befriended the solitary white man. Usually he slept on shore rolled in a buffalo-robe; but if Indian signs were fresh, he moored his canoe in mid-current and slept under hiding of the driftwood. Friendly Indians did not conceal themselves, but came to the river bank waving a buffalo-robe and spreading it out to signal a welcome to the white man; when the trapper would go ashore, whiff pipes with the chiefs and perhaps spend the night listening to the tales of exploits which each notch on the calumet typified. Incidents that meant nothing to other men were full of significance to the lone voyageur through hostile lands. Always the spring floods drifted down numbers of dead buffalo; and the carrion birds sat on the trees of the shore with their wings spread out to dry in the sun. The sudden flacker of a rising flock betrayed something prowling in ambush on the bank; so did the splash of a snake from over-hanging branches into the water.

Different sorts of dangers beset the free trapper crossing the plains to the mountains. The fur company brigades always had escort of armed guard and provision packers. The free trappers went alone or in pairs, picketing horses to the saddle overlaid with a buffalo-robe for a pillow, cooking meals on chip fires, using a slow-burning wormwood bark for matches, and trusting their horses or dog to give the alarm if the bands of coyotes hovering through the night dusk approached too near. On the high rolling plains, hostiles could be descried at a distance, coming over the horizon head and top first like the peak of a sail, or emerging from the "coolies"—dried sloughs—like wolves from the earth. Enemies could be seen soon enough; but where could the trapper hide on bare prairie? He didn't attempt to hide. He simply set fire to the prairie and took refuge on the lee side. That device failing, he was at his enemies' mercy.

On the plains, the greatest danger was from lack of water. At one season the trapper might know where to find good camping streams. The next year when he came to those streams they were dry.

—◦—

"After leaving the buffalo meadows a dreadful scarcity of water ensued," wrote Charles MacKenzie, of the famous MacKenzie clan. He was journeying north from the Missouri. "We had to alter our course and steer to a distant lake. When we got there we found the lake dry. However, we dug a pit which produced a kind of stinking liquid which we all drank. It was salt and bitter, caused an inflammation of the mouth, left a disagreeable roughness of the throat, and seemed to increase our thirst. . . . We passed the night under great uneasiness. Next day we continued our journey, but not a drop of water was to be found, . . . and our distress became insupportable. . . . All at once our horses became so unruly that we could not manage them. We observed that they showed an inclination towards a hill which was close by. It struck me that they might have scented water. . . . I ascended to the top, where, to my great joy, I discovered a small pool. . . . My horse plunged in before I could prevent him, . . . and all the horses drank to excess."

—◦—

"The plains across"—which was a western expression meaning the end of that part of the trip—there rose on the west rolling foothills and dark peaked profiles against the sky scarcely to be distinguished from gray cloud banks. These were the mountains; and the real hazards of free trapping began. No use to follow the easiest passes to the most frequented valleys. The fur company brigades marched through these, sweeping up game like a forest fire; so the free trappers sought out the hidden, inaccessible valleys, going where neither pack horse nor canot à bec d'esturgeon could follow. How did they do it? Very much the way Simon Fraser's hunters crawled down the river-course named after him. "Our shoes," said one trapper, "did not last a single day."

"We had to plunge our daggers into the ground, . . . otherwise we would slide into the river," wrote Fraser. "We cut steps into the declivity, fastened a line to the front of the canoe, with which some of the men ascended in order to haul it up. . . . Our lives hung, as it were, upon a thread, as the failure of the line or the false step of the man might have hurled us into eternity. . . . We had to pass where no human being should venture. . . . Steps were formed like a ladder on the shrouds of a ship, by poles hanging to one another and crossed at certain distances with twigs, the whole suspended from the top to the foot of immense precipices, and fastened at both extremities to stones and trees."

He speaks of the worst places being where these frail swaying ladders led up to the overhanging ledge of a shelving precipice.

Such were the very real adventures of the trapper's life . . .

CHAPTER 5

The Happy Mountain Man

By George Laycock

As you'll discover in this wonderful story from George Laycock's book, The Mountain Men, Joe Meek did not stand out from the crowd because he was happy. As a group, mountain men were boisterous fun-loving individuals, always ready for a good time, especially a "spree" as they called drunken parties. Meek became an iconic mountain man by experiencing dangerous situations in the wild many others never survived.

JOE MEEK WAS A BIG MAN WHO SMILED EASILY AND LIKED A GOOD TIME. He sometimes played jokes on his friends just for the hell of it. One fine day Meek and three other trappers were up on the Pryor's River in Yellowstone Country setting their traps when Meek had what he thought was a clever idea.

As they approached a narrow pass known as Pryor's Gap, where prudent men might logically expect an Indian ambush, Meek dashed ahead on his spirited white horse. He was only a short distance into the pass when he wheeled about, lowered his large frame close against his mount's neck, and, in a cloud of dust, raced back at breakneck speed, his horse under spur and quirt. Meek's companions knew the signals; old Joe had sure enough run into a passel of Injuns and the time had come to vacate this place if they hankered to keep their hair.

Meek had cried "wolf" without saying a word and was having a big chuckle watching the other trappers race off down the trail at top speed, until he glanced over his shoulder. There, sure enough, came a Blackfoot war party, whooping and yelling, and trying to get within range.

The Blackfeet, who had been waiting in ambush, were on foot, however, because their common practice in dose-quarter fighting was to hide their horses, slip about in the thick vegetation, and take their enemies by surprise. This tactic came within moments of working and, except for Joe Meek's love of a joke, the Blackfeet might have shot him from their ambush.

Meek's encounters with Indians sometimes took on a more serious complexion. On a May morning in 1834, when he and five other trappers were trespassing on Comanche hunting grounds near the Arkansas River in southern Colorado, they saw in the distance, across the open plain, a large party of Comanches riding hell-bent toward them. Meek and his party, a hundred and fifty miles from the main body of their group, knew they could expect neither help nor mercy.

Their problem was compounded by the fact that they were out in plain view and there was not a bush or ravine to hide them. Running would only delay the inevitable torture and death. The Comanche, known as excellent horsemen, were mounted on powerful animals.

Meek glanced at his companions, one of whom was Kit Carson. Almost without a word they leaped from their frightened mules and formed the animals into a tight circle. Then, holding the reins tightly, each man slipped his butcher knife from his belt and cut his mule's throat. The weakening animals soon slid to their knees and fell in a ring around them. Then, digging as fast as possible with their knives, the trappers prepared the best fort they could of dirt and warm horseflesh.

The screaming Comanches, more than a hundred strong, their head medicine man in the lead, drew closet; weapons waving above their heads, feathers flying in the breeze. Then, before they could get into range with their spears, their horses slid to a halt and milled about. They had caught the scent of the mules' fresh blood and would come no closer which was exactly what Meek and Carson expected.

The Indians had made the mistake of coming within reach of the trappers' deadly rifles. According to plan, three of the trappers shot while the others held their fire until the first three could reload. This put three dead Comanches on the ground, among them their medicine man. The Indians drew back, reformed, chose a new leader, attacked again, and three more Comanches were added to the dead.

All day the little party, surrounded by its dead mules, repulsed the Comanche attacks. According to Joe Meek's story, which was written down for him in 1870 by journalist Frances Fuller Victor in a book entitled The River of the West, "The burning sun of the plains shone on them, scorching them to faintness. Their faces were begrimed with powder and dust; their throats parched and tongues swollen with thirst, and their whole frames aching from their cramped positions, as well as the excitement and fatigue of the battle."

This was simply the price of survival. They knew their enemy well enough to understand the kind of death awaiting them if they were overrun. Time and again throughout that bright May day, the Indians repeated their attack. And time and again they left dead warriors behind. As darkness settled over the plain, the Indians drew back. Their women, who came to drag away the dead, had now recovered forty-two bodies, taking time meanwhile to taunt the mountain men for fighting like women behind dead mules.

That night the trappers slipped away, leaving behind their packs of furs. They carried only their guns and blankets as they started for camp a hundred and fifty miles away. Their task now was to put enough distance between themselves and the Comanche that the Indians would give up the pursuit. They settled down to a steady dog trot, and ran all night, then kept on going. According to Victor, they ran seventy-five miles before coming to water, then, after refreshing themselves, ran another seventy-five miles into camp.

This escape supplied fresh material for Meek's stories around the campfires and at rendezvous. Meek could hold an audience spellbound, for in a frontier society that developed storytelling to an art form, Joe Meek was a master.

Most mountain men came from poor backgrounds, but Joe Meek grew up on a Virginia plantation. He had resisted schooling but he had some education. He was tall, powerfully built, and considered handsome with his broad shoulders and dark eyes. As a young man he was filled with a longing for adventure and, unhappy under the stern eye of a stepmother, he left home for the frontier. Before long he was across the Mississippi and headed for the mountains and the headwaters of the Missouri. He spent the next eleven years in the mountains.

His frequent encounters with grizzly bears figured heavily in Meek's stories. The tale that brought the biggest laughs was Joe's account of the bear that he and another trapper spotted one day across the Yellowstone River. The temptation was too strong to resist. The two trappers took careful aim and shot the bear, dropping him on the spot. The only problem then was getting enough of the animal back to camp to prove that they had really shot another grizzly.

They tied their horses, stripped off their clothes, leaned their guns against a cottonwood, and wearing nothing but their belt knives, stepped into the frigid waters of the Yellowstone. They came dripping out on the far side, climbed the steep bank, and approached the bear just as it recovered its senses. The beast rose to its feet and, as Meek told Mrs. Victor, "took after us."

With the injured bear on their heels, the two naked trappers bolted for the river. "The bank war about fifteen feet high above the water," said Meek, "and the river ten or twelve feet deep; but we didn't halt. Overboard we went, the bar after us, and in the stream about as quick as we war."

The bear tried desperately to get at one of them, but the trappers went in opposite, directions and came out on the side of the stream where they had begun their swim, while the confused bear landed on the opposite shore. The strong current had carried the trappers a mile downstream, and they picked their way ·back barefoot through the cactus to their well-rested mules. Even then, they brought back nothing to prove their story.

An even closer call came for Meek on the late winter day that he and his companions discovered large grizzly bear tracks in front of a mountainside cave. It had been a harsh winter. Meat was scarce in the trappers' camp. The buffalo had moved out ahead of winter and other game was rare. Little bands of trappers scoured the surrounding countryside for meat to feed themselves, with perhaps some left over to bring back to camp. The hunting parties were sometimes out for a week or more at a time.

The trappers frequently faced hunger, even in summer. On one occasion, Meek, travelling with a brigade led by Milton Sublette, crossed an extensive plain where they could find no food for man or beast. As Meek later told Mrs. Victor, "I have held my hands in an ant-hill until they were covered with the ants, then greedily licked them off. I have taken the soles off my moccasins, crisped them in the fire, and eaten them." They also captured the large, black crickets, tossed them into a kettle of hot water, then ate them as soon as they stopped kicking. Or they would bleed a mule and sup on the blood, taking care not to drain too much because the mule was as weak as they were. On this day Meek and his companions climbed a long slope watching for bighorn sheep. They found no wild sheep, but along a rocky ledge discovered the footprints of the "enormous" grizzly. The bear sign told them that the grizzly had taken refuge in a nearby cavern after a brief appearance in the open, as wintering bears will sometimes do.

One of the trappers suggested that somebody should go into the cave and drive the bear out, and he would be waiting on a rock above so he could shoot the beast when it appeared. Meek said, "I'll send old grizz out or I wouldn't say so." Two other trappers, willing to prove their courage, joined him and they headed for the cave.

The entrance was high enough for them to walk in upright, and they moved slowly into the shadows, senses at full alert. As Meek told the story, their eyes adjusted to the dim light, and they saw an extremely large bear standing in the middle of the cave, staring at them. As the rest of the scene came into focus, they realized that two only slightly smaller bears flanked the big one. There were grizzlies enough to go around.

Inching closer, Meek's story claimed that he struck the big bear with his "wiping stick." This made it run past the trappers toward the entrance and as it emerged, the first trapper shot the bear, but not too well, so it wheeled about and dashed back into the cave where, in the half-light, the trappers finished it. The young bears were chased from the cave and promptly fell to the concentrated shots of the other hunters. That night there were fresh roasts over the fire for the whole camp-and a fresh round of storytelling.

Meek's most famous bear encounter occurred along the Yellowstone when he and two other trappers spotted a large bear busily digging roots beside the creek. Meek could not let the bear go its way without giving it one from Old Sally. His plan called for him to slip up and shoot the bear while his companions held his horse in readiness, in case he had to make a fast escape.

As he told Mrs. Victor, he slipped to within forty paces before bringing his gun up, but when he pulled the trigger, the cap burst. The sound was enough to alert the feeding bear. Baring her teeth, and growling from deep in her throat, the old bear rushed down on Meek, whose legs were pumping as fast as they could in his frantic effort to reach his horse, while attempting all the while to put another cap on the nipple of his gun. He was almost within reach of his jittery horse when all the horses and their riders bolted, leaving Meek alone with a maddened grizzly. The bear promptly ripped his belt off.

By now Meek's story is going very well. He explains that he had managed to put a new cap on his gun so he stuck the muzzle into the bear's mouth and pulled the trigger, but found that he had failed to set the double-triggered gun. The bear was angrier than ever. Just as Meek managed to set the triggers, the grizzly gave the gun a swat, knocking it from her mouth.

In that instant the gun fired but the bullet struck her well clear of her vitals, and this new injury added fuel to her anger. Then two large cubs, learning by example, joined their mother in attacking the trapper. The old bear knocked Meek's gun out of his hands, and he drew his knife. He stabbed her deeply behind the ear before she whipped a paw up, with lighting swiftness, and swatted that weapon from his hand also.

She was so angry that she next began abusing the cubs, which mother bears will often do under similar stressful circumstances, While she was engaged in this disciplinary action, Meek had time to get his tomahawk, his last weapon, into action. The bear now had him backed up against a rock ledge from which there was no escape. He was weaving and swaying like a boxer, following every movement of the old female grizzly until he saw his opportunity. With all his force he brought the tomahawk down behind her ear and sank the sharp blade into her brain. The mighty grizzly slumped to the ground and lay dead at his feet.

Another time, on Pryor's River, Meek and a companion went to run their beaver traps where the high banks above the river are lined with thickets of wild plum and willow. Meek had an uncanny feeling that there were strangers nearby. Two or three times he saw wild game running from the thicket. Osborne Russell recorded the event in his Journal of a Trapper.

Meek and his companion Dave Crow, a quiet little man who had been fifteen years in the Rockies, rode into Jim Bridger's camp where Russell was one of the brigade, and Russell heard Meek tell Bridger about the experience.

> *I have been, me and Dave, over on to Priors Fork to set our traps . . . Gabe, do you know where Prior leaves the cut bluffs going up it? . . . Well after you get out of the hills on the right hand fork there is scrubby box elders about 3 miles along the Creek up to where a little right hand spring branch puts in with lots and slivers of Plum trees about the mouth of it and some old beaver dams at the mouth on the main Creek? Well sir we went up there and yesterday morning I set two traps right below the mouth of that little branch and in them old dams and Dave set his down the creek apiece, so after we had got our traps set we cruised round and eat plums a while, the best plums I ever saw is there. The trees are loaded and breaking down to the ground with the finest kind as large as Pheasants eggs and sweet as sugar they almost melt in yo mouth no wonder them rascally Savages like that place so well—Well sir after we had eat what plums we wanted me and Dave took down the creek and staid all night on a little branch in the hills and this morning started to our traps we came up to Dave's traps in the first there was a 4 year old 'spade' the next was false lickt went to the next and it had cut a foot and none of the rest disturbed, we then went up to mine to the mouth of the branch I rode on 5 or 6 steps ahead of Dave and just as I got opposite the first trap I heard a rustling in the bushes within about five steps of me I looked round and pop pop pop went the guns covering me with smoke so close that I could see the blanket wads coming out of the muzzles. Well sir I wheeled and a ball struck Too shebit [Meek's horse] in the neck . . . and we pitched heels overhead but Too shebit raised runnin and I on his back and the savages just squattin and grabbin at me but I raised a fog for about half a mile till I overtook Dave.*

Even on his injured horse, Meek outdistanced the Indians, and he and Dave made it in to Bridger's camp.

In 1835, Meek's good friend and "booshway" Milt Sublette came down from the mountains and went east to get medical treatment for an old foot injury that was growing steadily more painful. The problem eventually claimed Sublette's life. As Meek tells it, Milt left behind his beautiful Indian wife, whom he called Isabel, and who was known among her people as Mountain Lamb. Meek had long admired her, and he told Mrs. Victor that Mountain Lamb was "the most beautiful Indian woman I ever saw." He described the dapple gray on which Mountain Lamb rode, her fine decorated clothing, and beautiful, braided black hair. Once Sublette was gone, said Meek, Mountain Lamb became Joe Meek's wife. Her life thereafter seems so filled with turbulence that one suspects Joe of story enhancement again.

One day when the camp was moving, she failed to keep up and a dozen Crow warriors swooped in and captured her. The enraged Meek and half a dozen friends took chase. He rode right in among the enemy shooting as fast as he could load. He and his companions killed two of the kidnappers, the rest fled, and Meek proudly led his wife back to camp.

Another day a few Crow warriors were visiting the trapper's camp when one of them made a serious error in etiquette. The records do not tell us why it happened. We learn only that this Crow warrior slapped the Mountain Lamb on her backside and Meek, as anyone might have predicted, shot him on the spot. "Nobody slaps Joe Meek's wife," he said. But Mountain Lamb did not have much time left. She and Meek had been together for only one year when, as the story goes, she died from a wound inflicted by a Bannock arrow.

With the fur business winding down, Meek, after eleven years in the mountains, began looking toward Oregon. He moved out with a wagon train of settlers, preachers, and gamblers. With him was his new wife, Virginia, a Nez Perce. They arrived in the Willamette Valley late in 1840.

In Oregon, Meek's Indian wife and half-blood children met frequent prejudice, but the family became prominent and Meek became a frontier leader. He farmed for a while, was elected sheriff, and was appointed United States Marshal of the new Territory. He later held other offices. Joe Meek, the happy mountain man, died proud of the fact that, "I never tried to act like anybody but myself."

CHAPTER 6

The Snow Tramp

By Lewis H. Garrard

This excerpt from Garrard's Wah-To-Yah and the Taos Trail *(1850)
is a veritable showcase for the author's talent for describing the action
in language that makes the experiences real. The life we feel resonating
from Garrard's prose comes from our sense of being beside a camp-
fire with the narrator, hearing him speak as a mountain man telling
his story. Were they tall tales? Sometimes. But often they were as real
as life could make them, and in Garrard's case that meant gripping
adventures, having his audience hanging on every word. In this story
his companion referred to simply as "Smith" is John Smith, whose
explorations became well documented in mountain man literature.*

On the 8th, we packed our robes, and possibles,
and, by eleven o'clock, the wagon, with its two yoke
of half-famished oxen attached, ready for a start,
was on the top of the hill. The sun shone clear,
reflecting, in the intense cold, from the incrusted
snow points, millions of miniature diamonds. We
parted cheerfully with our kind-hearted Indian host,
Se-ne-mone ; and, I did not omit to take the hand
of his daughter, "red-dress," to tell her "goodbye."
At the same instant, the recollections of the gay dan-
ces around scalps in her company, with other grace-
ful Houris, enveloped in the same blanket, and our
commingled hay-he-a-hay (scalp chorus) rising

above the other voices, sent a momentary pang vibrating through me. I half wanted to stay. The poor, shivering Indians, standing in the deep snow, saw us off.

The surface of the country, on this (the south) side of the river, was greatly broken. Large sandhills sloped to the river's very edge : others, with a strip of land intervening, were frequent; the loose, slippy nature of which made the footing uncertain, the travel laborious. The poor oxen, toiling through snow up to the briskets, were to be pitied. The Bent's Fort trail was on the opposite side.

We went on for some hours ; now on the steep side of a glazed sand butte, now on top, with the freezing wind shooting pains through our heads ; now again stretching across a low bottom, at a tediously slow rate. On the exclamation by the blue-lipped squaw, of " Po-ome ! na-wa 'sst," we looked the direction she pointed, to perceive an Indian urging his animal through the snow with all speed.

Ten-o-wast ("What is it?") asked Smith, making " sign," as the savage drew rein along side, most opportunely for his panting animal.

The amount of the conversation was, that he had a "big heart" for Pinto; he loved him very much, and, in a few moments, his saddle was changed to Pinto, and, shaking hands with us, he urged him back toward the village, while we kept out way.

We talked of the battle of New Orleans (this was the anniversary)—of the bravery evinced—the probability' of another war : but, plowing through the snow, and the tingling cold, were no aids to prolonged dissertations on the merits and demerits of Jackson and his army. A little more severe weather would have dismounted us.

With all our steady travel, we made no more
than five or six miles, and encamped, as the sun was
waning beyond the snowbanks ahead, sheltered
in rear by a sparse growth of stunted willows.

We felt with our feet, on the river's edge, for pieces
of wood, and, with numbed fingers, knocked the snow
from them. These, with the aid of a few handfuls of
dead willow twigs, served as fuel. Watering the animals through a hole in the ice-bound river, they
were hobbled in a hollow, and left exposed to the
"storm's pitiless peltings," to eke a scanty meal
from the weeds and stray blades of grass laid bare
by the frame-pervading blasts. We cut brush, and
clearing a small space of the snow, laid our robes
and blankets on the boughs, and, sitting, with crossed
legs, stared at the flickering blaze, rising through
the still and piercing air, our pipes charged
with fragrant "honeydew," or "single twist;" the
holders every moment blowing out blue clouds of
smoke, calculated, at most any other time, to sicken,
but now, not a bit too strong. By turning our eyes
to the darkness, we could see the dusky forms of our
congregated caballada, with backs bowed, and tails
to the blast, too cold to paw for grass, now snorting
as a hungry wolf crossed the wind, or feebly an-
swering an inquiring whinney from a timid mule,
scared at its own tramping in the dry, frosty snow.

It is strange how self-satisfied one is, when safely
in camp. There we, almost at an unapproachable
distance from anywhere, amid snowstorms, with
scarce a hearty meal, in a barren country, and too
freezing cold to hunt, sat on our soft robes, acknow-
ledging the grateful warmth of the coals (shuddering, perhaps, as a cold puff of wind, coursing on
the crusted snow, struck our backs, and caused us

*to pull the blankets more closely to our necks)—
chatting as unconcernedly, as if surrounded by luxu-
ries, such as large fires, and plenty to eat. It is by
some experience in a prairie voyageur s life, that I
can say, never was I more contented, silently happy
than when, with snow wreaths drifted interminably
for miles and miles around, with a choice companion or two, cozily seated by a small comfortable fire, with plenty of tobacco, and a modicum of
meat to sustain life, I have listened to the baying of
wolves, and have imagined the Hamadryads' tune-
ful sighs, mingling with the crackling of the frosted
tree branches, while the mournful cadences of the
wind, sweeping up the vale with wild fury, would
burst over our heads, with shrieks of crazy delight
—now dying away in harmonious deflections, anon
increasing in vigor, yet never ending.*

*And, on composing oneself to sleep, with what
care does he place his feet, well-covered by thick
moccasins, to the broadest blaze. Then, sitting on
his robe, he tucks it around his legs and body, high
as the waist, and falls back with his face from rude
Boreas, retaining his soft wool hat, to serve as a
breakwind to his head, resting on the saddle for
pillow. There he is, warm, comfortable, and selfish
—nothing short of Indians, or fire on the dear robe,
would stir him an inch. Then, in the morning, how
hard he is to rouse. His cold blue nose, exposed to
the weather, is sensitive enough, in its gradations
from warm to cold, to serve as thermometer—
"b 'low zero, wagh ! too cold," and he draws within
himself, shuddering at the bare idea of facing the
breeze. "Darn breakfast, when a feller's fixed; I
would 'nt git up for the fattest meat as runs on the per-
aira ; t'aint't often this buffler is comfortable, an' when
he is, he knows it," and oft' he drops in dreamland,*

"Chasing the stag
From crag to crag,"

indicating, by convulsive twitchings of the hands,
or contortions of the face, the contending passions
by which he is actuated when in quest of game, or
"raising the hair" of a skulking Pawnee, who
has been audacious and unfortunate enough to steal
his animals.

Our Mexican was up first, and kindled a fire.
All soon rising, we drove the caballada to camp,
from the leeward of a bank, whither they had
retreated, standing with low, drooping heads, and
indicating, by a glance at their hollow flanks, the
scanty meal they had eaten; choosing rather to
starve, than push away with aching noses, or paw
with balled feet, the cold snow from the withered
herbage of this region, at no time remarkable in
excellency.

The morning was bitter, bitter cold. The exhaled
breath rapidly condensed; which, with the blowing
of the animals as they were forced over the deep
snow, enveloped us in a cloud of vapor. We
strung out, one or the other in front; the Mexican
with his ox team following. In the wake was our
squaw, astride of a large sorrel horse, muffled in
robes. Clinging to her back was the boy, Wo-pe-
kon-ne ["White Eyes], with his lint white locks, grayish-white
eyes, and sallow face, visible through an opening—
an airhole—in the hairy covering.

About eleven o'clock, in the morning, we saw a
party of men trailing toward the States. Urging
our mules through the snow, nearly breast high, to
the river, we were met by one of them, who crossed
the ice on foot. He was almost hid in the folds of a
robe overcoat, extra moccasins, heavy hat, and his

*right hand grasped a thick, large-bored rifle. On
nearing, he shouted—"How are ye. Smith, old coon.
Whar now—are ye makin' tracks to Fort William?"*

*"Why, Boggs, old hos," rejoined Smith, "what's
up? you've got so much 'fofaraw' stuck 'bout you,
this child didn't savy at fust! Which way?"*

*"Well, old Kurnel Price wanted some one to take
the trail fur the States on express; and, as none
but mountain men can 'come in' now, he gave me
six hundred dollars to 'travel' with letters and
dispatches. But, I tell 'ee it '11 be a chargin' time,
fur the snow is bad some, now."*

*"Who's with you; right sort of stuff for this
season?"*

*"Oh ! a lot of darned gover'ment men ; but as
I'm 'bugheway' [bourgeoise—master] they do pretty well.
Well, I must break—how are ye off for cow meat?"*

*"H—! cow meat, this freezin' time? You've bin
down to Santy Fee too long. Why, 'poor bull' is
hard to git, boudin out of the question, and 'gras'
so scarce we don't think of it. Howsomever, if
you want to chaw on lean buffler dryed, you can
have it 'on the prairie.' Hombre, Pedro, mira!
Venica cary por carne, poquita! " Pedro, look here,
want a little meat," shouted Smith to our Mexican.*

*"Na-ioa ! o-ne-a-voke veheo. (" Quick, some meat
for the whiteman")—to his squaw.*

*He took about half—not much to be sure, but
seemingly a great deal—and crossed the river,
while we started the team, the wagon wheels creak-
ing and singing as they pressed the stalagmitic
snow. We were thoroughly benumbed, and rode
in a state nearly amounting to torpidity. How
I silently wished for the warm and pleasant home
left but a few months previous. How we longed*

for fire—no wood to be had—even coffee would
have given comfort. Our pipes were the only
solace in this trying time, but one tires of that, or
sickens by too frequent use. As far as the eye
could reach, on all sides, was a boundless expanse
of snow, snow, snow ! above, the dreary, dull-gray
winter sky ; no sun to cheer us, or to impart warmth.
Every step, every motion, every glance, bore down
instead of relieving us. I shut my eyes, wearied and
sick of the white monotonous drapery ; which, in
my bewildered fancy, seemed to look on unmoved
at us stiffening by degrees ; and, by mocking, freezing
placidity, to check all buoyant hope or retrospect.
To add to the wretchedness of mind, large, gaunt
white wolves, attracted through keen hunger, stealthily followed, or dashed across our way like specters
—spirits of the storm wind—and burst, hell-hound
like, into prolonged, fearful howls, rousing us from
our apathy, to cause shudders to pervade our chilled
and weakened frames.

Camp at night and its few duties soon were completed, for our provision (if a little dried meat,
without bread, coffee, or salt could be called provision) was scanty, requiring no cooking or preparation but thorough mastication.

Sunrise saw us on the tramp. It was so cold,
Smith left his gun (a most foolish thing, not to be
expected of a mountaineer) in the wagon. Though
I hardly had the sense of feeling , I retained my rifle
in front of the saddle. In the afternoon we were
finding a practicable route in the drifts, for the
team; and, in so doing, strayed several hundred
yards ahead, and out of sight of the wagon. Seeing
a party approaching. Smith called my attention to
it with—

"Look ahead ! there's white men."

I gave a shout, at the same moment digging my
spurs into the mule's side—"Hooray, we'll have
meat and coffee tonight ; but look ! they wear
Mexican hats."

"So they do," replied he, after a scrutiny ; " but
they wont bother us, they know me too well to cut
shines'—John Smith's a name not to be grinned at
by a darned carahoing 'palou'—Wagh! Indians,
'by beaver !' "hurriedly said he, changing his tone,
" keep your eye skinned ; I have left my gun in
the wagon, and have nothing but a knife."

I put on a fresh cap without changing its position,
so as not to excite the attention of the coming-
party, though one gun was as nothing against thirty
Arapahoes. We met them with as little show of
trepidation as could be helped, and advancing to
the foremost grim savage, offered our hands. The
fellow took the proffered advance of amity with
coldness, and stopped still. We dared not pass by,
and asked him—

"Ten-o-wast ?" [What is it you wish?]

He looked silently at us, and again we chidingly
asked, in the Cheyenne tongue, "Ten-o-wast?"

"Ni-hi-ni, veheo, rnatsebo, esvone Arapaho," answered
he. The amount of his answer was, that the
" white man was bad, that he ran the buffalo out of
the country, and starved the Arapaho."

Smith explained, that he had been trading a long
time with the Cheyenne, whom he loved, and who
was brother to the Arapaho ; that he only took
what meat he wanted, and, pointing to his squaw,
that his wife was a Cheyenne. The Arapaho must
not blame him. It was the white man from the
States (Government men) with wagons, who scared
the buffalo from him and his children. It was always his intention to live and die with the Che-

68

*yenne, for he had thrown away his brothers in the
States. The Cheyenne lodge was his home—they
smoked the same pipe—the broad prairie supported
them both.*

*"The white man has a forked tongue," replied the
chief, impatiently, raising his hand to his mouth,
and sending it in a direct line with two of the fingers open, and stretched far apart, to signify a fork
or divergence from a point.*

"I-sto-mct, wah-hein." (p'shaw, no) said Smith.

*"Ni-hi-ni, ni-hi-ni, Hook-ah-hay." (Yes, yes. Good-
Bye.) and, off they rode, trying, yet, without much
open manifestation, to drive our little band of horses
with theirs, but, by a dexterous interposition of
Smith, he turned their heads, preventing the quiet
trick of our brothers, the Arapahoes.*

*Smith told me, after they left, that they were just
returning from a successful marauding expedition
into New Mexico, with several scalps, two prisoners,
and thirty, or more, horses and mules, which they
then had with them. Happily was it for us, that
their vengeance was wreaked on other unfortunates
than ourselves. We, however, feared for our
swarthy son of Mexico, the ox driver—as he was of
the same stripe, as those to whom the scalps, dangling from the Arapaho lance points, originally belonged. We waited, with some doubts, as to his
safety, until he made his appearance.*

*The poor wretch ! there he came, plying the whip
vigorously to his tired yoke. When, within hearing
distance, we distinguished the fierce spoken words,
"Geet up—caraho ! Wo-o ha-ha—los Rapaho."*

"Did you see the Indians, Pedro ?"

*"Si Senor, a-a-h Caraho ! los Rapaho ; muchos
diablos—grandote, muchos, muchos, muchos. Damn the
Arapahoes—big devils."*

"Did they touch you, the darned niggurs ?"

"Si !" replied he, in a tone of vexation, "Si, mucho, dis a way," jerking himself to and fro by the hair, " dis a way, pull me bout, de damn Rapaho ; dey want carne (meat), want carabine, dey want mucho ; and," added he, ready to burst into tears, " dey want my hair. Me feel for my cuchillo (knife), but de one lancero grandote, he luk mad—he raise his lance. By by dey mount de cavallos (horses), dey go way—"

"Yes !" said Smith, " but, it's too cold here to talk—start up your team, we must be to a good camp before night, for it'll freeze the nose off a feller's face in the morning."

The queerest part of this meeting with the Indians, was, that after their departure, Smith upbraided me for turning pale, and showing fear, while his face was blanched, and wore a peculiar rigidity of features, and nervous twinkling of the eyelids. The fact is, we were both scared badly.

An hour before the sun set, saw us stopping on an island, for the sake of a little dry grass for the animals, and the twisted, partly decayed stump of a fallen cottonwood for ourselves—both things quite essential this inclement season.

My mule was an obstinate, foolish animal, and, to keep her from returning to the village, a hobble was necessary every night. The rest of the caballada was as usual, snorting and pawing for grass, or wandering around, before mine was let loose ; and while I, in the snow, was adjusting the hobble, she was impatiently stamping, and frettingly held by the bridle. So soon as I rose to my feet, and pulled the headstall from her brow, off she started, with a squeal, the rein still on her neck. To prevent her

*trampling on the bit, I caught it in my hand and
kept up alongside. She rushed in the water,
splashing my moccasins and buckskins to the knee ;
by the time she hauled me in the ripple, to her satisfaction, and jerked me down several times, my
scalp knife was out of its sheath.*

*To keep my limbs from freezing, from the effects
of the already congealed water, with which my moccasins and pants were saturated, while Smith and
Pedro were making a fire, I took a sheet-iron camp-
kettle—an Indian article of trade—to the river for
water, which labor might restore the circulation.
Under a bank, several springs kept the water from
freezing hard ; I broke it with but little difficulty,
and, reaching down the bucket to dip and fill it, in I
followed. Scrambling out, I hm'ried to camp with
the water in frozen pellets on my clothes and
hair.*

*Smith, standing with back to the fire, shouted as
I approached, "Ho, boy ! wet ? you 're more like a
ducked beaver 'an anything this hos has seen yet.
Cold, eh?"*

*"Caraho!" cried Pedro, looking up from the
ground, where he was seated, drying his torn moccasins. "Senor, tu muy freo ?" (Are you very cold ?)*

*We cleared the snow for several feet around the
fire, so as not to melt and make a muddy camp.
Spreading down my robe, I wrung and dried my
clothes.*

*For supper each took a little piece of dried buf-
falo meat, and chewed on it until the strength was
gone ; then, smoking, we went to bed, to dream of
the many good things some persons have and know
not how to appreciate. Being now not at all
fastidious, Pedro and I shared the same robes.*

*In the morning, seeing that the caballada had
had but little to eat, and the cold being so intense,
a day in camp was thought best. A snowstorm,
with all its blustering fury, burst upon us during the
morning, and lasted half the day, driving the rotten-
wood smoke in our eyes, so that small comfort was
gained by the fire. We would sit in one position
until nearly stifled; a change to the opposite side,
was only for the wind to veer and drive us again
away. We had no tent of course, and the shifting
wind monopolized every good position.*

*What a prospect was in advance! Snow twenty-
two to twenty-eight inches deep; our mules starving;
the oxen broken down with fatigue; and not more
than one day's scanty portion of dried meat, and
nothing else; an attempt at hunting almost certain
death; and, at least, two days' travel to William
Bent's village; although there were but forty miles
between the two (one day's trip in pleasant weather;
now five for us). Verily, this is the dark side of
prairie life!*

*We ventured to start the following morning, but
dared not ride for fear of freezing to the saddles,
though tramping in the snow was severely fatiguing.*

*The few pairs of socks brought with me from the
States were long before worn out, and my moccasins
coming only to the anklebone, left bare part of the
foot and leg. The snow soon filled the hollow
under the instep, which I, at first, raked out with
my forefinger; but, becoming so benumbed, I forgot
it, and it congealed, unheeded, in a solid mass.*

*We kept on foot all that day, without stopping,
dragging one weary foot after the other, until near
night, and encamped on an island, with plenty of*

*wood and high grass. Our mules procured their
food only by pawing, in which mode they became
adepts. With tobacco, and a stinted ration of
"poor bull," we managed to pass the evening.*

*We left camp, the next sunrise, with keen appe-
tites and nothing to eat, and traveled the entire day
without stopping. An hour or two- before dark,
Smith approached some antelope, leaving his bridle-
rein in the squaw's hand. The band, afar off,
scented us, though they scarcely moved; while we
anxiously watched Smith, stealthily drawing nigh.
Hunger rendered him cautious ; and, when within
two hundred yards, he fired, bringing down a doe.
The others ran across the river, stopping once to
gaze back at their fallen companion. I imagined
the teardrops glistening in their big dark eyes.
Our hearts were now made glad, for we had a
prospect of plenty ; and, as Fortune never comes
single-handed, the snow decreased in depth, enabling
us to travel in a fast walk. At camp, we used part
of the rather unmasticable and poor goat ; which,
however, was better than nothing ; and, to make
up for the deficiency of our larder of the past few
days, we lingered by the red coals late.*

*Did anyone ever hear of the Gros Ventres Indians ?
Well, we were the same, so far as the name goes,
about the hour for retiring.*

*The travel improved ; snow not more than twelve
or fourteen inches in depth. The oxen labored less
heavily. Smith's gravity relaxed in a degree ; and
I, being crammed with goatmeat, felt finely.*

*Near noon the squaw cried out—Po-ome,na-wa
Chcyennes! "Blackfoot (Smith), look ahead, Chey-*

*enne !" pointing to an approaching body of men,
women, children, horses, and lodges. It was part
of the upper village, on the march.*

*The first few we merely saluted en passant. Then
came the "Morning Mist" and her father, Vip-
po-nah; and, after them, "Smiling Moon," riding
on a lodge dray. Her kind eyes beamed with tem-
pered rays of affection ; but Smith marred the
pleasurableness of our meeting by informing me
that she had, during my absence, married—run off
with one of the village exquisites. I was quite
unhappy for an hour, and rode, in silence, apart
from the joking Smith; but, finally, consoled myself
with the idea that there was more than one pretty
Indian girl left in the world.*

*We found William Bent in his lodge, with hia
squaws, children, and goods for trading. A few
steps distant was another cone, in which were
Fisher and Long Lade, traders, and Pierre, and one
other, employees. We abode in the back part.
The village was a quarter of a mile off—a de
sirable distance—for we could trade without the
usual bother and throng. No snow, but on the
shady declivities, chilled us with the sight ; the sun
shone joyously ; the horses capered on the green
sward, and the dull, but comfort-recalling drum-
notes, in honor of fresh scalps, were heard once
more. We reclined that night in the warm lodge,
with feet to the fire, new faces to look at, and
stomachs filled with "fat cow" and coffee. A
casual observer could have seen, by the smoke,
which so gracefully curled from our pipes, that
contentment reigned within.*

CHAPTER 7

Beaver Country:
Skills and Lore of the Mountain Men

By A. C. Laut

The mountain men weren't out there to pan for gold. Hunting was an everyday affair, made something glorious when buffalo herd were around. Also an everyday affair was eluding Indians, or negotiating with them if possible when in their country. To make a living, however, to pay for the supplies they would need to stay in the high country, the mountain man had to trap beaver and prepare the pelts. Here's how they did it, as told by A. C. Laut in his book The Story of the Trapper, *1902.*

ALL SUMMER LONG HE HAD HUNG ABOUT THE FUR COMPANY TRADING-posts waiting for the signs.

And now the signs had come.

Foliage crimson to the touch of night-frosts. Crisp autumn days, spicy with the smell of nuts and dead leaves. Birds flying away southward, leaving the woods silent as the snow-padded surface of a frozen pond. Hoar-frost heavier every morning; and thin ice edged round stagnant pools like layers of mica.

Then he knew it was time to go. And through the Northern forests moved a new presence—the trapper.

Of the tawdry, flash clothing in which popular fancy is wont to dress him he has none. Bright colours would be a danger-signal to game. If his costume has any colour, it is a waist-belt or neck-scarf, a toque or bright handkerchief round his head to keep distant hunters from mistaking him for a moose. For the rest, his clothes are as ragged as any old, weather-worn garments. Sleeping on balsam boughs or cooking over a smoky fire will reduce the newness of blanket coat and buckskin jacket to the dun shades of the grizzled forest. A few days in the open and the trapper has the complexion of a bronzed tree-trunk.

Like other wild creatures, this foster-child of the forest gradually takes on the appearance and habits of woodland life. Nature protects the ermine by turning his russet coat of the grass season to spotless white for midwinter—except the jet tail-tip left to lure hungry enemies and thus, perhaps, to prevent the little stoat degenerating into a sloth. And the forest looks after her foster-child by transforming the smartest suit that ever stepped out of the clothier's bandbox to the dull tints of winter woods.

This is the seasoning of the man for the work. But the trapper's training does not stop here.

When the birds have gone south the silence of a winter forest on a windless day becomes tense enough to be snapped by either a man's breathing or the breaking of a small twig; and the trapper acquires a habit of moving through the brush with noiseless stealth. He must learn to see better than the caribou can hear or the wolf smell—which means that in keenness and accuracy his sight outdistances the average field-glass. Besides, the trapper has learned how to look, how to see, and seeing—discern; which the average man cannot do even through a field-glass. Then animals have a trick of deceiving the enemy into mistaking them for inanimate things by suddenly standing stock-still in closest peril, unflinching as stone; and to match himself against them the trapper must also get the knack of instantaneously becoming a statue, though he feel the clutch of bruin's five-inch claws.

And these things are only the a b c of the trapper's woodcraft.

One of the best hunters in America confessed that the longer he trapped the more he thought every animal different enough from the fellows of its kind to be a species by itself. Each day was a fresh page in the book of forest-lore.

It is in the month of May-goosey-geezee, the Ojibways' trout month, corresponding to the late October and early November of the white man, that the trapper sets out through the illimitable stretches of the forest land and waste prairie south of Hudson Bay, between Labrador and the Upper Missouri.

His birch canoe has been made during the summer. Now, splits and seams, where the bark crinkles at the gunwale, must be filled with rosin and pitch. A light sled, with only runners and cross frame, is made to haul the canoe over still water, where the ice first forms. Sled, provisions, blanket, and fish-net are put in the canoe, not forgetting the most important part of his kit—the trapper's tools. Whether he hunts from point to point all winter, travelling light and taking nothing but absolute necessaries, or builds a central lodge, where he leaves full store and radiates out to the hunting-grounds, at least four things must be in his tool-bag: a woodman's axe; a gimlet to bore holes in his snow-shoe frame; a crooked knife—not the sheathed dagger of fiction, but a blade crooked hook-shape, somewhat like a farrier's knife, at one end—to smooth without splintering, as a carpenter's plane; and a small chisel to use on the snow-shoe frames and wooden contrivances that stretch the pelts.

If accompanied by a boy, who carries half the pack, the hunter may take more tools; but the old trapper prefers to travel light. Fire-arms, ammunition, a common hunting-knife, steel-traps, a cotton-factory tepee, a large sheet of canvas, locally known as abuckwan, for a shed tent, complete the trapper's equipment. His dog is not part of the equipment: it is fellow-hunter and companion.

From the moose must come the heavy filling for the snow-shoes; but the snow-shoes will not be needed for a month, and there is no haste about shooting an unfound moose while mink and musk-rat and otter and beaver are waiting to be trapped. With the dog showing his wisdom by sitting motionless as an Indian bowman, the trapper steps into his canoe and pushes out.

Eye and ear alert for sign of game or feeding-place, where traps would be effective, the man paddles silently on. If he travels after night-fall, the chances are his craft will steal unawares close to a black head above a swimming body. With both wind and current meeting the canoe, no suspicion of his presence catches the scent of the sharp-nosed swimmer. Otter or beaver, it is shot from the canoe. With a leap over bow or stern—over his master's shoulder if necessary, but never sideways, lest the rebound cause an upset—the dog brings back his quarry. But this is only an aside, the hap-hazard shot of an amateur hunter, not the sort of trapping that fills the company's lofts with fur bales.

While ranging the forest the former season the trapper picked out a large birch-tree, free of knots and underbranching, with the full girth to make the body of a canoe from gunwale to gunwale without any gussets and seams. But birch-bark does not peel well in winter. The trapper scratched the trunk with a mark of "first-finder-first-owner," honoured by all hunters; and came back in the summer for the bark.

Perhaps it was while taking the bark from this tree that he first noticed the traces of beaver. Channels, broader than runnels, hardly as wide as a ditch, have been cut connecting pool with pool, marsh with lake. Here are runways through the grass, where beaver have dragged young saplings five times their own length to a winter storehouse near the dam. Trees lie felled miles away from any chopper. Chips are scattered about marked by teeth which the trapper knows—knows, perhaps, from having seen his dog's tail taken off at a nip, or his own finger amputated almost before he felt it. If the bark of a tree has been nibbled around, like the line a chopper might make before cutting, the trapper guesses whether his coming has not interrupted a beaver in the very act.

All these are signs which spell out the presence of a beaver-dam within one night's travelling distance; for the timid beaver frequently works at night, and will not go so far away that forage cannot be brought in before daylight. In which of the hundred water-ways in the labyrinth of pond and stream where beavers roam is this particular family to be found?

Realizing that his own life depends on the life of the game, no true trapper will destroy wild creatures when the mothers are caring for their young. Besides, furs are not at their prime when birch-bark is peeled, and the trapper notes the place, so that he may come back when the fall hunt begins. Beaver kittens stay under the parental roof for three years, but at the end of the first summer are amply able to look after their own skins. Free from nursery duties, the old ones can now use all the ingenuity and craft which nature gave them for self-protection. When cold weather comes the beaver is fair game to the trapper. It is wit against wit. To be sure, the man has superior strength, a gun, and a treacherous thing called a trap. But his eyes are not equal to the beaver's nose. And he hasn't that familiarity with the woods to enable him to pursue, which the beaver has to enable it to escape. And he can't swim long enough under water to throw enemies off the scent, the way the beaver does.

Now, as he paddles along the network of streams which interlace Northern forests, he will hardly be likely to stumble on the beaver-dam of last summer. Beavers do not build their houses, where passers-by will stumble upon them. But all the streams have been swollen by fall rains; and the trapper notices the markings on every chip and pole floating down the full current. A chip swirls past white and fresh cut. He knows that the rains have floated it over the beaver-dam. Beavers never cut below their houses, but always above, so that the current will carry the poles down-stream to the dam.

Leaving his canoe-load behind, the trapper guardedly advances within sight of the dam. If any old beaver sentinel be swimming about, he quickly scents the man-smell, upends and dives with a spanking blow of his trowel tail on the water, which heliographs danger to the whole community. He swims with his webbed hind feet, the little fore paws being used as carriers or hanging limply, the flat tail acting the faintest bit in the world like a rudder; but that is a mooted question. The only definitely ascertained function of that bat-shaped appendage is to telegraph danger to comrades. The beaver neither carries things on his tail, nor plasters houses with it; for the simple reason that the joints of his caudal appur-tenance admit of only slight sidelong wigglings and a forward sweep between his hind legs, as if he might use it as a tray for food while he sat back spooning up mouthfuls with his fore paws.

Having found the wattled homes of the beaver, the trapper may pro-ceed in different ways. He may, after the fashion of the Indian hunter, stake the stream across above the dam, cut away the obstruction lowering the water, break the conical crowns of the houses on the south side, which is thinnest, and slaughter the beavers indiscriminately as they rush out. But such hunting kills the goose that lays the golden egg; and explains why it was necessary to prohibit the killing of beaver for some years. In the con-fusion of a wild scramble to escape and a blind clubbing of heads there was bootless destruction. Old and young, poor and in prime, suffered the same fate. The house had been destroyed; and if one beaver chanced to escape into some of the bank-holes under water or up the side channels, he could be depended upon to warn all beaver from that country. Only the degenerate white man practices bad hunting. The skilled hunter has other methods.

If unstripped saplings be yet about the bank of the stream, the beavers have not finished laying up their winter stores in adjacent pools. The trapper gets one of his steel-traps. Attaching the ring of this to a loose trunk heavy enough to hold the beaver down and drown him, he places the trap a few inches under water at the end of a runway or in one of the channels. He then takes out a bottle of castoreum. This is a substance from the glands of a beaver which destroys all traces of the man-smell. For it the beavers have a curious infatuation, licking everything touched by it, and said, by some hunters, to be drugged into a crazy stupidity by the very smell. The hunter daubs this on his own foot-tracks.

Or, if he finds tracks of the beaver in the grass back from the bank, he may build an old-fashioned deadfall, with which the beaver is still taken in Labrador. This is the small lean-to, with a roof of branches and bark—usually covered with snow—slanting to the ground on one side, the ends either posts or logs, and the front an opening between two logs wide enough to admit half the animal's body. Inside, at the back, on a rectangular stick, one part of which bolsters up the front log, is the bait. All traces of the hunter are smeared over with the elusive castoreum. One tug at the bait usually brings the front log crashing down across the animal's back, killing it instantly.

But neither the steel-trap nor the deadfall is wholly satisfactory. When the poor beaver comes sniffing along the castoreum trail to the steel-trap and on the first splash into the water feels a pair of iron jaws close on his feet, he dives below to try and gain the shelter of his house. The log plunges after him, holding him down and back till he drowns; and his whereabouts are revealed by the upend of the tree.

But several chances are in the beaver's favour. With the castoreum licks, which tell them of some other beaver, perhaps looking for a mate or lost cub, they may become so exhilarated as to jump clear of the trap. Or, instead of diving down with the trap, they may retreat back up the bank and amputate the imprisoned foot with one nip, leaving only a mutilated paw for the hunter. With the deadfall a small beaver may have gone entirely inside the snare before the front log falls; and an animal whose teeth saw through logs eighteen inches in diameter in less than half an hour can easily eat a way of escape from a wooden trap. Other things are against the hunter. A wolverine may arrive on the scene before the trapper and eat the finest beaver ever taken; or the trapper may discover that his victim is a poor little beaver with worthless, ragged fur, who should have been left to forage for three or four years.

———

All these risks can be avoided by waiting till the ice is thick enough for the trapper to cut trenches. Then he returns with a woodman's axe and his dog. By sounding the ice, he can usually find where holes have been hollowed out of the banks. Here he drives stakes to prevent the beaver taking refuge in the shore vaults. The runways and channels, where the beaver have dragged trees, may be hidden in snow and iced over; but the man and his dog will presently find them.

The beaver always chooses a stream deep enough not to be frozen solid, and shallow enough for it to make a mud foundation for the house without too much work. Besides, in a deep, swift stream, rains would carry away any house the beaver could build. A trench across the upper stream or stakes through the ice prevent escape that way.

The trapper then cuts a hole in the dam. Falling water warns the terrified colony that an enemy is near. It may be their greatest foe, the wolverine, whose claws will rip through the frost-hard wall as easily as a bear delves for gophers; but their land enemies cannot pursue them into water; so the panic-stricken family—the old parents, wise from many such alarms; the young three-year-olds, who were to go out and rear families for themselves in the spring; the two-year-old cubbies, big enough to be saucy, young enough to be silly; and the baby kittens, just able to forage for themselves and know the soft alder rind from the tough old bark unpalatable as mud—pop pell-mell from the high platform of their houses into the water. The water is still falling. They will presently be high and dry. No use trying to escape up-stream. They see that in the first minute's wild scurry through the shallows. Besides, what's this across the creek? Stakes, not put there by any beaver; for there is no bark on. If they only had time now they might cut a passage through; but no—this wretched enemy, whatever it is, has ditched the ice across.

They sniff and listen. A terrible sound comes from above—a low, exultant, devilish whining. The man has left his dog on guard above the dam. At that the little beavers—always trembling, timid fellows—tumble over each other in a panic of fear to escape by way of the flowing water below the dam. But there a new terror assails them. A shadow is above the ice, a wraith of destruction—the figure of a man standing at the dam with his axe and club—waiting.

Where to go now? They can't find their bank shelters, for the man has staked them up. The little fellows lose their presence of mind and their heads and their courage, and with a blind scramble dash up the remaining open runway. It is a cul-de-sac. But what does that matter? They run almost to the end. They can crouch there till the awful shadow goes away. Exactly. That is what the man has been counting on. He will come to them afterward.

The old beavers make no such mistake. They have tried the hollow-log trick with an enemy pursuing them to the blind end, and have escaped only because some other beaver was eaten.

The old ones know that water alone is safety.

That is the first and last law of beaver life. They, too, see that phantom destroyer above the ice; but a dash past is the last chance. How many of the beaver escape past the cut in the dam to the water below, depends on the dexterity of the trapper's aim. But certainly, for the most, one blow is the end; and that one blow is less cruel to them than the ravages of the wolf or wolverine in spring, for these begin to eat before they kill.

A signal, and the dog ceases to keep guard above the dam. Where is the runway in which the others are hiding? The dog scampers round aimlessly, but begins to sniff and run in a line and scratch and whimper. The man sees that the dog is on the trail of sagging snow, and the sag betrays ice settling down where a channel has run dry. The trapper cuts a hole across the river end of the runway and drives down stakes. The young beavers are now prisoners.

The human mind can't help wondering why the foolish youngsters didn't crouch below the ice above the dam and lie there in safe hiding till the monster went away. This may be done by the hermit beavers—fellows who have lost their mates and go through life inconsolable; or sick creatures, infested by parasites and turned off to house in the river holes; or fat, selfish ladies, who don't want the trouble of training a family. Whatever these solitaries are—naturalists and hunters differ—they have the wit to keep alive; but the poor little beavers rush right into the jaws of death. Why do they? For the same reason probably, if they could answer, that people trample each other to death when there is an alarm in a crowd.

—◆—

They cower in the terrible pen, knowing nothing at all about their hides being valued all the way from fifty cents to three dollars, according to the quality; nothing about the dignity of being a coin of the realm in the Northern wilderness, where one beaver-skin sets the value for mink, otter, marten, bear, and all other skins, one pound of tobacco, one kettle, five pounds of shot, a pint of brandy, and half a yard of cloth; nothing about the rascally Indians long ago bartering forty of their hides for a scrap of iron and a great company sending one hundred thousand beaver-skins in a single year to make hats and cloaks for the courtiers of Europe; nothing about the laws of man forbidding the killing of beaver till their number increase.

All the little beaver remembers is that it opened its eyes to daylight in the time of soft, green grasses; and that as soon as it got strong enough on a milk diet to travel, the mother led the whole family of kittens—usually three or four—down the slanting doorway of their dim house for a swim; and that she taught them how to nibble the dainty, green shrubs along the bank; and then the entire colony went for the most glorious, pell-mell splash up-stream to fresh ponds. No more sleeping in that stifling lodge; but beds in soft grass like a goose-nest all night, and tumbling in the water all day, diving for the roots of the lily-pads. But the old mother is always on guard, for the wolves and bears are ravenous in spring. Soon the cubs can cut the hardening bark of alder and willow as well as their two-year-old brothers; and the wonderful thing is—if a tooth breaks, it grows into perfect shape inside of a week.

By August the little fellows are great swimmers, and the colony begins the descent of the stream for their winter home. If unmolested, the old dam is chosen; but if the hated man-smell is there, new waterways are sought. Burrows and washes and channels and retreats are cleaned out. Trees are cut and a great supply of branches laid up for winter store near the lodge, not a chip of edible bark being wasted. Just before the frost they begin building or repairing the dam. Each night's frost hardens the plastered clay till the conical wattled roof—never more than two feet thick—will support the weight of a moose.

All work is done with mouth and fore paws, and not the tail. This has been finally determined by observing the Marquis of Bute's colony of beavers. If the family—the old parents and three seasons' offspring—be too large for the house, new chambers are added. In height the house is seldom more than five feet from the base, and the width varies. In building a new dam they begin under water, scooping out clay, mixing this with stones and sticks for the walls, and hollowing out the dome as it rises, like a coffer-dam, except that man pumps out water and the beaver scoops out mud. The domed roof is given layer after layer of clay till it is cold-proof. Whether the houses have one door or two is disputed; but the door is always at the end of a sloping incline away from the land side, with a shelf running round above, which serves as the living-room. Differences in the houses, breaks below water, two doors instead of one, platforms like an oven instead of a shelf, are probably explained by the continual abrasion of the current. By the time the ice forms the beavers have retired to their houses for the winter, only coming out to feed on their winter stores and get an airing.

But this terrible thing has happened; and the young beavers huddle together under the ice of the canal, bleating with the cry of a child. They are afraid to run back; for the crunch of feet can be heard. They are afraid to go forward; for the dog is whining with a glee that is fiendish to the little beavers. Then a gust of cold air comes from the rear and a pole prods forward.

The man has opened a hole to feel where the hiding beavers are, and with little terrified yelps they scuttle to the very end of the runway. By this time the dog is emitting howls of triumph. For hours he has been boxing up his wolfish ferocity, and now he gives vent by scratching with a zeal that would burrow to the middle of earth.

The trapper drives in more stakes close to the blind end of the channel, and cuts a hole above the prison of the beaver. He puts down his arm. One by one they are dragged out by the tail; and that finishes the little beaver—sacrificed, like the guinea-pigs and rabbits of bacteriological laboratories, to the necessities of man. Only, this death is swifter and less painful. A prolonged death-struggle with the beaver would probably rob the trapper of half his fingers. Very often the little beavers with poor fur are let go. If the dog attempts to capture the frightened runaways by catching at the conspicuous appendage to the rear, that dog is likely to emerge from the struggle minus a tail, while the beaver runs off with two.

Trappers have curious experiences with beaver kittens which they take home as pets. When young they are as easily domesticated as a cat, and become a nuisance with their love of fondling. But to them, as to the hunter, comes what the Indians call "the-sickness-of-long-thinking," the gipsy yearning for the wilds. Then extraordinary things happen. The beaver are apt to avenge their comrades' death. One old beaver trapper of New Brunswick related that by June the beavers became so restless, he feared their escape and put them in cages. They bit their way out with absurd ease.

He then tried log pens. They had eaten a hole through in a night. Thinking to get wire caging, he took them into his lodge, and they seemed contented enough while he was about; but one morning he wakened to find a hole eaten through the door, and the entire round of birch-bark, which he had staked out ready for the gunwales and ribbing of his canoe—bark for which he had travelled forty miles—chewed into shreds. The beavers had then gone up-stream, which is their habit in spring.

CHAPTER 8

The Way West

Lewis and Clark Reach the Pacific

From *The Journals of Lewis and Clark*

LIKE MOUNTAIN CLIMBERS WHO GAIN THE SUMMITS OF PEAKS LIKE MT. EVEREST, then perish on the route down, Meriwether Lewis and William Clark faced a similar fate after they reached the Pacific Ocean. Their journey across the continent, 4,102 miles Lewis figured, had started in St. Louis in May, 1804. Now, in November, 1805, within sight of the destination of their dreams, the waves of the Pacific splashing in their ears, they pondered the run for home. Making their way back across the Rocky Mountains, the Continental Divide, then beginning a downstream run—the tributaries of the Missouri, then the Missouri itself back to St. Louis. Another 4,000 miles. Their Corps of Discovery now carried maps and facts about the Rocky Mountains and the streams leading to the Columbia and the Pacific: There was no single waterway across the continent; the Missouri River came from the Rockies not the country beyond them. Lewis and Clark were also eager to tell President Thomas Jefferson—who had so ardently conceived and sponsored their expedition—about the multitudinous wildlife and the Indian tribes they had encountered. They completed their epic voyage in 1806, arriving in St. Louis that September. The Journals of Lewis and Clark, *from which this excerpt is taken, have been compiled and translated in many different versions. In them, spelling is primitive; the descriptions often inadequate, leaving the reader hungry for more details. That can be clearly seen here, in the day the Pacific comes into view. Clark's description makes the event sound almost ordinary. All his journal entries are that way. Lewis, at that part of the journals, was writing no entries at all. So we are left with Clark, telling us about the difficulties the Corps faced on the edge of the Pacific. There are many books about Lewis and Clark, but if you want to follow their journey in a single great book, don't miss Stephen Ambrose's Undaunted Courage. It is a masterpiece, expanding on the day-by-day left by these two intrepid explorers.*

[Clark, November 3, 1805]
November 3rd Sunday 1805
The Fog So thick this morning that we could not See a man 50 Steps off, this fog detained us untill 10 oClock at which time we Set out, accompanied by our Indian friends who are from a village near the great falls, previous to our Setting out Collins killed a large Buck, and Labiech killed 3 Geese flying. I walked on the Sand beech Lard. Side, opposit the canoes as they passed allong. The under groth rushes, vines &c. in the bottoms too thick to pass through, at 3 miles I arrived at the enterance of a river which appeared to Scatter over a Sand bar, the bottom of which I could See quite across and did not appear to be 4 Inches deep in any part; I attempted to wade this Stream and to my astonishment found the bottom a quick Sand, and impassable—I called to the Canoes to put to Shore, I got into the Canoe and landed below the mouth, & Capt Lewis and my Self walked up this river about 11/2 miles to examine this river which we found to be a verry Considerable Stream Dischargeing its waters through 2 Chanels which forms an Island of about 3 miles in length on the river and 1 1/2 miles wide, composed of Corse Sand which is thrown out of this quick Sand river Compressing the waters of the Columbia and throwing the whole Current of its waters against its Northern banks, within a Chanel of 1/2 a mile wide, Several Small Islands 1 mile up this river, This Stream has much the appearance of the River Plait; roleing its quick Sands into the bottoms with great velocity after which it is divided into 2 Chanels by a large Sand bar before mentioned, the narrowest part of this River is 120 yards-on the Opposit Side of the Columbia a falls in above this Creek on the Same Side is a Small prarie. extensive low country on each Side thickly timbered.

The Quick Sand river appears to pass through the low countrey at the
foot of those high range of mountains in a Southerly direction,—The
large Creeks which fall into the Columbia on the Stard. Side rise in
the Same range of mountains to the N. N. E. and pass through Some
ridgey land—A Mountain which we Suppose to be Mt. Hood is S. 85 E
about 47 miles distant from the mouth of quick sand river This mtn. is
Covered with Snow and in the range of mountains which we have passed
through and is of a Conical form but rugid—after takeing dinner at the
mouth of this river we proceeded on passed the head of a Island near
the lard Side back of which on the Same Side and near the head a large
Creek falls in, and nearly opposit & 3 miles below the upper mouth of
quick Sand river is the lower mouth, This Island is 31/2 miles long,
has rocks at the upper point, Some timber on the borders of this Island
in the middle open and ponney. Some rugid rocks in the middle of the
Stream opposit this Island. proceeded in to Center of a large Island in
the middle of the river which we call Dimond Isld. from its appearance,
here we met 15 Indn men in 2 canoes from below, they informed us they
Saw 3 vestles below &c. &c. we landed on the North Side of this Dimond
Island and Encamped, Capt. L walked out with his gun on the Island,
Sent out hunters & fowlers—below quick Sand River the Countrey is low
rich and thickly timbered on each Side of the river, the Islands open &
Some ponds river wide and emence numbers of fowls flying in every
direction Such as Swan, geese, Brants, Cranes, Stalks, white guls,
comerants & plevers &c. also great numbers of Sea Otter in the river—a
Canoe arrived from the village below the last rapid with a man his wife
and 3 children, and a woman whome had been taken prisoner from the
Snake Inds. on Clarks River I Sent the Interpreters wife who is a So So
ne or Snake Indian of the Missouri, to Speake to this Squar, they Could
not understand each other Sufficiently to Converse. This familey and
the Inds. we met from below continued with us Capt Lewis borrowed a
Small Canoe of those Indians & 4 men took her across to a Small lake in
the Isld. Cap L. and 3 men Set out after night in this Canoe in Serch
of the Swans, Brants Ducks &c. &c. which appeared in great numbers in
the Lake, he Killed a Swan and Several Ducks which made our number of

fowls this evening 3 Swan, 8 brant and 5 Ducks, on which we made a Sumptious Supper. We gave the Indian-who lent the Canoe a brant, and Some meat to the others. one of those Indians, the man from the village near the lower Rapids has a gun with a brass barrel & Cock of which he prises highly—note the mountain we Saw from near the forks proves to be Mount Hood

[Clark, November 4, 1805]
Novr. 4th Monday 1805 A Cloudy Cool morning, wind West, we Set out at 1/2 past 8 oClock having dispatched 4 men in the Small canoe to hunt

(Those people men & women heads are flat)

We landed at a village 200 men of Flatheads of 25 houses 50 canoes built of Straw, we were treated verry kindly by them, they gave us round root near the Size of a hens egg roasted which they call Wap-to to eate

I walked out on the Stard. Side found the country fine, an open Prarie for 1 mile back of which the wood land comence riseing back, the timber on the edge of the Prarie is white oke, back is Spruce pine & other Species of Pine mixed Some under groth of a wild crab & a Specis of wood I'm not acquainted, a Specis of maple & Cotton wood grow near this river, Some low bushes

Indians continue to be with us, Several Canoes Continue with us, The Indians at the last village have more Cloth and uriopian trinkets than above I Saw Some Guns, a Sword, maney Powder flasks, Salers jackets, overalls, hats & Shirts, Copper and Brass trinkets with few Beeds only. dureing the time I was at Dinner the Indians Stold my tomahawk which I made use of to Smoke I Serched but Could not find it, a Pond on the Stard Side, off from the river. Raspberries and _____ are also in the bottoms—met a large and Small canoe with 12 men from below the men were dressed with a variety of articles of European manufactory the large Canoe had emeges on the bow & Stern handsomly Carved in wood &

painted with the figur of a Bear in front & man in a Stern. Saw white geese with black wings—Saw a Small Crab-apple with all the taste & flavor of the Common—Those Indians were all armed with Pistols or bows and arrows ready Sprung war axes &c.

Mount Hellen bears N. 25° E about 80 miles, this is the mountain we Saw near the foks of this river. it is emensely high and covered with Snow, riseing in a kind of Cone perhaps the highest pinecal from the common leavel in america passed a village of 4 hs. on the Stard Side at 2 mils, one at 3 mls.

One deer 2 Ducks & Brant killed

[Clark, November 4, 1805]
November 4th Monday 1805
A cloudy cool morning wind from the West we Set out at 1/2 past 8 oClock, one man Shannon Set out early to walk on the Island to kill Something, he joined us at the lower point with a Buck. This Island is 6 miles long and near 3 miles wide thinly timbered (Tide rose last night 18 inches perpndicular at Camp) near the lower point of this dimond Island is The head of a large Island Seperated from a Small one by a narrow chanel, and both Situated nearest the Lard Side, those Islands as also the bottoms are thickly Covered with Pine &c. river wide, Country low on both Sides; on the Main Lard Shore a Short distance below the last Island we landed at a village of 25 Houses; 24 of those houses were thached with Straw, and covered with bark, the other House is built of boards in the form of those above, except that it is above ground and about 50 feet in length and covered with broad Split boards This village contains about 200 men of the Skil-loot nation I counted 52 canoes on the bank in front of this village maney of them verry large and raised in bow. we recognised the man who over took us last night, he invited us to a lodge in which he had Some part and gave us a roundish roots about the Size of a Small Irish potato which they roasted in the embers until they became Soft, This root they call Wap-pa-to which the Bulb of the Chinese cultivate in great

95

quantities called the Sa-git ti folia or common arrow head-. it has an agreeable taste and answers verry well in place of bread. we purchased about 4 bushels of this root and divided it to our party, at 7 miles below this village passed the upper point of a large Island nearest the Lard Side, a Small Prarie in which there is a pond opposit on the Stard. here I landed and walked on Shore, about 3 miles a fine open Prarie for about 1 mile, back of which the countrey rises gradually and wood land comencies Such as white oake, pine of different kinds, wild crabs with the taste and flavour of the common crab and Several Species of undergroth of which I am not acquainted, a few Cottonwood trees & the Ash of this countrey grow Scattered on the river bank, Saw Some Elk and Deer Sign and Joined Capt. Lewis at a place he had landed with the party for Diner. Soon after Several Canoes of Indians from the village above came down dressed for the purpose as I Supposed of Paying us a friendly visit, they had Scarlet & blue blankets Salors jackets, overalls, Shirts and Hats independant of their Usial dress; the most of them had either war axes Spears or Bows Sprung with quivers of arrows, Muskets or pistols, and tin flasks to hold their powder; Those fellows we found assumeing and disagreeable, however we Smoked with them and treated them with every attention & friendship.

dureing the time we were at dinner those fellows Stold my pipe Tomahawk which They were Smoking with, I imediately Serched every man and the canoes, but Could find nothing of my Tomahawk, while Serching for the Tomahawk one of those Scoundals Stole a Cappoe of one of our interpreters, which was found Stufed under the root of a treer, near the place they Sat, we became much displeased with those fellows, which they discovered and moved off on their return home to their village, except 2 canoes which had passed on down—we proceeded on met a large & a Small Canoe from below, with 12 men the large Canoe was orniminted with Images carved in wood the figures of a Bear in front & a man in Stern, Painted & fixed verry netely on the of the Canoe, rising to near the hight of a man two Indians verry finely Dressed & with hats on was in this canoe passed the lower point of the Island which is nine miles in length haveing passed 2 Islands on the Stard Side of this large

Island, three Small Islands at its lower point. the Indians make Signs
that a village is Situated back of those Islands on the Lard. Side and
I believe that a Chanel is Still on the Lrd, Side as a Canoe passed in
between the Small Islands, and made Signs that way, probably to
traffick with Some of the nativs liveing on another Chanel, at 3 miles
lower, and 12 Leagues below quick Sand river passed a village of four
large houses on The Lard. Side, near which we had a full view of Mt.
Helien which is perhaps the highest pinical in America from their base
it bears N. 25° E about 90 miles—This is the mountain I Saw from the
Muscle Shell rapid on the 19th of October last Covered with Snow, it
rises Something in the form of a Sugar lofe—about a mile lower passed
a Single house on the Lard. Side, and one on the Stard. Side, passed a
village on each Side and Camped near a house on the Stard. Side we
proceeded on untill one hour after dark with a view to get clear of the
nativs who was constantly about us, and troublesom, finding that we
could not get Shut of those people for one night, we landed and
Encamped on the Stard. Side Soon after 2 canoes Came to us loaded with
Indians, we purchased a fiew roots of them.

This evening we Saw vines much resembling the raspberry which is verry
thick in the bottoms. A range of high hills at about 5 miles on the
Lard Side which runs S. E. & N. W. Covered with tall timber the bottoms
below in this range of hills and the river is rich and leavel, Saw
White geese with a part of their wings black. The river here is 1 1/2
miles wide, and current jentle. opposit to our camp on a Small Sandy
Island the brant & geese make Such a noise that it will be impossible
for me to Sleap. we made 29 miles to day Killed a Deer and Several
brant and ducks. I Saw a Brarow tamed at the 1st village to day The
Indians which we have passd to day of the Scil-loot nation in their
language from those near & about the long narrows of the
Che-luc-it-te-quar or E-chee-lute, their dress differ but little,
except they have more of the articles precured from the white traders,
they all have flatened heads both men and women, live principally on
fish and Wap pa toe roots, they also kill Some fiew Elk and Deer,
dureing the Short time I remained in their village they brought in

*three Deer which they had killed with their Bow & arrows. They are
thievishly inclined as we have experienced.*

[Clark, November 5, 1805]
Novr. 5th Tuesday 1805
*a Cloudy morning Som rain the after part of last night & this morning.
I could not Sleep for the noise kept by the Swans, Geese, white & black
brant, Ducks &c. on a opposit base, & Sand hill Crane, they were
emensely numerous and their noise horrid. We Set out at Sun rise & our
hunters killed 10 Brant 4 of which were white with black wings 2 Ducks,
and a Swan which were divided, we Came too and Encamped on the Lard.
Side under a high ridgey land, the high land come to the river on each
Side. the river about 1 1/2 mile wide. those high lands rise gradually
from the river & bottoms—we are all wet Cold and disagreeable, rain
Continues & encreases. I killed a Pheasent which is very fat—my feet
and legs cold. I saw 17 Snakes to day on a Island, but little
appearance of Frost at this place.*

[Clark, November 5, 1805]
November 5th Tuesday 1805
*Rained all the after part of last night, rain continues this morning, I
slept but verry little last night for the noise Kept dureing the whole
of the night by the Swans, Geese, white & Grey Brant Ducks &c. on a
Small Sand Island close under the Lard. Side; they were emensely
noumerous, and their noise horid—we Set out early here the river is
not more than 3/4 of a mile in width, passed a Small Prarie on the
Stard. Side passed 2 houses about 1/2 a mile from each other on the
Lard. Side a Canoe came from the upper house, with 3 men in it mearly
to view us, passed an Isld. Covered with tall trees & green briers
Seperated from the Stard. Shore by a narrow Chanel at 9 miles I
observed on the Chanel which passes on the Stard Side of this Island a
Short distance above its lower point is Situated a large village, the
front of which occupies nearly 1/4 of a mile fronting the Chanel, and
closely Connected, I counted 14 houses in front here the river widens
to about 1 1/2 miles. Seven canoes of Indians came out from this large*

village to view and trade with us, they appeared orderly and well disposed, they accompanied us a fiew miles and returned back. about 11 1/2 miles below this village on the Lard Side behind a rockey Sharp point, we passed a Chanel 1/4 of a mile wide, which I take to be the one the Indian Canoe entered yesterday from the lower point of Immage Canoe Island a Some low clifts of rocks below this Chanel, a large Island Close under the Stard Side opposit, and 2 Small Islands, below, here we met 2 canoes from below,—below those Islands a range of high hills form the Stard. Bank of the river, the Shore bold and rockey, Covered with a thick groth of Pine an extensive low Island, Seperated from the Lard side by a narrow Chanel, on this Island we Stoped to Dine I walked out found it open & covered with grass interspersed with Small ponds, in which was great numbr. of foul, the remains of an old village on the lower part of this Island, I saw Several deer our hunters killed on this Island a Swan, 4 white 6 Grey brant & 2 Ducks all of them were divided, below the lower point of this Island a range of high hills) which runs S. E. forms the Lard. bank of the river the Shores bold and rockey & hills Covered with pine, The high hills leave the river on the Stard. Side a high bottom between the hill & river. We met 4 Canoes of Indians from below, in which there is 26 Indians, one of those Canoes is large, and orniminted with Images on the bow & Stern. That in the Bow the likeness of a Bear, and in Stern the picture of a man—we landed on the Lard. Side & camped a little below the mouth of a creek on the Stard. Side a little below the mouth of which is an Old Village which is now abandaned; here the river is about one and a half miles wide, and deep, The high Hills which run in a N. W. & S. E. derection form both banks of the river the Shore boald and rockey, the hills rise gradually & are Covered with a thick groth of pine &c. The valley which is from above the mouth of Quick Sand River to this place may be computed at 60 miles wide on a Derect line, & extends a great Distanc to the right & left rich thickly Covered with tall timber, with a fiew Small Praries bordering on the river and on the Islands; Some fiew Standing Ponds & Several Small Streams of running water on either Side of the river; This is certainly a fertill and a handsom valley, at this time Crouded with Indians. The day proved Cloudy with rain the greater

part of it, we are all wet cold and disagreeable—I Saw but little
appearance of frost in this valley which we call Wap-pa-loo Columbia
from that root or plants growing Spontaneously in this valley only In
my walk of to Day I saw 17 Striped Snakes I killed a grouse which was
verry fat, and larger than Common. This is the first night which we
have been entirely clear of Indians Since our arrival on the waters of
the Columbia River. We made 32 miles to day by estimation-

[Clark, November 6, 1805]
November 6th Wednesday a cold wet morning. rain Contd. untill _____
oClock we Set out early & proceeded on the Corse of last night &c.

[Clark, November 6, 1805]
November 6th Wednesday 1805
A cool wet raney morning we Set out early at 4 miles pass 2 Lodges of
Indians in a Small bottom on the Lard Side I believe those Indians to
be travelers. opposit is the head of a long narrow Island close under
the Starboard Side, back of this Island two Creeks fall in about 6
miles apart, and appear to head in the high hilley countrey to the N.
E. opposit this long Island is 2 others one Small and about the middle
of the river. the other larger and nearly opposit its lower point, and
opposit a high clift of Black rocks on the Lard. Side at 14 miles: here
the Indians of the 2 Lodges we passed to day came in their canoes with
Sundery articles to Sell, we purchased of them Wap-pa-too roots, Salmon
trout, and I purchased 2 beaver Skins for which I gave 5 Small fish
hooks. here the hills leave the river on the Lard. Side, a butifull
open and extensive bottom in which there is an old Village, one also on
the Stard. Side a little above both of which are abandened by all their
inhabitents except Two Small dogs nearly Starved, and an unreasonable
portion of flees—The Hills and mountains are covered with Sever kinds
of Pine-Arber Vitea or white Cedar, red Loril, alder and Several
Species of under groth, the bottoms have common rushes, nettles, &
grass the Slashey parts have Bull rushes & flags—Some willow on the
waters edge, passed an Island 3 miles long and one mile wide, close
under the Stard. Side below the long narrow Island below which the

*Stard Hills are verry from the river bank and Continues high and rugid
on that Side all day, we over took two Canoes of Indians going down to
trade one of the Indians Spoke a fiew words of english and Said that
the principal man who traded with them was Mr. Haley, and that he had a
woman in his Canoe who Mr. Haley was fond of &c. he Showed us a Bow of
Iron and Several other things which he Said Mr. Haley gave him. we came
too to Dine on the long narrow Island found the woods So thick with
under groth that the hunters could not get any distance into the Isld.
the red wood, and Green bryors interwoven, and mixed with pine, alder,
a Specis of Beech, ash &c. we killed nothing to day The Indians leave
us in the evening, river about one mile wide hills high and Steep on
the Std. no place for Several Miles suffcently large and leavil for our
camp we at length Landed at a place which by moveing the Stones we made
a place Suffcently large for the party to lie leavil on the Smaller
Stones Clear of the Tide Cloudy with rain all day we are all wet and
disagreeable, had large fires made on the Stone and dried our bedding
and Kill the flees, which collected in our blankets at every old
village we encamped near I had like to have forgotten a verry
remarkable Knob riseing from the edge of the water to about 80 feet
high, and about 200 paces around at its Base and Situated on the long
narrow Island above and nearly opposit to the 2 Lodges we passed to
day, it is Some distance from the high land & in a low part of the
Island*

*[Clark, November 7, 1805]
November 7th Thursday 1805
a Cloudy fogey morning, a little rain. Set out at 8 oClock proceeded on*

*The womens peticoat is about 15 Inches long made of arber vita or the
white Cedar bark wove to a String and hanging down in tossles and tied
So as to cover from their hips as low as the peticoat will reach and
only Covers them when Standing, as in any other position the Tosels
Seperate. Those people Sold us otter Skins for fish hooks of which they
wer fond*

We delayed 1 1/2 hour & Set out the tide being up in & the river So Cut with Islands we got an Indian to pilot us into the main chanel one of our Canoes Seperated from us this morning in the fog—great numbers of water fowls of every descriptn. common to this river

[Clark, November 7, 1805]
November 7th Thursday 1805
A cloudy foggey morning Some rain. we Set out early proceeded under the Stard Shore under a high rugid hills with Steep assent the Shore boalt and rockey, the fog So thick we could not See across the river, two Canos of Indians met and returned with us to their village which is Situated on the Stard Side behind a cluster of Marshey Islands, on a narrow chanl. of the river through which we passed to the Village of 4 Houses, they gave us to eate Some fish, and Sold us, fish, Wap pa to roots three dogs and 2 otter Skins for which we gave fish hooks principally of which they were verry fond.

Those people call themselves War-ci-a-cum and Speake a language different from the nativs above with whome they trade for the Wapato roots of which they make great use of as food. their houses differently built, raised entirely above ground eaves about 5 feet from the ground Supported and covered in the same way of those above, dotes about the Same size but in the Side of the house in one Corner, one fire place and that near the opposit end; around which they have their beads raised about 4 feet from the fore which is of earth, under their beads they Store away baskets of dried fish Berries & wappato, over the fire they hang the flesh as they take them and which they do not make immediate use. Their Canoes are of the Same form of those above. The Dress of the men differ verry little from those above, The womin altogether different, their robes are Smaller only Covering their Sholders & falling down to near the hip—and Sometimes when it is Cold a piec of fur curiously plated and connected So as to meet around the body from the arms to the hips The garment which occupies the waist and thence as low as the knee before and mid leg behind, cannot properly be called a petticoat, in the common acception of the word; it is a Tissue

*formed of white Cedar bark bruised or broken into Small Straps, which
are interwoven in their center by means of Several cords of the Same
materials which Serves as well for a girdle as to hold in place the
Straps of bark which forms the tissue, and which Strans, Confined in
the middle, hang with their ends pendulous from the waiste, the whole
being of Suffcent thickness when the female Stands erect to conceal
those parts useally covered from familiar view, but when she stoops or
places herself in any other attitudes this battery of Venus is not
altogether impervious to the penetrating eye of the amorite. This
tissue is Sometims formed of little Strings of the Silk grass twisted
and knoted at their ends &c. Those Indians are low and ill Shaped all
flat heads*

*after delaying at this village one hour and a half we Set out piloted
by an Indian dressed in a Salors dress, to the main Chanel of the
river, the tide being in we Should have found much dificuelty in
passing into the main Chanel from behind those islands, without a
pilot, a large marshey Island near the middle of the river near which
Several Canoes Came allong Side with Skins, roots fish &c. to Sell, and
had a temporey residence on this Island, here we See great numbers of
water fowls about those marshey Islands; here the high mountanious
Countrey approaches the river on the Lard Side, a high mountn. to the S.
W. about 20 miles, the high mountans. Countrey Continue on the Stard
Side, about 14 miles below the last village and 18 miles of this day we
landed at a village of the Same nation. This village is at the foot of
the high hills on the Stard Side back OF 2 Small Islands it contains 7
indifferent houses built in the Same form of those above, here we
purchased a Dog Some fish, wappato roots and I purchased 2 beaver Skins
for the purpose of makeing me a roab, as the robe I have is rotten and
good for nothing. opposit to this Village the high mountaneous Countrey
leave the river on the Lard Side below which the river widens into a
kind of Bay & is Crouded with low Islands Subject to be Covered by the
tides—we proceeded on about 12 miles below the Village under a high
mountaneous Countrey on the Stard. Side. Shore boald and rockey and
Encamped under a high hill on the Stard. Side opposit to a rock*

Situated half a mile from the Shore, about 50 feet high and 20 feet Diamieter, we with dificuelty found a place Clear of the tide and Sufficiently large to lie on and the only place we could get was on round Stones on which we lay our mats rain Continud. moderately all day & Two Indians accompanied us from the last village, they we detected in Stealing a knife and returned, our Small Canoe which got Seperated in the fog this morning joined us this evening from a large Island Situated nearest the Lard Side below the high hills on that Side, the river being too wide to See either the form Shape or Size of the Islands on the Lard Side.

Great joy in camp we are in View of the Ocian, this great Pacific Octean which we been So long anxious to See. and the roreing or noise made by the waves brakeing on the rockey Shores (as I Suppose) may be heard distictly

we made 34 miles to day as Computed

[Editor's Note: As written in Clark's diary, the climactic moment of the Voyage of Discovery comes to us without emotion and celebration. The words "Great joy" are all we have to share the triumph of the expedition. Lewis at the time was not writing in his diary at all.]

[Clark, November 8, 1805]
Novr. 8th Friday 1805 a cloudy morning Some rain and wind we Changed our Clothes and Set out at 9 oClock proceeded on Close under the Stard. Side

R. Fields Killed a goose & 2 Canvis back Ducks in this bay after Dinner we took the advantage of the returning tide & proceeded on to the 2d point, at which place we found the Swells too high to proceed we landed and drew our canoes up So as to let the tide leave them. The three Indians after Selling us 4 fish for which we gave Seven Small fishing hooks, and a piece of red Cloth. Some fine rain at intervales all this day. the Swells Continued high all the evening & we are Compelled to

form an Encampment on a Point Scercely room Sufficent for us all to lie
Clear of the tide water. hills high & with a Steep assent, river wide &
at this place too Salt to be used for Drink. we are all wet and
disagreeable, as we have been Continually for Severl. days past, we are
at a loss & cannot find out if any Settlement is near the mouth of this
river.

The Swells were So high and the Canoes roled in Such a manner as to
cause Several to be verry Sick. Reuben fields, Wiser McNeal & the Squar
wer of the number

[Clark, November 8, 1805]
November 8th Friday 1805
A Cloudy morning Some rain, we did not Set out untill 9 oClock, haveing
Changed our Clothing—proceeded on Close under the Stard. Side, the
hills high with Steep assent, Shore boald and rockey Several low
Islands in a Deep bend or Bay to the Lard Side, river about 5 or 7
miles wide. three Indians in a Canoe overtook us, with Salmon to Sell,
passed 2 old villages on the Stard. Side and at 3 miles entered a nitch
of about 6 miles wide and 5 miles deep with Several Creeks makeing into
the Stard Hills, this nitch we found verry Shallow water and Call it
the Shallow nitch we came too at the remains of an old village at the
bottom of this nitch and dined, here we Saw great numbers of fowl, Sent
out 2 men and they killed a Goose and two Canves back Ducks here we
found great numbers of Hees which we treated with the greatest caution
and distance; after Diner the Indians left us and we took the advantage
of a returning tide and proceeded on to the Second point on the Std.
here we found the Swells or waves So high that we thought it imprudent
to proceed; we landed unloaded and drew up our Canoes. Some rain all
day at intervales; we are all wet and disagreeable, as we have been for
Several days past, and our present Situation a verry disagreeable one
in as much; as we have not leavel land Sufficient for an encampment and
for our baggage to lie Cleare of the tide, the High hills jutting in So
Close and Steep that we cannot retreat back, and the water of the river
too Salt to be used, added to this the waves are increasing to Such a

hight that we cannot move from this place, in this Situation we are compelled to form our Camp between the hite of the Ebb and flood tides, and rase our baggage on logs—We are not certain as yet if the whites people who trade with those people or from whome they precure ther goods are Stationary at the mouth, or visit this quarter at Stated times for the purpose of trafick &c. I believe the latter to be the most probable conjucture—The Seas roled and tossed the Canoes in Such a manner this evening that Several of our party were Sea Sick.

[Clark, November 9, 1805]
Novr. 9th Saturday 1805
The tide of last night obliged us to unload all the Canoes one of which Sunk before She was unloaded by the high waves or Swells which accompanied the returning tide, The others we unloaded, and 3 others was filled with water Soon after by the Swells or high Sees which broke against the Shore imediately where we lay, rained hard all the fore part of the day, the tide which rose untill 2 oClock P M to day brought with it Such emence Swells or waves, added to a hard wind from the South which Loosened the Drift trees which is verry thick on the Shores, and tossed them about in Such a manner, as to endanger our Canoes very much, with every exertion and the Strictest attention by the party was Scercely Suffient to defend our Canoes from being Crushed to pieces between those emensely large trees maney of them 200 feet long and 4 feet through. The tide of this day rose about ____ feet & 15 Inches higher than yesterday this is owing to the wind which Sets in from the ocian, we are Compelled to move our Camp from the water, as also the loading every man as wet all the last night and this day as the rain Could make them which Contind. all day. at 4 oClock the wind Shifted about to the S. W. imediately from the ocian and blew a Storm for about 2 hours, raised the tide verry high all wet & cold Labiech killed 4 Ducks very fat & R. Fields Saw Elk Sign.

not withstanding the disagreeable time of the party for Several days past they are all Chearfull and full of anxiety to See further into the ocian. the water is too Salt to Drink, we use rain water. The Salt

water has acted on some of the party already as a Pergitive. rain
continus.

[Clark, November 9, 1805]
November 9th Saturday 1805
The tide of last night did not rise Sufficintly high to come into our
camp, but the Canoes which was exposed to the mercy of the waves &c.
which accompanied the returning tide, they all filled, and with great
attention we Saved them untill the tide left them dry—wind Hard from
the South and rained hard all the fore part of the day, at 2 oClock P M
the flood tide came in accompanied with emence waves and heavy winds,
floated the trees and Drift which was on the point on which we Camped
and tosed them about in Such a manner as to endanger the Canoes verry
much, with every exertion and the Strictest attention by every
individual of the party was Scercely Sufficient to Save our Canoes from
being crushed by those monsterous trees maney of them nearly 200 feet
long and from 4 to 7 feet through. our camp entirely under water
dureing the hight of the tide, every man as wet as water could make
them all the last night and to day all day as the rain Continued all
day, at 4 oClock P M the wind Shifted about to the S. W. and blew with
great violence imediately from the Ocian for about two hours,
notwithstanding the disagreeable Situation of our party all wet and
Cold (and one which they have experienced for Several days past) they
are chearfull and anxious to See further into the Ocian, The water of
the river being too Salt to use we are obliged to make use of rain
water—Some of the party not accustomed to Salt water has made too free
a use of it on them it acts as a pergitive.

at this dismal point we must Spend another night as the wind & waves
are too high to proceed.

[Clark, November 10, 1805]
November 10th Sunday 1805 rained verry hard the greater part of the
last night & Continus this morning, the wind has layed and the Swells
are fallen. we loaded our Canoes and proceeded on, passed a Deep Bay on

the Stard. Side I Call _____ The wind rose from the N. W. and the Swells became So high, we were Compelled to return about 2 miles to a place where we Could unld. our Canoes, which was in a Small Bay on Driftwood, on which we had also to make our fires to dry our Selves as well as we could the Shore being either a Clift of Purpendicular rocks or Steep assents to the hight of 4 or 500 feet, we continued on this drift wood untill about 3 oClock when the evening appearing favourable we loaded & Set out in hopes to turn the Point below and get into a better harber, but finding the waves & Swells continue to rage with great fury below, we got a Safe place for our Stores & a much beter one for the Canoes to lie and formed a Campment on Drift logs in the Same little Bay under a high hill at the enterence of a Small drean which we found verry convt. on account of its water, as that of the river is Brackish—The logs on which we lie is all on flote every high tide—The rain Continud all day—we are all wet, also our beding and many other articles. we are all employed untill late drying our bedding. nothing to eate but Pounded fish

[Clark, November 10, 1805]
November 10th Sunday 1805
Rained verry hard the greater part of last night and continues this morning. the wind has luled and the waves are not high; we loaded our canoes and proceeded on passed Several Small and deep nitch on the Stard. Side, we proceeded on about 10 miles Saw great numbers of Sea Guls, the wind rose from the N. W. and the waves became So high that we were compelled to return about 2 miles to a place we Could unload our Canoes, which we did in a Small nitch at the mouth of a Small run on a pile of drift logs where we Continued untill low water, when the river appeared calm we loaded and Set out; but was obliged to return finding the waves too high for our Canoes to ride, we again unloaded the Canoes, and Stoed the loading on a rock above the tide water, and formed a camp on the Drift Logs which appeared to be the only Situation we could find to lie, the hills being either a perpendicular Clift, or Steep assent, riseing to about 500 feet—our Canoes we Secured as well as we could—we are all wet the rain haveing continued all day, our

beding and maney other articles, employ our Selves drying our blankets
—nothing to eate but dried fish pounded which we brought from the falls.
we made 10 miles today

[Clark, November 11, 1805]
November 11th Monday 1805
a hard rain all the last night we again get wet the rain continue at
intervals all day. Wind verry high from S. W. and blew a Storm all day
Sent out Jo. Fields & Collins to hunt. at 12 oClock at a time the wind
was verry high and waves tremendeous five Indians Came down in a Canoe
loaded with fish of Salmon Spes. Called Red Charr, we purchased of
those Indians 13 of these fish, for which we gave, fishing hooks & some
trifling things. we had Seen those Indians at a village behind Some
marshey Islands a few days ago. they are on their way to trade those
fish with white people which they make Signs live below round a point,
those people are badly Clad, one is dressd. in an old Salors Jacket &
Trouses, the others Elk Skin robes. we are truly unfortunate to be
Compelled to lie 4 days nearly in the Same place at a time that our day
are precious to us, The Wind Shifted to _____ the Indians left us and
Crossed the river which is about 5 miles wide through the highest Sees
I ever Saw a Small vestle ride, their Canoe is Small, maney times they
were out of Sight before the were 2 miles off Certain it is they are
the best canoe navigators I ever Saw The tide was 3 hours later to day
than yesterday and rose much higher, the trees we camped on was all on
flote for about 2 hours from 3 untill 5 oClock P M, the great
quantities of rain which has fallen losenes the Stones on the Side of
the hill & the Small ones fall on us, our Situation is truly a
disagreeable one our Canoes in one place at the mercy of the waves our
baggage in another and our Selves & party Scattered on drift trees of
emense Sizes, & are on what dry land they can find in the Crevices of
the rocks & hill Sides

[Clark, November 11, 1805]
November 11th Monday 1805
A hard rain all the last night, dureing the last tide the logs on which

we lay was all on float Sent out Jo Fields to hunt, he Soon returned and informed us that the hills was So high & Steep, & thick with undergroth and fallen Timber that he could not get out any distance; about 12 oClock 5 Indians came down in a canoe, the wind verry high from the S. W. with most tremendious waves brakeing with great violence against the Shores, rain falling in torrents, we are all wet as usial and our Situation is truly a disagreeable one; the great quantites of rain which has loosened the Stones on the hill Sides, and the Small Stones fall down upon us, our canoes at one place at the mercy of the waves, our baggage in another and our Selves and party Scattered on floating logs and Such dry Spots as can be found on the hill Sides, and Crivices of the rocks. we purchased of the Indians 13 red chary which we found to be an excellent fish we have Seen those Indians above and are of a nation who reside above and on the opposit Side who call themselves Call-har-ma they are badly clad & illy made, Small and Speak a language much resembling the last nation, one of those men had on a Salors Jacket and Pantiloons and made Signs that he got those Clothes from the white people who lived below the point &c. those people left us and Crossed the river (which is about 5 miles wide at this place) through the highest waves I ever Saw a Small vestles ride. Those Indians are Certainly the best Canoe navigaters I ever Saw. rained all day

[Clark, November 12, 1805]
November 12th Tuesday 1805
a tremendious thunder Storm abt. 3 oClock this morning accompanied by wind from the S. W. and Hail, this Storm of hard Clap's thunder Lighting and hail untill about 6 oClock at intervals it then became light for a Short time when the heavens became darkined by a black Cloud from the S. W. & a hard rain Suckceeded which lasted untill 12 oClock with a hard wind which raised the Seas tremendiously high braking with great force and fury against the rocks & trees on which we lie, as our Situation became Seriously dangerous, we took the advantage of a low tide & moved our Camp around a point a Short distance to a Small wet bottom at the mouth of a Small Creek, which we had not observed when we first Came to this Cove, from its being very thick and obscured by

*drift trees & thick bushes, Send out men to hunt they found the woods
So thick with Pine & timber and under Broth that they could not get
through, Saw Some Elk tracks, I walked up this creek & killed 2 Salmon
trout, the men killd. 13 of the Salmon Species, The Pine of fur Specs,
or Spruc Pine grow here to an emense Size & hight maney of them 7 & 8
feet through and upwards of 200 feet high. It would be distressing to a
feeling person to See our Situation at this time all wet and cold with
our bedding &c. also wet, in a Cove Scercely large nough to Contain us,
our Baggage in a Small holler about 1/2 a mile from us, and Canoes at
the mercy of the waves & drift wood, we have Scured them as well as it
is possible by Sinking and wateing them down with Stones to prevent the
emence waves dashing them to pices against the rocks—one got loose
last night & was left on a rock by the tide Some distance below without
recving much damage. fortunately for us our Men are helthy. It was
clear at 12 for a Short time. I observed the Mountains on the opposit
Side was covered with Snowour party has been wet for 8 days and is
truly disagreeable, their robes & leather Clothes are rotten from being
Continually wet, and they are not in a Situation to get others, and we
are not in a Situation to restore them—I observe great numbers of Sea
guls, flying in every derection—Three men Gibson Bratten & Willard
attempted to decend in a Canoe built in the Indian fashion and abt. the
Size of the one the Indians visited us in yesterday, they Could not
proceed, as the waves tossed them about at will, they returned after
proceeding about 1 mile—we got our Selves tolerable Comfortable by
drying our Selves & bedding Cought 3 salmon this evining in a Small
branch above about 1 mile*

[Clark, November 12, 1805]
November 12th Tuesday 1805
*A Tremendious wind from the S. W. about 3 oClock this morning with
Lightineng and hard claps of Thunder, and Hail which Continued untill 6
oClock a.m. when it became light for a Short time, then the heavens
became Sudenly darkened by a black Cloud from the S. W. and rained with
great violence untill 12 oClock, the waves tremendious brakeing with
great fury against the rocks and trees on which we were encamped. our
Situation is dangerous. we took the advantage of a low tide and moved*

*our camp around a point to a Small wet bottom at the mouth of a Brook,
which we had not observed when we Came to this cove; from it being
verry thick and obscured by drift trees and thick bushes It would be
distressing to See our Situation, all wet and Colde our bedding also
wet, (and the robes of the party which Compose half the bedding is
rotten and we are not in a Situation to supply their places) in a wet
bottom Scercely large enough to contain us, our baggage half a mile
from us and Canoes at the mercy of the waves, altho Secured as well as
possible, Sunk with emence parcels of Stone to wate them down to
prevent their dashing to pieces against the rocks; one got loose last
night and was left on a rock a Short distance below, without rciving
more daminage than a Split in her bottom—Fortunately for us our men
are healthy. 3 men Gibson Bratten & Willard attempted to go aroud the
point below in our Indian Canoe, much Such a canoe as the Indians
visited us in yesterday, they proceeded to the point from which they
were oblige to return, the waves tossing them about at will I walked up
the branch and giged 3 Salmon trout. the party killed 13 Salmon to day
in a branch about 2 miles above. rain Continued*

[Clark, November 13, 1805]
*November 13th Wednesday 1805 Some intervales of fair weather last
night, rain and wind Continue this morning, as we are in a Cove & the
Mountains verry high & Pine Spruce verry high & thick Cannot deturmine
the procise course of the winds. I walked to the top of the first part
of the mountain with much fatigue as the distance was about 3 miles
thro intolerable thickets of Small Pine, arrow wood a groth much
resembling arrow wood with briers, growing to 10 & 15 feet high
interlocking with each other & Furn, aded to this difficulty the hill
was So Steep that I was obliged to drawing my Self up in many places by
the bowers, the Countrey Continues thick and hilley as far back a I
could See. Some Elk Sign, rained all day moderately. I am wet &c. &c.
The Hail which fell 2 night past is yet to be Seen on the mountain on
which I was to day. I Saw a Small red Berry which grows on a Stem of
about 6 or 8 Inches from the Ground, in bunches and in great quantity
on the Mountains, the taste insiped. I saw a number of verry large
Spruce Pine one of which I measured 14 feet around and verry tall. My*

principal objects in assdg. this mountain was to view the river below, the weather being So Cloudey & thick that I could not See any distance down, discovered the wind high from the N. W. and waves high at a Short distance below our Encampment, (Squar displeased with me for not sin &c &c. Wap-lo a excellent root which is rosted and tastes like a potato I Cut my hand despatched 3 men in a Indian canoe (which is calculated to ride high Swells) down to examine if they can find the Bay at the mouth & good barbers below for us to proceed in Safty. The fides at every Hud come in with great Swells & Breake against the rocks & Drift trees with great fury—the rain Continue all the evening nothing to eate but Pounded fish which we have as a reserve See Store, and what Pore fish we can kill up the branch on which we are encamped our canoe and the three men did not return this evening—if we were to have cold weather to accompany the rain which we have had for this 6 or 8 days passed we must eneviatilbly Suffer verry much as Clothes are Scerce with us.

[Clark, November 13, 1805]
November 13th Wednesday 1805
Some intervales of fair weather last night, rain continue this morning. I walked up the Brook & assended the first Spur of the mountain with much fatigue, the distance about 3 miles, through an intolerable thickets of Small pine, a groth much resembling arrow wood on the Stem of which there is thorns; this groth about 12 or 15 feet high inter lockd into each other and Scattered over the high fern & fallen timber, added to this the hills were So Steep that I was compelled to draw my Self up by the assistance of those bushes—The Timber on those hills are of the pine Species large and tall maney of them more than 200 feet high & from 8 to 10 feet through at the Stump those hills & as far back as I could See, I Saw Some Elk Sign, on the Spur of the mountain tho not fresh. I killed a Salmon trout on my return. The Hail which fell 2 nights past is yet to be Seen on the mountains; I Saw in my ramble to day a red berry resembling Solomons Seal berry which the nativs call Sol-me and use it to eate. my principal object in assending this mountain was to view the countrey below, the rain continuing and weather proved So Cloudy that I could not See any distance on my return we dispatched 3 men Colter, Willard and Shannon in the Indian canoe to

*get around the point if possible and examine the river, and the Bay
below for a god barber for our Canoes to lie in Safty &c. The tide at
every floot tide Came with great swells brakeing against the rocks &
Drift trees with great fury The rain Continue all day. nothing to eate
but pounded fish which we Keep as a reserve and use in Situations of
this kind.*

[Clark, November 14, 1805]
Novr. 14th Thursday 1805
*Rained last night without intermission and this morning the wind blew
hard from the _____ We Could not move, one Canoe was broken last night
against the rocks, by the waves dashing her against them in high tide
about 10 oClock 5 Indians Come up in a Canoe thro emence waves &
Swells, they landed and informed us they Saw the 3 men we Sent down
yesterday, at Some distance below Soon after those people Came Colter
one of the 3 men returned and informed us that he had proceeded with
his Canoe as far as they Could, for the waves and Could find no white
people, or Bay, he Saw a good Canoe barber & 2 Camps of Indians at no
great distance below and that those with us had taken his gig & knife
&c. which he forcably took from them & they left us, after our treating
them well. The rain Continue all day all wet as usial, killed only 2
fish to day for the whole Party, at 3 oClock Capt. Lewis Drewyer Jo. &
R. Fields & Frasure Set out down on the Shore to examine if any white
men were below within our reach, they took a empty Canoe & 5 men to Set
them around the Point on a Gravelley Beech which Colter informed was at
no great distance below. The Canoe returned at dusk half full of water,
from the waves which dashed over in passing the point Capt Lewis is
object is also to find a Small Bay as laid down by Vancouver just out
of the mouth of the Columbia River. rained as usial all the evening,
all wet and disagreeable Situated*

[Clark, November 14, 1805]
November 14th Thursday 1805
*rained all the last night without intermition, and this morning. wind
blows verry hard but our Situation is Such that we Cannot tell from*

*what point it comes—one of our Canoes is much broken by the waves
dashing it against the rocks—5 Indians Came up in a Canoe, thro the
waves, which is verry high and role with great fury—They made Signs to
us that they Saw the 3 men we Sent down yesterday. only 3 of those
Indians landed, the other 2 which was women played off in the waves,
which induced me to Suspect that they had taken Something from our men
below, at this time one of the men Colter returnd by land and informed
us that those Indians had taken his Gigg & basket, I called to the
Squars to land and give back the gigg, which they would not doe untill
a man run with a gun, as if he intended to Shute them when they landed,
and Colter got his gig & basket I then ordered those fellows off, and
they verry readily Cleared out they are of the War-ci-a-cum N. Colter
informed us that "it was but a Short distance from where we lay around
the point to a butifull Sand beech, which continud for a long ways,
that he had found a good harber in the mouth of a creek near 2 Indian
Lodgesthat he had proceeded in the Canoe as far as he could for the
waves, the other two men Willard & Shannon had proceeded on down"*

*Capt Lewis concluded to proceed on by land & find if possible the white
people the Indians Say is below and examine if a Bay is Situated near
the mouth of this river as laid down by Vancouver in which we expect,
if there is white traders to find them &c. at 3 oClock he Set out with
4 men Drewyer Jos. & Reu. Fields & R. Frasure, in one of our large
canoes and 5 men to Set them around the point on the Sand beech. this
canoe returned nearly filled with water at Dark which it receved by the
waves dashing into it on its return, haveing landed Capt. Lewis & his
party Safe on the Sand beech. The rain Continues all day all wet. The
rain &c. which has continued without a longer intermition than 2 hours
at a time for ten days past has distroyd. the robes and rotted nearly
one half of the fiew Clothes the party has, perticularley the leather
Clothes,—fortunately for us we have no very Cold weather as yet and if
we have Cold weather before we Can kill & Dress Skins for Clothing the
bulk of the party will Suffer verry much.*

CHAPTER 9

Trails, Camps and Fights for Life
In the High Country
(Part One)

By George Frederick Ruxton

As with all my favorite books, and even movies I have seen, I'm never happy using the word "best" without qualifying the expression. I like "Among the best." And George Frederick Ruxton's Life in the Far West *certainly makes that list. A mountain man named Killbuck and his companion La Bonté are followed in third-person narrative far more detailed, clear and covering more landscapes than most mountain men epics. Ruxton was born and educated in England. He travelled widely in the American west before he died in St. Louis at the age of 28 in 1848, the same year his tales were first published in* Blackwood's Edinburgh *Magazine. They were first published in book form in 1849 and have been republished many times since. In this excerpt, we enter the action as the two mountain men are part of a trapping party on their way north of the Platte headed deep into the mountain vastness and the New Mexico paradise beyond.*

With the Yutas, Killbuck and La Bonté remained during the winter; and when the spring sun had opened the ice-bound creeks, and melted the snow on the mountains, and its genial warmth had expanded the earth and permitted the roots of the grass to "live" once more, and throw out green and tender shoots, the two trappers bade adieu to the hospitable Indians, who broke up their village in order to start for the valleys of the Del Norte. As they followed the trail from the bayou, at sundown, just as they thought of camping, they observed

*ahead of them a solitary horseman riding along, followed by three
mules. His hunting-frock of fringed buckskin, and the rifle resting
across the horn of his saddle, at once proclaimed him white; but as he
saw the mountaineers winding through the canyon, driving before them
half a dozen horses, he judged they might possibly be Indians and
enemies, the more so as their dress was not the usual costume of the
whites. The trappers, therefore, saw the stranger raise the rifle in
the hollow of his arm, and, gathering up his horse, ride steadily to
meet them, as soon as he observed they were but two; two to one in
mountain calculation being scarcely considered odds, if red skin to
white.*

*However, on nearing them, the stranger discovered his mistake; and,
throwing his rifle across the saddle once more, reined in his horse
and waited their approach; for the spot where he then stood presented
an excellent camping-ground, with abundance of dry wood and convenient
water.*

"Where from, stranger?"

"The divide, and to the bayou for meat; and you are from there, I see.
Any buffalo come in yet?"

"Heap, and seal-fat at that. What's the sign out on the plains?"

"War-party of Rapahos passed Squirrel at sundown yesterday, and nearly
raised my animals. Sign, too, of more on left fork of Boiling Spring.
No buffalo between this and Bijou. Do you feel like camping?"

"Well, we do. But whar's your companyeros?"

"I'm alone."

"Alone! Wagh! How do you get your animals along?"

"I go ahead, and they follow the horse."

"Well, that beats all! That's a smart-looking hos now; and runs some,
I'm thinking."

"Well, it does."

"Whar's them mules from? They look like Californy."

"Mexican country—away down south."

"H—! Whar's yourself from?"

"There away, too."

"What's beaver worth in Taos?"

"Dollar."

"In Saint Louiy?"

"Same."

"H——! Any call for buckskin?"

"A heap! The soldiers in Santa Fé are half froze for leather; and moccasins fetch two dollars, easy."

"Wagh! How's trade on Arkansa, and what's doin to the Fort?"

"Shians at Big Timber, and Bent's people trading smart. On North Fork, Jim Waters got a hundred pack right off, and Sioux making more."

"Whar's Bill Williams?"

"Gone under, they say: the Diggers took his hair."

"How's powder goin?"

"Two dollars a pint."

"Bacca?"

"A plew a plug."

"Got any about you?"

"Have so."

"Give us a chaw; and now let's camp."

Whilst unpacking their own animals, the two trappers could not refrain from glancing, every now and then, with no little astonishment, at the solitary stranger they had so unexpectedly encountered. If truth be told, his appearance not a little perplexed them. His hunting-frock of buckskin, shining with grease, and fringed pantaloons, over which the well-greased butcher-knife had evidently been often wiped after cutting his food, or butchering the carcass of deer and buffalo, were of genuine mountain make. His face, clean shaved, exhibited in its well-tanned and weather-beaten complexion, the effects of such natural cosmetics as sun and wind; and under the mountain hat of felt which covered his head, long uncut hair hung in Indian fashion on his shoulders. All this would have passed muster, had it not been for the most extraordinary equipment of a double-barrelled rifle; which, when it had attracted the eyes of the mountaineers, elicited no little astonishment, not to say derision. But, perhaps, nothing excited their admiration so much as the perfect docility of the stranger's animals; which, almost like dogs, obeyed his voice and call; and albeit that one, in a small sharp head and pointed ears, expanded nostrils, and eye twinkling and malicious, exhibited the personification of a "lurking devil," yet they could not but admire the perfect ease with which even this one, in common with the rest, permitted herself to be handled.

Dismounting, and unhitching from the horn of his saddle the coil of skin rope, one end of which was secured round the neck of the horse, he proceeded to unsaddle; and whilst so engaged, the three mules, two of which were packed, one with the unbutchered carcass of a deer, the other with a pack of skins, &c., followed leisurely into the space chosen for the camp, and, cropping the grass at their ease, waited until a whistle called them to be unpacked.

The horse was a strong square-built bay; and, although the severities of a prolonged winter, with scanty pasture and long and trying travel, had robbed his bones of fat and flesh, tucked up his flank, and "ewed" his neck; still his clean and well-set legs, oblique shoulder, and withers fine as a deer's, in spite of his gaunt half-starved appearance, bore ample testimony as to what he had been; while his clear cheerful eye, and the hearty appetite with which he fell to work on the coarse grass of the bottom, proved that he had something in him still, and was game as ever. His tail, gnawed by the mules in days of strait, attracted the observant mountaineers.

"Hard doins when it come to that," remarked La Bonté.

Between the horse and two of the mules a mutual and great affection appeared to subsist, which was no more than natural, when their master observed to his companions that they had travelled together upwards of two thousand miles.

One of these mules was a short, thick-set, stumpy animal, with an enormous head surmounted by proportionable ears, and a pair of unusually large eyes, beaming the most perfect good temper and docility (most uncommon qualities in a mule.) Her neck was thick, and rendered more so in appearance by reason of her mane not being roached, (or, in English, hogged), which privilege she alone enjoyed of the trio; and her short, strong legs, ending in small, round, cat-like hoofs, were feathered with a profusion of dark brown hair.

*As she stood stock-still, whilst the stranger removed the awkwardly
packed deer from her back, she flapped her huge ears backward and
forward, occasionally turning her head, and laying her cold nose
against her master's cheek. When the pack was removed, he advanced
to her head, and resting it on his shoulder, rubbed her broad and
grizzled cheeks with both his hands for several minutes, the old
mule laying her ears, like a rabbit, back upon her neck, and with
half-closed eyes enjoyed mightily the manipulation. Then, giving her a
smack upon the haunch, and a "hep-a" well known to the mule kind, the
old favourite threw up her heels and cantered off to the horse, who
was busily cropping the buffalo grass on the bluff above the stream.*

*Great was the contrast between the one just described and the next
which came up to be divested of her pack. She, a tall beautifully
shaped Mexican mule, of a light mouse colour, with a head like a
deer's, and long springy legs, trotted up obedient to the call, but
with ears bent back and curled up nose, and tail compressed between
her legs. As her pack was being removed, she groaned and whined like a
dog, as a thong or loosened strap touched her ticklish body, lifting
her hind-quarters in a succession of jumps or preparatory kicks, and
looking wicked as a panther. When nothing but the fore pack-saddle
remained, she had worked herself into the last stage; and as the
stranger cast loose the girth of buffalo hide, and was about to lift
the saddle and draw the crupper from the tail, she drew her hind legs
under her, more tightly compressed her tail, and almost shrieked with
rage.*

*"Stand clear," he roared (knowing what was coming), and raised the
saddle, when out went her hind legs, up went the pack into the
air, and, with it dangling at her heels, away she tore, kicking
the offending saddle as she ran. Her master, however, took this as
matter of course, followed her and brought back the saddle, which he
piled on the others to windward of the fire one of the trappers was
kindling. Fire-making is a simple process with the mountaineers. Their
bullet-pouches always contain a flint and steel, and sundry pieces of
"punk" or tinder; and pulling a handful of dry grass, which they
screw into a nest, they place the lighted punk in this, and, closing*

the grass over it, wave it in the air, when it soon ignites, and readily kindles the dry sticks forming the foundation of the fire.

The tit-bits of the deer the stranger had brought in were soon roasting over the fire; whilst, as soon as the burning logs had deposited a sufficiency of ashes, a hole was raked in them, and the head of the deer, skin, hair, and all, placed in this primitive oven, and carefully covered with the hot ashes.

A "heap" of "fat meat" in perspective, our mountaineers enjoyed their ante-prandial pipes, recounting the news of the respective regions whence they came; and so well did they like each other's company, so sweet was the "honey-dew" tobacco of which the strange hunter had good store, so plentiful the game about the creek, and so abundant the pasture for their winter-starved animals, that before the carcass of the "two-year" buck had been more than four-fifths consumed; and, although rib after rib had been picked and chucked over their shoulders to the wolves, and one fore leg and the "bit" of all, the head, were still cooked before them,—the three had come to the resolution to join company, and hunt in their present locality for a few days at least—the owner of the "two-shoot" gun volunteering to fill their horns with powder, and find tobacco for their pipes.

Here, on plenty of meat, of venison, bear, and antelope, they merrily luxuriated; returning after their daily hunts to the brightly burning camp-fire, where one always remained to guard the animals, and unloading their packs of meat, (all choicest portions), ate late into the night, and, smoking, wiled away the time in narrating scenes in their hard-spent lives, and fighting their battles o'er again.

The younger of the trappers, he who has figured under the name of La Bonté, had excited, by scraps and patches from his history, no little curiosity in the stranger's mind to learn the ups and downs of his career; and one night, when they assembled earlier than usual at the fire, he prevailed upon the modest trapper to "unpack" some passages in his wild adventurous life.

"Maybe," commenced the mountaineer, "you both remember when old Ashley went out with the biggest kind of band to trap the Columbia, and head-waters of Missoura and Yellow Stone. Well, that was the time this niggur first felt like taking to the mountains."

CHAPTER 10

Trails, Camps and Fights for Life
In the High Country
(Part Two)

By George Frederick Ruxton

As Killbuck and La Bonté press on into the high country as part of a trapping party, La Bonté continues with the details of how he became a trapper and a mountain man. Ruxton's accounts of mountain man life are among the greatest ever written.

This brings us back to the year of our Lord 1825; and perhaps it will be as well, in order to render La Bonté's mountain language intelligible, to translate it at once into tolerable English, and to tell in the third person, but from his own lips, the scrapes which befell him in a sojourn of more than twenty years in the Far West, and the causes that impelled him to quit the comfort and civilization of his home, to seek the perilous but engaging life of a trapper of the Rocky Mountains.

La Bonté was raised in the state of Mississippi, not far from Memphis, on the left bank of that huge and snag-filled river. His father was a Saint Louis Frenchman, his mother a native of Tennessee. When a boy, our trapper was "some," he said, with the rifle, and always had a hankering for the west; particularly when, on accompanying his father to Saint Louis every spring, he saw the different bands of traders and hunters start upon their annual expeditions to the mountains. Greatly did he envy the independent, insouciant trappers, as, in all the glory of beads and buckskin, they shouldered their rifles at Jake Hawkin's door (the rifle-maker of St Louis), and bade adieu to the cares and trammels of civilized life.

La Bonté, on his arrival at St Louis, found himself one day in no less a place than this; and here he made acquaintance with an old trapper about to start for the mountains in a few days, to hunt on the head waters of Platte and Green River. With this man he resolved to start, and, having still some hundred dollars in cash, he immediately set about equipping himself for the expedition. To effect this, he first of all visited the gun-store of Hawken, whose rifles are renowned in the mountains, and exchanged his own piece, which was of very small bore, for a regular mountain rifle. This was of very heavy metal, carrying about thirty-two balls to the pound, stocked to the muzzle, and mounted with brass, its only ornament being a buffalo bull, looking exceedingly ferocious, which was not very artistically engraved upon the trap in the stock. Here, too, he laid in a few pounds of powder and lead, and all the necessaries for a long hunt.

His next visit was to a smith's store, which smith was black by trade and black by nature, for he was a nigger, and, moreover, celebrated as being the best maker of beaver-traps in St Louis, and of him he purchased six new traps, paying for the same twenty dollars—procuring, at the same time, an old trap-sack, made of stout buffalo skin, in which to carry them.

We next find La Bonté and his companion—one Luke, better known as Grey-Eye, one of his eyes having been "gouged" in a mountain fray—at Independence, a little town situated on the Missouri, several hundred miles above St Louis, and within a short distance of the Indian frontier.

Independence may be termed the "prairie port" of the western country. Here the caravans destined for Santa Fé, and the interior of Mexico, assemble to complete their necessary equipment. Mules and oxen are purchased, teamsters hired, and all stores and outfit laid in here for the long journey over the wide expanse of prairie ocean. Here, too, the Indian traders and the Rocky-Mountain trappers rendezvous, collecting in sufficient force to ensure their safe passage through the Indian country. At the seasons of departure and arrival of these bands, the little town presents a lively scene of bustle and confusion. The wild and dissipated mountaineers get rid of their last

*dollars in furious orgies, treating all comers to galore of drink,
and pledging each other, in horns of potent whisky, to successful
hunts and "heaps of beaver." When every cent has disappeared from
their pouches, the free trapper often makes away with rifle, traps,
and animals, to gratify his "dry" (for your mountaineer is never
"thirsty"); and then, "hos and beaver" gone, is necessitated to hire
himself to one of the leaders of big bands, and hypothecate his
services for an equipment of traps and animals. Thus La Bonté picked
up three excellent mules for a mere song, with their accompanying
pack-saddles, apishamores, and lariats, and the next day, with
Luke, "put out" for Platte.*

*As they passed through the rendezvous, which was encamped on a little
stream beyond the town, even our young Mississippian was struck with
the novelty of the scene. Upwards of forty huge wagons, of Conostoga
and Pittsburg build, and covered with snow-white tilts, were ranged in
a semicircle, or rather a horse-shoe form, on the flat open prairie,
their long "tongues" (poles) pointing outwards; with the necessary
harness for four pairs of mules, or eight yoke of oxen, lying on the
ground beside them, spread in ready order for "hitching up." Round
the wagons groups of teamsters, tall stalwart young Missourians,
were engaged in busy preparation for the start, greasing the wheels,
fitting or repairing harness, smoothing ox-bows, or overhauling their
own moderate kits or "possibles." They were all dressed in the same
fashion: a pair of "homespun" pantaloons, tucked into thick boots
reaching nearly to the knee, and confined round the waist by a broad
leather belt, which supported a strong butcher-knife in a sheath. A
coarse checked shirt was their only other covering, with a fur cap on
the head.*

*Numerous camp-fires surrounded the wagons, and near them lounged
wild-looking mountaineers, easily distinguished from the "greenhorn"
teamsters by their dresses of buckskin, and their weather-beaten
faces. Without an exception, these were under the influence of the
rosy god; and one, who sat, the picture of misery, at a fire by
himself—staring into the blaze with vacant countenance, his long
matted hair hanging in unkempt masses over his face, begrimed with*

the dirt of a week, and pallid with the effects of ardent drink—was
suffering from the usual consequences of having "kept it up" beyond
the usual point, paying the penalty in a fit of "horrors"—as delirium
tremens is most aptly termed by sailors and the unprofessional.

In another part, the merchants of the caravan and the Indian traders
superintended the lading of the wagons, or mule packs. They were
dressed in civilised attire, and some were even bedizened in St Louis
or Eastern City dandyism, to the infinite disgust of the mountain men,
who look upon a bourge-way (bourgeois) with most undisguised contempt,
despising the very simplest forms of civilisaton. The picturesque
appearance of the encampment was not a little heightened by the
addition of several Indians from the neighbouring Shawnee settlement,
who, mounted on their small active horses, on which they reclined,
rather than sat, in negligent attitudes, quietly looked on at the
novel scene, indifferent to the "chaff" in which the thoughtless
teamsters indulged at their expense. Numbers of mules and horses were
picketed at hand, whilst a large herd of noble oxen were being driven
towards the camp—the wo-ha of the teamsters sounding far and near, as
they collected the scattered beasts in order to yoke up.

As most of the mountain men were utterly unable to move from camp,
Luke and La Bonté, with three or four of the most sober, started in
company, intending to wait on "Blue," a stream which runs into the Caw
or Kanzas River, until the "balance" of the band came up. Mounting
their mules, and leading the loose animals, they struck at once into
the park-like prairie, and were speedily out of sight of civilization in an instant.

It was the latter end of May, towards the close of the season of
heavy rains, which in early spring render the climate of this country
almost intolerable, at the same time that they fertilise and thaw the
soil, so long bound up by the winter's frosts. The grass was every
where luxuriantly green, and gaudy flowers dotted the surface of the
prairie. This term, however, should hardly be applied to the beautiful
undulating scenery of this park-like country. Unlike the flat monotony
of the Grand Plains, here well wooded uplands, clothed with forest
trees of every species, and picturesque dells, through which run
clear bubbling streams belted with gay-blossomed shrubs, every where

present themselves; whilst on the level meadow-land, topes of trees with spreading foliage afford a shelter to the game and cattle, and well-timbered knolls rise at intervals from the plain.

Many clear streams dashing over their pebbly beds intersect the country, from which, in the noon-day's heat, the red-deer jump, shaking their wet sides, as the noise of approaching man disturbs them; and booming grouse rise from the tall luxuriant herbage at every step. Where the deep escarpments of the river banks exhibit the section of the earth, a rich alluvial soil of surprising depth appears to court the cultivation of civilised man; and in every feature it is evident that here nature has worked with kindliest and most bountiful hand.

For hundreds of miles along the western or right bank of the Missouri does a country extend, with which, for fertility and natural resources, no part of Europe can stand comparison. Sufficiently large to contain an enormous population, it has, besides, every advantage of position, and all the natural capabilities which should make it the happy abode of civilised man. Through this unpeopled country the United States pours her greedy thousands, to seize upon the barren territories of her feeble neighbour.

Camping the first night on "Black Jack," our mountaineers here cut each man a spare hickory wiping-stick for his rifle; and La Bonté, who was the only greenhorn of the party, witnessed a savage ebullition of rage on the part of one of his companions, exhibiting the perfect unrestraint which these men impose upon their passions, and the barbarous anger which the slightest opposition to their will excites. One of the trappers, on arriving at the camping-place, dismounted from his horse, and, after divesting it of the saddle, endeavoured to lead his mule by the rope up to the spot where he wished to deposit his pack. Mule-like, however, the more he pulled the more stubbornly she remained in her tracks, planting her fore-legs firmly, and stretching out her neck with provoking obstinacy. Truth to tell, it does require the temper of a thousand Jobs to manage a mule; and in no case does the willful mulishness of the animal stir up one's choler more than in the very trick this one played, and which is a daily occurrence. After tugging ineffectually for several minutes, winding the rope round his body, and throwing himself suddenly forward with all his strength, the trapper actually foamed with passion; and although he might have subdued the animal at once by fastening the rope with a half-hitch round its nose, this, with an obstinacy equal to that of the mule itself, he refused to attempt it, preferring to vanquish her by main strength. Failing so to do, the mountaineer, with a volley of blasphemous imprecations, suddenly seized his rifle, and levelling it at the mule's head, shot her dead.

Passing the Wa-ka-rasha, a well-timbered stream, they met a band of Osages going "to buffalo." These Indians, in common with some tribes of the Pawnees, shave the head, with the exception of a ridge from the forehead to the centre of the scalp, which is "roached" or hogged like the mane of a mule, and stands erect, plastered with unguents, and ornamented with feathers of the hawk and turkey. The naked scalp is often painted in mosaic with black and red, the face with shining vermilion. This band were all naked to the breech-clout, the warmth of the sun having made them throw their dirty blankets from their shoulders. These Indians not unfrequently levy contributions on the strangers they accidentally meet; but they easily distinguish the determined mountaineer from the incautious greenhorn, and think it better to let the former alone.

Crossing Vermilion, the trappers arrived on the fifth day at "Blue," where they encamped in the broad timber belting the creek, and there awaited the arrival of the remainder of the party.

It was two days before they came up; but the following day they started for the mountains, fourteen in number, striking a trail which follows the "Big Blue" in its course through the prairies, which, as they advanced to the westward, gradually smoothed away into a vast unbroken expanse of rolling plain. Herds of antelope began to show themselves, and some of the hunters, leaving the trail, soon returned with plenty of their tender meat. The luxuriant but coarse grass they had hitherto seen now changed into the nutritious and curly buffalo grass, and their animals soon improved in appearance on the excellent pasture. In a few days, without any adventure, they struck the Platte River, its shallow waters (from which it derives its name) spreading over a wide and sandy bed, numerous sand bars obstructing the sluggish current, nowhere sufficiently deep to wet the forder's knee.

By this time, but few antelope having been seen, the party ran entirely out of meat; and, one whole day and part of another having passed without so much as a stray rabbit presenting itself, not a few objurgations on the buffalo grumbled from the lips of the hunters, who expected ere this to have reached the land of plenty. La Bonté killed a fine deer, however, in the river bottom, after they had encamped, not one particle of which remained after supper that night, but which hardly took the rough edge off their keen appetites. Although already in the buffalo range, no traces of these animals had yet been seen; and as the country afforded but little game, and the party did not care to halt and lose time in hunting for it, they moved along hungry and sulky, the theme of conversation being the well remembered merits of good buffalo meat,—of "fat fleece," "hump rib," and "tender loin;" of delicious "boudins," and marrow bones too good to think of. La Bonté had never seen the lordly animal, and consequently but half believed the accounts of the mountaineers, who described their countless bands as covering the prairie far as the eye could reach, and requiring days of travel to pass through; but the visions of such dainty and abundant feeding as they descanted on set his mouth watering, and danced before his eyes as he slept supperless, night after night, on the banks of the hungry Platte.

One morning he had packed his animals before the rest, and was riding a mile in advance of the party, when he saw on one side the trail, looming in the refracted glare which mirages the plains, three large dark objects without shape or form, which rose and fell in the exaggerated light like ships at sea. Doubting what it could be, he approached the strange objects; and as the refraction disappeared before him, the dark masses assumed a more distinct form, and clearly moved with life. A little nearer, and he made them out—they were buffalo. Thinking to distinguish himself, the greenhorn dismounted from his mule, and quickly hobbled her, throwing his lasso on the ground to trail behind when he wished to catch her. Then, rifle in hand, he approached the huge animals, and, being a good hunter, knew *well to take advantage of the inequalities of the ground and face the wind; by which means he crawled at length to within forty yards of the buffalo, which quietly cropped the grass, unconscious of danger. Now, for the first time, he gazed upon the noble beast he had so often heard of, and longed to see. With coal-black beard sweeping the ground as he fed, an enormous bull was in advance of the others, his wild brilliant eyes peering from an immense mass of shaggy hair, which covered his neck and shoulder. From this point his skin was smooth as one's hand, a sleek and shining dun, and his ribs were well covered with shaking flesh. Whilst leisurely cropping the short curly grass he occasionally lifted his tail into the air, and stamped his foot as a fly or mosquito annoyed him—flapping the intruder with his tail, or snatching at the itching part with his ponderous head.*

When La Bonté had sufficiently admired the buffalo, he lifted his rifle, and, taking steady aim, and certain of his mark, pulled the trigger, expecting to see the huge beast fall over at the report. What was his surprise and consternation, however, to see the animal only flinch when the ball struck him, and then gallop off, followed by the others, apparently unhurt. As is generally the case with greenhorns, he had fired too high, ignorant that the only certain spot to strike a buffalo is but a few inches above the brisket, and that a higher shot is rarely fatal. When he rose from the ground, he saw all the party halting in full view of his discomfiture; and when he joined them, loud were the laughs, and deep the regrets of the hungry at his first attempt.

However, they now knew that they were in the country of meat; and a few miles farther, another band of stragglers presenting themselves, three of the hunters went in pursuit, La Bonté taking a mule to pack in the meat. He soon saw them crawling towards the band, and shortly two puffs of smoke, and the sharp cracks of their rifles, showed that they had got within shot; and when he rode up, two fine buffaloes were stretched upon the ground. Now, for the first time, he was initiated in the mysteries of "butchering." He watched the hunters as they turned the carcass on the belly, stretching out the legs to support it on each side. A transverse cut was then made at the nape of the neck,

and, gathering the long hair of the boss in one hand, the skin was
separated from the shoulder. It was then laid open from this point to
the tail, along the spine, and then, freed from the sides and pulled
down to the brisket, but still attached to it, was stretched upon
the ground to receive the dissected portions. Then the shoulder was
severed, the fleece removed from along the backbone, and the hump-ribs
cut off with a tomahawk. All this was placed upon the skin; and after
the "boudins" had been withdrawn from the stomach, and the tongue—a
great dainty—taken from the head, the meat was packed upon the mule,
and the whole party hurried to camp rejoicing.

There was merry-making in the camp that night, and the way they
indulged their appetites—or, in their own language, "throw'd" the
meat "cold"—would have made the heart of a dyspeptic leap for joy or
burst with envy. Far into the "still watches of the tranquil night"
the fat-clad "depouille" saw its fleshy mass grow small by degrees
and beautifully less, before the trenchant blades of the hungry
mountaineers; appetizing yards of well-browned "boudin" slipped glibly
down their throats; rib after rib of tender hump was picked and flung
to the wolves; and when human nature, with helpless gratitude, and
confident that nothing of superexcellent comestibility remained, was
lazily wiping the greasy knife that had done such good service,—a
skillful hunter was seen to chuckle to himself as he raked the deep
ashes of the fire, and drew therefrom a pair of tongues so admirably
baked, so soft, so sweet, and of such exquisite flavour, that a veil
is considerately drawn over the effects their discussion produced in
the mind of our greenhorn La Bonté, and the raptures they excited in
the bosom of that, as yet, most ignorant mountaineer. Still, as he
ate he wondered, and wondering admired, that nature, in giving him
such profound gastronomic powers, and such transcendant capabilities
of digestion, had yet bountifully provided an edible so peculiarly
adapted to his ostrich-like appetite, that after consuming nearly his
own weight in rich and fat buffalo meat, he felt as easy and as little
incommoded as if he had lightly supped on strawberries and cream.

Sweet was the digestive pipe after such a feast; soft was the sleep
and deep, which sealed the eyes of the contented trappers that night.

It felt like the old thing, they said, to be once more amongst the "meat;" and, as they were drawing near the dangerous portion of the trail, they felt at home; although they now could never be confident, when they lay down at night upon their buffalo robes, of awaking again in this life, knowing, as they did, full well, that savage men lurked near, thirsting for their blood.

However, no enemies showed themselves as yet, and they proceeded quietly up the river, vast herds of buffaloes darkening the plains around them, affording them more than abundance of the choicest meat; but, to their credit be it spoken, no more was killed than was absolutely required,—unlike the cruel slaughter made by most of the white travellers across the plains, who wantonly destroy these noble animals, not even for the excitement of sport, but in cold-blooded and insane butchery. La Bonté had practice enough to perfect him in the art, and, before the buffalo range was passed, he was ranked as a first-rate hunter. One evening he had left the camp for meat, and was approaching a band of cows for that purpose, crawling towards them along the bed of a dry hollow in the prairie, when he observed them suddenly jump towards him, and immediately afterwards a score of mounted Indians appeared, whom, by their dress, he at once knew to be Pawnees and enemies. Thinking they might not discover him, he crouched down in the ravine; but a noise behind caused him to turn his head, and he saw some five or six advancing up the bed of the dry creek, whilst several more were riding on the bluffs. The cunning savages had cut off his retreat to his mule, which he saw in the possession of one of them. His presence of mind, however, did not desert him; and seeing at once that to remain where he was would be like being caught in a trap (as the Indians could advance to the edge of the bluff and shoot him from above), he made for the open prairie, determined at least to sell his scalp dearly, and make "a good fight." With a yell the Indians charged, but halted when they saw the sturdy trapper deliberately kneel, and, resting his rifle on the wiping-stick, take a steady aim as they advanced. Full well the Pawnees know, to their cost, that a mountaineer seldom pulls his trigger without sending a bullet to the mark; and, certain that one at least must fall, they hesitated to make the onslaught. Steadily the white retreated with his face to the foe, bringing the rifle to his shoulder the instant that one advanced within shot, the Indians galloping round, firing the few guns they had amongst them at long distances, but without effect. One young "brave," more daring than the rest, rode out of the crowd, and dashed at the hunter, throwing himself, as he passed within a few yards, from the saddle, and hanging over the opposite side of his horse, thus presenting no other mark than his left foot. As he crossed La Bonté, he discharged his bow from under his horse's neck, and with such good aim, that the arrow, whizzing through the air, struck the stock of the hunter's rifle, which was at his shoulder, and, glancing off, pierced his arm, inflicting, luckily, but a slight wound. Again the Indian turned in his course, the others encouraging him with loud war-whoops, and, once more passing at still less distance, he drew his arrow to the head. This time, however, the eagle eye of the white detected the action, and suddenly rising from his knee as the Indian approached (hanging by his foot alone over the opposite side of the horse), he jumped towards the animal with outstretched arms and a loud yell, causing it to start suddenly, and swerve from its course. The Indian lost his foot-hold, and, after a fruitless struggle to regain his position, fell to the ground; but instantly rose upon his feet and gallantly confronted the mountaineer, striking his hand upon his brawny chest and shouting a loud whoop of defiance. In another instant the rifle of La Bonté had poured forth its contents; and the brave savage, springing into the air, fell dead to the ground, just as the other trappers, who had heard the firing, galloped up to the spot. At sight of them the Pawnees, with yells of disappointed vengeance, hastily retreated.

That night La Bonté first lifted hair!

A few days later the mountaineers reached the point where the Platte divides into two great forks: the northern one, stretching to the north-west, skirts the eastern base of the Black Hills, and sweeping round to the south rises in the vicinity of the mountain valley called the New Park, receiving the Laramie, Medicine Bow, and Sweet-Water creeks. The other, or "South Fork," strikes towards the mountains

*in a south-westerly direction, hugging the base of the main chain
of the Rocky Mountains; and, fed by several small creeks, rises in
the uplands of the Bayou Salade, near which is also the source of
the Arkansa. To the forks of the Platte the valley of that river
extends from three to five miles on each side, enclosed by steep sandy
bluffs, from the summits of which the prairies stretch away in broad
undulating expanse to the north and south. The "bottom," as it is
termed, is but thinly covered with timber, the cotton-woods being
scattered only here and there; but some of the islands in the broad
bed of the stream are well wooded, leading to the inference that the
trees on the banks have been felled by Indians who formerly frequented
the neighbourhood of this river as a chosen hunting-ground. As, during
the long winters, the pasture in the vicinity is scarce and withered,
the Indians feed their horses on the bark of the sweet cotton-wood,
upon which they subsist, and even fatten. Thus, wherever a village
has encamped, the trunks of these trees strew the ground, their upper
limbs and smaller branches peeled of their bark, and looking as white
and smooth as if scraped with a knife.*

*On the forks, however, the timber is heavier and of greater variety,
some of the creeks being well wooded with ash and cherry, which break
the monotony of the everlasting cotton-wood.*

*Dense masses of buffalo still continued to darken the plains, and
numerous bands of wolves hovered round the outskirts of the vast
herds, singling out the sick and wounded animals, and preying upon
such calves as the rifles and arrows of the hunters had bereaved of
their mothers. The white wolf is the invariable attendant upon the
buffalo; and when one of these persevering animals is seen, it is
certain sign that buffalo are not far distant. Besides the buffalo
wolf, there are four distinct varieties common to the plains, and
all more or less attendant upon the buffalo. These are, the black,
the gray, the brown, and last and least the coyote, or cayeute
of the mountaineers, the "wach-unka-mănet," or "medicine wolf" of
the Indians, who hold the latter animal in reverential awe. This
little wolf, whose fur is of great thickness and beauty, is of
diminutive size, but wonderfully sagacious, making up by cunning
what it wants in physical strength. In bands of from three to thirty*

they not unfrequently station themselves along the "runs" of the deer and the antelope, extending their line for many miles—and the quarry being started, each wolf follows in pursuit until tired, when it relinquishes the chase to another relay, following slowly after until the animal is fairly run down, when all hurry to the spot and speedily consume the carcass. The cayeute, however, is often made a tool of by his larger brethren, unless, indeed, he acts from motives of spontaneous charity. When a hunter has slaughtered game, and is in the act of butchering it, these little wolves sit patiently at a short distance from the scene of operations, while at a more respectful one the larger wolves (the white or gray) lope hungrily around, licking their chops in hungry expectation. Not unfrequently the hunter throws a piece of meat towards the smaller one, who seizes it immediately, and runs off with the morsel in his mouth. Before he gets many yards with his prize, the large wolf pounces with a growl upon him, and the cayeute, dropping the meat, returns to his former position, and will continue his charitable act as long as the hunter pleases to supply him.

Wolves are so common on the plains and in the mountains, that the hunter never cares to throw away a charge of ammunition upon them, although the ravenous animals are a constant source of annoyance to him, creeping to the camp-fire at night, and gnawing his saddles and apishamores, eating the skin ropes which secure the horses and mules to their pickets, and even their very hobbles, and not unfrequently killing or entirely disabling the animals themselves.

Round the camp, during the night, the cayeute keeps unremitting watch, and the traveller not unfrequently starts from his bed with affright, as the mournful and unearthly chiding of the wolf breaks suddenly upon his ear: the long-drawn howl being taken up by others of the band, until it dies away in the distance, or some straggler passing within hearing answers to the note, and howls as he lopes away.

Our party crossed the south fork about ten miles from its juncture with the main stream, and then, passing the prairie, struck the north fork a day's travel from the other. At the mouth of an ash-timbered creek they came upon Indian "sign," and, as now they were in the vicinity of the treacherous Sioux, they moved along with additional caution, Frapp and Gonneville, two experienced mountaineers, always heading the advance.

About noon they had crossed over to the left bank of the fork, intending to camp on a large creek where some fresh beaver "sign" had attracted the attention of some of the trappers; and as, on further examination, it appeared that two or three lodges of that animal were not far distant, it was determined to remain here a day or two, and set their traps.

Gonneville, old Luke, and La Bonté, had started up the creek, and were carefully examining the banks for "sign," when the former, who was in front, suddenly paused, and looking intently up the stream, held up his hand to his companions to signal them to stop.

Luke and La Bonté both followed the direction of the trapper's intent and fixed gaze. The former uttered in a suppressed tone the expressive exclamation, Wagh!—the latter saw nothing but a wood-duck swimming swiftly down the stream, followed by her downy progeny.

Gonneville turned his head, and extending his arm twice with a forward motion up the creek, whispered—"Les sauvages."

"Injuns, sure, and Sioux at that," answered Luke.

Still La Bonté looked, but nothing met his view but the duck with her brood, now rapidly approaching; and as he gazed, the bird suddenly took wing, and, flapping on the water, flew a short distance down the stream and once more settled on it.

"Injuns?" he asked; "where are they?"

"Whar?" repeated old Luke, striking the flint of his rifle, and opening the pan to examine the priming. "What brings a duck a-streakin it down stream, if humans aint behint her? And who's thar in these diggins but Injuns, and the worst kind? And we'd better push to camp, I'm thinking, if we mean to save our hair."

"Sign" sufficient, indeed, it was to all the trappers, who, on being apprised of it, instantly drove in their animals, and picketed them; and hardly had they done so when a band of Indians made their appearance on the banks of the creek, from whence they galloped to the bluff which overlooked the camp at the distance of about six hundred yards; and crowning this, in number some forty or more, commenced brandishing their spears and guns, and whooping loud yells of defiance. The trappers had formed a little breast-work of their packs, forming a semicircle, the chord of which was made by the animals standing in a line, side by side, closely picketed and hobbled. Behind this defence stood the mountaineers, rifle in hand, and silent and determined. The Indians presently descended the bluff on foot, leaving their animals in charge of a few of the party, and, scattering, advanced under cover of the sage bushes which dotted the bottom, to about two hundred yards of the whites. Then a chief advanced before the rest, and made the sign for a talk with the Long-knives, which led to a consultation amongst the latter, as to the policy of acceding to it. They were in doubts as to the nation these Indians belonged to, some bands of the Sioux being friendly, and others bitterly hostile to the whites.

Gonneville, who spoke the Sioux language, and was well acquainted with the nation, affirmed they belonged to a band called the Yanka-taus, well known to be the most evil-disposed of that treacherous nation; another of the party maintained they were Brulés, and that the chief advancing towards them was the well-known Tah-sha-tunga or Bull Tail, a most friendly chief of that tribe. The majority, however, trusted to Gonneville, and he volunteered to go out to meet the Indian, and hear what he had to say. Divesting himself of all arms save his butcher-knife, he advanced towards the savage, who awaited his approach, enveloped in the folds of his blanket. At a glance he knew him to be a Yanka-tau, from the peculiar make of his moccasins, and the way in which his face was daubed with paint.

"Howgh!" exclaimed both as they met; and, after a silence of a few moments, the Indian spoke, asking—"Why the Long-knives hid behind their packs, when his band approached? Were they afraid, or were they preparing a dog-feast to entertain their friends?" The whites were passing through his country, burning his wood, drinking his water, and killing his game; but he knew they had now come to pay for the mischief they had done, and that the mules and horses they had brought with them were intended as a present to their red friends.

"He was Mah-to-ga-shane," he said, "the Brave Bear: his tongue was short, but his arm long; and he loved rather to speak with his bow and his lance than with the weapon of a squaw. He had said it: the

Long-knives had horses with them and mules; and these were for him, he knew, and for his 'braves.' Let the White-face go back to his people and return with the animals, or he, the 'Brave Bear,' would have to come and take them; and his young men would get mad and would feel blood in their eyes; and then he would have no power over them; and the whites would have to 'go under.'"

The trapper answered shortly.—"The Long-knives," he said, "had brought the horses for themselves—their hearts were big, but not towards the Yanka-taus: and if they had to give up their animals, it would be to men and not squaws. They were not 'wah-keitcha,' (French engages), but Long-knives; and, however short were the tongues of the Yanka-taus, theirs were still shorter, and their rifles longer. The Yanka-taus were dogs and squaws, and the Long-knives spat upon them."

Saying this, the trapper turned his back and rejoined his companions; whilst the Indian slowly proceeded to his people, who, on learning the contemptuous way in which their threats had been treated, testified their anger with loud yells; and, seeking whatever cover was afforded, commenced a scattering volley upon the camp of the mountaineers. The latter reserved their fire, treating with cool indifference the balls which began to rattle about them; but as the Indians, emboldened by this apparent inaction, rushed for a closer position, and exposed their bodies within a long range, half-a-dozen rifles rang from the assailed, and two Indians fell dead, one or two more being wounded. As yet, not one of the whites had been touched, but several of the animals had received wounds from the enemy's fire of balls and arrows. Indeed, the Indians remained at too great a distance to render the volleys from their crazy fusees any thing like effectual, and had to raise their pieces considerably to make their bullets reach as far as the camp. After three of their band had been killed outright, and many more wounded, their fire began to slacken, and they drew off to a greater distance, evidently resolved to beat a retreat. Retiring to the bluff, they discharged their pieces in a last volley, mounted their horses and galloped off, carrying their wounded with them. This last volley, however, although intended as a mere bravado, unfortunately proved fatal to one of the whites. Gonneville, at the moment, was standing on a pack, to get an uninterrupted sight for a

last shot, when one of the random bullets struck him in the breast.
La Bonté caught him in his arms as he was about to fall, and laying
the wounded trapper gently on the ground, stripped him of his buckskin
hunting-frock, to examine the wound. A glance was sufficient to
convince his companions that the blow was mortal. The ball had passed
through the lungs; and in a few moments the throat of the wounded
man swelled and turned to a livid blue colour, as the choking blood
ascended. Only a few drops of purple blood trickled from the wound,—a
fatal sign,—and the eyes of the mountaineer were already glazing with
death's icy touch. His hand still grasped the barrel of his rifle,
which had done good service in the fray. Anon he essayed to speak,
but, choked with blood, only a few inarticulate words reached the ears
of his companions, as they bent over him.

"Rubbed—out—at—last," they heard him say, the words gurgling in his
blood-filled throat; and opening his eyes once more, and turning them
upwards for a last look at the bright sun, the trapper turned gently
on his side and breathed his last sigh.

With no other tools than their scalp-knives, the hunters dug a grave
on the banks of the creek; and whilst some were engaged in this work,
others sought the bodies of the Indians they had slain in the attack,
and presently returned with three reeking scalps, the trophies of the
fight. The body of the mountaineer was wrapped in a buffalo robe,
the scalps being placed on his breast, and the dead man was then laid
in the shallow grave, and quickly covered—without a word of prayer,
or sigh of grief; for, however much his companions may have felt, not
a word escaped them. The bitten lip and frowning brow told of anger
rather than of sorrow, as they vowed—what they thought would better
please the spirit of the dead man than vain regrets—bloody and lasting
revenge.

Trampling down the earth which filled the grave, they raised upon
it a pile of heavy stones; and packing their mules once more, and
taking a last look at their comrade's lonely resting-place, they
turned their backs upon the stream, which has ever since been known as
"Gonneville's Creek."

If the reader casts his eye over any of the recent maps of the western country, which detail the features of the regions embracing the Rocky Mountains, and the vast prairies at their bases, he will not fail to observe that many of the creeks or smaller streams which feed the larger rivers,—as the Missouri, Platte, and Arkansa,—are called by familiar proper names, both English and French. These are invariably christened after some unfortunate trapper, killed there in Indian fight; or treacherously slaughtered by the lurking savages, while engaged in trapping beaver on the stream. Thus alone is the memory of these hardy men perpetuated, at least of those whose fate is ascertained: for many, in every season, never return from their hunting expeditions, but meet a sudden death from Indians, or a more lingering fate from accident or disease in some lonely gorge of the mountains where no footfall save their own, or the heavy tread of grizzly bear, disturbs the unbroken silence of the awful solitude. Then, as many winters pass without some old familiar faces making their appearance at the merry rendezvous, their long protracted absence may perhaps elicit a remark, as to where such and such a mountain worthy can have betaken himself, to which the casual rejoinder of "Gone under, maybe," too often gives a short but certain answer.

In all the philosophy of hardened hearts, our hunters turned from the spot where the unmourned trapper met his death. La Bonté, however, not yet entirely steeled by mountain life to a perfect indifference to human feeling, drew his hard hand across his eye, as the unbidden tear rose from his rough but kindly heart. He could not forget so soon the comrade he had lost, the companion in the hunt or over the cheerful camp-fire, the narrator of many a tale of dangers past, of sufferings from hunger, cold, thirst, and untended wounds, of Indian perils, and other vicissitudes. One tear dropped from the young hunter's eye, and rolled down his cheek—the last for many a long year.

In the forks of the northern branch of the Platte, formed by the junction of the Laramie, they found a big village of the Sioux encamped near the station of one of the fur companies. Here the party broke up; many, finding the alcohol of the traders an impediment to their further progress, remained some time in the vicinity, while La Bonté, Luke, and a trapper named Marcelline, started in a few days to the mountains, to trap on Sweet Water and Medicine Bow. They had leisure, however, to observe all the rascalities connected with the Indian trade, although at this season (August) hardly commenced. However, a band of Indians having come in with several packs of last year's robes, and being anxious to start speedily on their return, a trader from one of the forts had erected his lodge in the village. Here he set to work immediately, to induce the Indians to trade. First, a chief appoints three "soldiers" to guard the trader's lodge from intrusion; and these sentries amongst the thieving fraternity can be invariably trusted. Then the Indians are invited to have a drink—a taste of the fire-water being given to all to incite them to trade. As the crowd presses upon the entrance to the lodge, and those in rear become impatient, some large-mouthed savage who has received a portion of the spirit, makes his way, with his mouth full of the liquor and cheeks distended, through the throng, and is instantly surrounded by his particular friends. Drawing the face of each, by turns, near his own, he squirts a small quantity into his open mouth, until the supply is exhausted, when he returns for more, and repeats the generous distribution.

When paying for the robes, the traders, in measuring out the liquor in a tin half-pint cup, thrust their thumbs or the four fingers of the hand into the measure, in order that it may contain the less, or not unfrequently fill the bottom with melted buffalo fat, with the same object. So greedy are the Indians, that they never discover the cheat, and, once under the influence of the liquor, cannot distinguish between the first cup of comparatively strong spirit, and the following ones diluted five hundred per cent, and poisonously drugged to boot.

Scenes of drunkenness, riot, and bloodshed last until the trade is over. In the winter it occupies several weeks, during which period the Indians present the appearance, under the demoralizing influence of the liquor, of demons rather than of men.

CHAPTER 11

Captain Bonneville
Among the Blackfeet

By Washington Irving

Noted American writer Washington Irving is said to have shelled out $1,000 (big hard-earned money back then) to buy a manuscript written by a certain Captain Benjamin Louis Eulalie de Bonneville. The author was a professional soldier, educated at West Point, who had taken leave from the Army in 1831 for a life of travel and adventure in the Rocky Mountains. He called his journal A Tour on the Prairies, *but apparently his skills in the outdoors were not matched by his skills with the pen. Deemed unpublishable by publishing gate-keepers of that time, the manuscript caught the eye of Washington Irving, who shared Bonneville's passion for western adventure. Irving rewrote the book, using both his own experiences and material from other sources, in conjunction with Bonneville's original work. The completed work,* The Adventures of Captain Bonneville U.S.A. in the Rocky Mountains of the Far West *was a big success. In this excerpt, we join Captain Bonneville as he heads for the Wind River Range.*

IT WAS ON THE 20ᵀᴴ OF JULY THAT CAPTAIN BONNEVILLE FIRST CAME in sight of the grand region of his hopes and anticipations, the Rocky Mountains. He had been making a bend to the south, to avoid some obstacles along the river, and had attained a high, rocky ridge, when a magnificent prospect burst upon his sight. To the west rose the Wind River Mountains, with their bleached and snowy summits towering into the clouds. These stretched far to the north-northwest, until they melted away into what appeared to be faint clouds, but which the experienced eyes of the veteran hunters of the party recognized for the rugged mountains of the Yellowstone; at the feet of which extended the wild Crow country: a perilous, though profitable region for the trapper.

To the southwest, the eye ranged over an immense extent of wilderness, with what appeared to be a snowy vapor resting upon its horizon. This, however, was pointed out as another branch of the Great Chippewyan, or Rocky chain; being the Eutaw Mountains, at whose basis the wandering tribe of hunters of the same name pitch their tents. We can imagine the enthusiasm of the worthy captain when he beheld the vast and mountainous scene of his adventurous enterprise thus suddenly unveiled before him. We can imagine with what feelings of awe and admiration he must have contemplated the Wind River Sierra, or bed of mountains; that great fountainhead from whose springs, and lakes, and melted snows some of those mighty rivers take their rise, which wander over hundreds of miles of varied country and clime, and find their way to the opposite waves of the Atlantic and the Pacific.

The Wind River Mountains are, in fact, among the most remarkable of the whole Rocky chain; and would appear to be among the loftiest. They form, as it were, a great bed of mountains, about eighty miles in length, and from twenty to thirty in breadth; with rugged peaks, covered with eternal snows, and deep, narrow valleys full of springs, and brooks, and rock-bound lakes. From this great treasury of waters issue forth limpid streams, which, augmenting as they descend, become main tributaries of the Missouri on the one side, and the Columbia on the other; and give rise to the Seeds-ke-dee Agie, or Green River, the great Colorado of the West, that empties its current into the Gulf of California.

The Wind River Mountains are notorious in hunters' and trappers' stories: their rugged defiles, and the rough tracts about their neighbourhood, having been lurking places for the predatory hordes of the mountains, and scenes of rough encounter with Crows and Blackfeet. It was to the west of these mountains, in the valley of the Seeds-ke-dee Agie, or Green River, that Captain Bonneville intended to make a halt for the purpose of giving repose to his people and his horses after their weary journeying; and of collecting information as to his future course. This Green River valley, and its immediate neighbourhood, as we have already observed, formed the main point of rendezvous, for the present year, of the rival fur companies, and the motley populace, civilized and savage, connected with them. Several days of rugged travel, however, yet remained for the captain and his men before they should encamp in this desired resting-place.

On the 21st of July, as they were pursuing their course through one of the meadows of the Sweet Water, they beheld a horse grazing at a little distance. He showed no alarm at their approach, but suffered himself quietly to be taken, evincing a perfect state of tameness. The scouts of the party were instantly on the look-out for the owners of this animal; lest some dangerous band of savages might be lurking in the vicinity. After a narrow search, they discovered the trail of an Indian party, which had evidently passed through that neighbourhood but recently. The horse was accordingly taken possession of, as an estray; but a more vigilant watch than usual was kept round the camp at nights, lest his former owners should be upon the prowl.

The travellers had now attained so high an elevation that on the 23d of July, at daybreak, there was considerable ice in the waterbuckets, and the thermometer stood at twenty-two degrees. The rarefy of the atmosphere continued to affect the wood-work of the wagons, and the wheels were incessantly falling to pieces. A remedy was at length devised. The tire of each wheel was taken off; a band of wood was nailed round the exterior of the felloes, the tire was then made red hot, replaced round the wheel, and suddenly cooled with water. By this means, the whole was bound together with great compactness.

The extreme elevation of these great steppes, which range along the feet of the Rocky Mountains, takes away from the seeming height of their peaks, which yield to few in the known world in point of altitude above the level of the sea.

On the 24th, the travellers took final leave of the Sweet Water, and keeping westwardly, over a low and very rocky ridge, one of the most southern spurs of the Wind River Mountains, they encamped, after a march of seven hours and a half, on the banks of a small clear stream, running to the south, in which they caught a number of fine trout.

The sight of these fish was hailed with pleasure, as a sign that they had reached the waters which flow into the Pacific; for it is only on the western streams of the Rocky Mountains that trout are to be taken. The stream on which they had thus encamped proved, in effect, to be tributary to the Seeds-ke-dee Agie, or Green River, into which it flowed at some distance to the south.

Captain Bonneville now considered himself as having fairly passed the crest of the Rocky Mountains; and felt some degree of exultation in being the first individual that had crossed, north of the settled provinces of Mexico, from the waters of the Atlantic to those of the Pacific, with wagons. Mr. William Sublette, the enterprising leader of the Rocky Mountain Fur Company, had, two or three years previously, reached the valley of the Wind River, which lies on the northeast of the mountains; but had proceeded with them no further.

A vast valley now spread itself before the travellers, bounded on one side by the Wind River Mountains, and to the west, by a long range of high hills. This, Captain Bonneville was assured by a veteran hunter in his company, was the great valley of the Seedske-dee; and the same informant would have fain persuaded him that a small stream, three feet deep, which he came to on the 25th, was that river. The captain was convinced, however, that the stream was too insignificant to drain so wide a valley and the adjacent mountains: he encamped, therefore, at an early hour, on its borders, that he might take the whole of the next day to reach the main river; which he presumed to flow between him and the distant range of western hills.

On the 26th of July, he commenced his march at an early hour, making directly across the valley, toward the hills in the west; proceeding at as brisk a rate as the jaded condition of his horses would permit. About eleven o'clock in the morning, a great cloud of dust was descried in the rear, advancing directly on the trail of the party. The alarm was given; they all came to a halt, and held a council of war. Some conjectured that the band of Indians, whose trail they had discovered in the neighbourhood of the stray horse, had been lying in wait for them in some secret fastness of the mountains; and were about to attack them on the open plain, where they would have no shelter. Preparations were immediately made for defence; and a scouting party sent off to reconnoitre. They soon came galloping back, making signals that all was well. The cloud of dust was made by a band of fifty or sixty mounted trappers, belonging to the American Fur Company, who soon came up, leading their pack-horses. They were headed by Mr. Fontenelle, an experienced leader, or "partisan," as a chief of a party is called in the technical language of the trappers.

Mr. Fontenelle informed Captain Bonneville that he was on his way from the company's trading post on the Yellowstone to the yearly rendezvous, with reinforcements and supplies for their hunting and trading parties beyond the mountains; and that he expected to meet, by appointment, with a band of free trappers in that very neighbourhood. He had fallen upon the trail of Captain Bonneville's party, just after leaving the Nebraska; and, finding that they had frightened off all the game, had been obliged to push on, by forced marches, to avoid famine: both men and horses were, therefore, much travel-worn; but this was no place to halt; the plain before them he said was destitute of grass and water, neither of which would be met with short of the Green River, which was yet at a considerable distance. He hoped, he added, as his party were all on horseback, to reach the river, with hard travelling, by nightfall: but he doubted the possibility of Captain Bonneville's arrival there with his wagons before the day following. Having imparted this information, he pushed forward with all speed.

Captain Bonneville followed on as fast as circumstances would permit. The ground was firm and gravelly; but the horses were too much fatigued to move rapidly. After a long and harassing day's march, without pausing for a noontide meal, they were compelled, at nine o'clock at night, to encamp in an open plain, destitute of water or pasturage. On the following morning, the horses were turned loose at the peep of day; to slake their thirst, if possible, from the dew collected on the sparse grass, here and there springing up among dry sand-banks. The soil of a great part of this Green River valley is a whitish clay, into which the rain cannot penetrate, but which dries and cracks with the sun. In some places it produces a salt weed, and grass along the margins of the streams; but the wider expanses of it are desolate and barren. It was not until noon that Captain Bonneville reached the banks of the Seeds-ke-dee, or Colorado of the West; in the meantime, the sufferings of both men and horses had been excessive, and it was with almost frantic eagerness that they hurried to allay their burning thirst in the limpid current of the river.

Fontenelle and his party had not fared much better; the chief part had managed to reach the river by nightfall, but were nearly knocked up by the exertion; the horses of others sank under them, and they were obliged to pass the night upon the road.

On the following morning, July 27th, Fontenelle moved his camp across the river; while Captain Bonneville proceeded some little distance below, where there was a small but fresh meadow yielding abundant pasturage. Here the poor jaded horses were turned out to graze, and take their rest: the weary journey up the mountains had worn them down in flesh and spirit; but this last march across the thirsty plain had nearly finished them.

The captain had here the first taste of the boasted strategy of the fur trade. During his brief, but social encampment, in company with Fontenelle, that experienced trapper had managed to win over a number of Delaware Indians whom the captain had brought with him, by offering them four hundred dollars each for the ensuing autumnal hunt. The captain was somewhat astonished when he saw these hunters, on whose services he had calculated securely, suddenly pack up their traps, and go over to the rival camp. That he might in some measure, however, be even with his competitor, he dispatched two scouts to look out for the band of free trappers who were to meet Fontenelle in this neighbourhood, and to endeavour to bring them to his camp.

As it would be necessary to remain some time in this neighbourhood, that both men and horses might repose, and recruit their strength; and as it was a region full of danger, Captain Bonneville proceeded to fortify his camp with breastworks of logs and pickets.

These precautions were, at that time, peculiarly necessary, from the bands of Blackfeet Indians which were roving about the neighbourhood. These savages are the most dangerous banditti of the mountains, and the inveterate foe of the trappers. They are Ishmaelites of the first order, always with weapon in hand, ready for action. The young braves of the tribe, who are destitute of property, go to war for booty; to gain horses, and acquire the means of setting up a lodge, supporting a family, and entitling themselves to a seat in the public councils. The veteran warriors fight merely for the love of the thing, and the consequence which success gives them among their people.

They are capital horsemen, and are generally well mounted on short, stout horses, similar to the prairie ponies to be met with at St. Louis. When on a war party, however, they go on foot, to enable them to skulk through the country with greater secrecy; to keep in thickets and ravines, and use more adroit subterfuges and stratagems. Their mode of warfare is entirely by ambush, surprise, and sudden assaults in the night time. If they succeed in causing a panic, they dash forward with headlong fury: if the enemy is on the alert, and shows no signs of fear, they become wary and deliberate in their movements.

Some of them are armed in the primitive style, with bows and arrows; the greater part have American fusees, made after the fashion of those of the Hudson's Bay Company. These they procure at the trading post of the American Fur Company, on Marias River, where they traffic their peltries for arms, ammunition, clothing, and trinkets. They are extremely fond of spirituous liquors and tobacco; for which nuisances they are ready to exchange not merely their guns and horses, but even their wives and daughters. As they are a treacherous race, and have cherished a lurking hostility to the whites ever since one of their tribe was killed by Mr. Lewis, the associate of General Clarke, in his exploring expedition across the Rocky Mountains, the American Fur Company is obliged constantly to keep at that post a garrison of sixty or seventy men.

Under the general name of Blackfeet are comprehended several tribes: such as the Surcies, the Peagans, the Blood Indians, and the Gros Ventres of the Prairies: who roam about the southern branches of the Yellowstone and Missouri Rivers, together with some other tribes further north.

The bands infesting the Wind River Mountains and the country adjacent at the time of which we are treating, were Gros Ventres of the Prairies, which are not to be confounded with Gros Ventres of the Missouri, who keep about the lower part of that river, and are friendly to the white men.

This hostile band keeps about the headwaters of the Missouri, and numbers about nine hundred fighting men. Once in the course of two or three years they abandon their usual abodes, and make a visit to the Arapahoes of the Arkansas. Their route lies either through the Crow country, and the Black Hills, or through the lands of the Nez Perces, Flatheads, Bannacks, and Shoshonies. As they enjoy their favorite state of hostility with all these tribes, their expeditions are prone to be conducted in the most lawless and predatory style; nor do they hesitate to extend their maraudings to any party of white men they meet with; following their trails; hovering about their camps; waylaying and dogging the caravans of the free traders, and murdering the solitary trapper. The consequences are frequent and desperate fights between them and the "mountaineers," in the wild defiles and fastnesses of the Rocky Mountains.

The band in question was, at this time, on their way homeward from one of their customary visits to the Arapahoes; and in the ensuing chapter we shall treat of some bloody encounters between them and the trappers, which had taken place just before the arrival of Captain Bonneville among the mountains.

Leaving Captain Bonneville and his band ensconced within their fortified camp in the Green River valley, we shall step back and accompany a party of the Rocky Mountain Fur Company in its progress, with supplies from St. Louis, to the annual rendezvous at Pierre's Hole. This party consisted of sixty men, well mounted, and conducting a line of packhorses. They were commanded by Captain William Sublette, a partner in the company, and one of the most active, intrepid, and renowned leaders in this half military kind of service. He was accompanied by his associate in business, and tried companion in danger, Mr. Robert Campbell, one of the pioneers of the trade beyond the mountains, who had commanded trapping parties there in times of the greatest peril.

As these worthy compeers were on their route to the frontier, they fell in with another expedition, likewise on its way to the mountains. This was a party of regular "down-easters," that is to say, people of New England, who, with the all-penetrating and all-pervading spirit of their race, were now pushing their way into a new field of enterprise with which they were totally unacquainted. The party had been fitted out and was maintained and commanded by Mr. Nathaniel J. Wyeth, of Boston. This gentleman had conceived an idea that a profitable fishery for salmon might be established on the Columbia River, and connected with the fur trade. He had, accordingly, invested capital in goods, calculated, as he supposed, for the Indian trade, and had enlisted a number of eastern men in his employ, who had never been in the Far West, nor knew anything of the wilderness. With these, he was bravely steering his way across the continent, undismayed by danger, difficulty, or distance, in the same way that a New England coaster and his neighbours will coolly launch forth on a voyage to the Black Sea, or a whaling cruise to the Pacific.

With all their national aptitude at expedient and resource, Wyeth and his men felt themselves completely at a loss when they reached the frontier, and found that the wilderness required experience and habitudes of which they were totally deficient. Not one of the party, excepting the leader, had ever seen an Indian or handled a rifle; they were without guide or interpreter, and totally unacquainted with "wood craft" and the modes of making their way among savage hordes, and subsisting themselves during long marches over wild mountains and barren plains.

In this predicament, Captain Sublette found them, in a manner becalmed, or rather run aground, at the little frontier town of Independence, in Missouri, and kindly took them in tow. The two parties travelled amicably together; the frontier men of Sublette's party gave their Yankee comrades some lessons in hunting, and some insight into the art and mystery of dealing with the Indians, and they all arrived without accident at the upper branches of the Nebraska or Platte River.

In the course of their march, Mr. Fitzpatrick, the partner of the company who was resident at that time beyond the mountains, came down from the rendezvous at Pierre's Hole to meet them and hurry them forward. He travelled in company with them until they reached the Sweet Water; then taking a couple of horses, one for the saddle, and the other as a pack-horse, he started off express for Pierre's Hole, to make arrangements against their arrival, that he might commence his hunting campaign before the rival company.

Fitzpatrick was a hardy and experienced mountaineer, and knew all the passes and defiles. As he was pursuing his lonely course up the Green

River valley, he described several horsemen at a distance, and came to a halt to reconnoitre. He supposed them to be some detachment from the rendezvous, or a party of friendly Indians. They perceived him, and setting up the war-whoop, dashed forward at full speed: he saw at once his mistake and his peril—they were Blackfeet. Springing upon his fleetest horse, and abandoning the other to the enemy, he made for the mountains, and succeeded in escaping up one of the most dangerous defiles. Here he concealed himself until he thought the Indians had gone off, when he returned into the valley. He was again pursued, lost his remaining horse, and only escaped by scrambling up among the cliffs. For several days he remained lurking among rocks and precipices, and almost famished, having but one remaining charge in his rifle, which he kept for self-defence.

In the meantime, Sublette and Campbell, with their fellow traveller, Wyeth, had pursued their march unmolested, and arrived in the Green River valley, totally unconscious that there was any lurking enemy at hand. They had encamped one night on the banks of a small stream, which came down from the Wind River Mountains, when about midnight, a band of Indians burst upon their camp, with horrible yells and whoops, and a discharge of guns and arrows. Happily no other harm was done than wounding one mule, and causing several horses to break loose from their pickets. The camp was instantly in arms; but the Indians retreated with yells of exultation, carrying off several of the horses under cover of the night.

This was somewhat of a disagreeable foretaste of mountain life to some of Wyeth's band, accustomed only to the regular and peaceful life of New England; nor was it altogether to the taste of Captain Sublette's men, who were chiefly creoles and townsmen from St. Louis. They continued their march the next morning, keeping scouts ahead and upon their flanks, and arrived without further molestation at Pierre's Hole.

The first inquiry of Captain Sublette, on reaching the rendezvous, was for Fitzpatrick. He had not arrived, nor had any intelligence been received concerning him. Great uneasiness was now entertained, lest he should have fallen into the hands of the Blackfeet who had made the midnight attack upon the camp. It was a matter of general joy, therefore, when he made his appearance, conducted by two half-breed Iroquois hunters. He had lurked for several days among the mountains, until almost starved; at length he escaped the vigilance of his enemies in the night, and was so fortunate as to meet the two Iroquois hunters, who, being on horseback, conveyed him without further difficulty to the rendezvous. He arrived there so emaciated that he could scarcely be recognized.

The valley called Pierre's Hole is about thirty miles in length and fifteen in width, bounded to the west and south by low and broken ridges, and overlooked to the east by three lofty mountains, called the three Tetons, which domineer as landmarks over a vast extent of country.

A fine stream, fed by rivulets and mountain springs, pours through the valley toward the north, dividing it into nearly equal parts. The meadows on its borders are broad and extensive, covered with willow and cottonwood trees, so closely interlocked and matted together as to be nearly impassable.

In this valley was congregated the motley populace connected with the fur trade. Here the two rival companies had their encampments, with their retainers of all kinds: traders, trappers, hunters, and half-breeds, assembled from all quarters, awaiting their yearly supplies, and their orders to start off in new directions. Here, also, the savage tribes connected with the trade, the Nez Perces or Chopunnish Indians, and Flatheads, had pitched their lodges beside the streams, and with their squaws, awaited the distribution of goods and finery. There was, moreover, a band of fifteen free trappers, commanded by a gallant leader from Arkansas, named Sinclair, who held their encampment a little apart from the rest. Such was the wild and heterogeneous assemblage, amounting to several hundred men, civilized and savage, distributed in tents and lodges in the several camps.

The arrival of Captain Sublette with supplies put the Rocky Mountain Fur Company in full activity. The wares and merchandise were quickly opened, and as quickly disposed of to trappers and Indians; the usual excitement and revelry took place, after which all hands began to disperse to their several destinations.

On the 17th of July, a small brigade of fourteen trappers, led by Milton Sublette, brother of the captain, set out with the intention of proceeding to the southwest. They were accompanied by Sinclair and his fifteen free trappers; Wyeth, also, and his New England band of beaver hunters and salmon fishers, now dwindled down to eleven, took this opportunity to prosecute their cruise in the wilderness, accompanied with such experienced pilots. On the first day, they proceeded about eight miles to the southeast, and encamped for the night, still in the valley of Pierre's Hole. On the following morning, just as they were raising their camp, they observed a long line of people pouring down a defile of the mountains. They at first supposed them to be Fontenelle and his party, whose arrival had been daily expected. Wyeth, however, reconnoitred them with a spy-glass, and soon perceived they were Indians. They were divided into two parties, forming, in the whole, about one hundred and fifty persons, men, women, and children. Some were on horseback, fantastically painted and arrayed, with scarlet blankets fluttering in the wind. The greater part, however, were on foot. They had perceived the trappers before they were themselves discovered, and came down yelling and whooping into the plain. On nearer approach, they were ascertained to be Blackfeet.

One of the trappers of Sublette's brigade, a half-breed named Antoine Godin, now mounted his horse, and rode forth as if to hold a conference. He was the son of an Iroquois hunter, who had been cruelly murdered by the Blackfeet at a small stream below the mountains, which still bears his name. In company with Antoine rode forth a Flathead Indian, whose once powerful tribe had been completely broken down in their wars with the Blackfeet. Both of them, therefore, cherished the most vengeful hostility against these marauders of the mountains. The Blackfeet came to a halt. One of the chiefs advanced singly and unarmed, bearing the pipe of peace. This overture was certainly pacific; but Antoine and the Flathead were predisposed to hostility, and pretended to consider it a treacherous movement.

"Is your piece charged?" said Antoine to his red companion.

"It is."

"Then cock it, and follow me."

They met the Blackfoot chief half way, who extended his hand in friendship. Antoine grasped it.

"Fire!" cried he.

The Flathead levelled his piece, and brought the Blackfoot to the ground. Antoine snatched off his scarlet blanket, which was richly ornamented, and galloped off with it as a trophy to the camp, the bullets of the enemy whistling after him. The Indians immediately threw themselves into the edge of a swamp, among willows and cotton-wood trees, interwoven with vines. Here they began to fortify themselves; the women digging a trench, and throwing up a breastwork of logs and branches, deep hid in the bosom of the wood, while the warriors skirmished at the edge to keep the trappers at bay.

The latter took their station in a ravine in front, whence they kept up a scattering fire. As to Wyeth, and his little band of "downeasters," they were perfectly astounded by this second specimen of life in the wilderness; the men, being especially unused to bushfighting and the use of the rifle, were at a loss how to proceed. Wyeth, however, acted as a skillful commander. He got all his horses into camp and secured them; then, making a breastwork of his packs of goods, he charged his men to remain in garrison, and not to stir out of their fort. For himself, he mingled with the other leaders, determined to take his share in the conflict.

In the meantime, an express had been sent off to the rendezvous for reinforcements. Captain Sublette, and his associate, Campbell, were at their camp when the express came galloping across the plain, waving his cap, and giving the alarm; "Blackfeet! Blackfeet! A fight in the upper part of the valley!—to arms! To arms!"

The alarm was passed from camp to camp. It was a common cause. Every one turned out with horse and rifle. The Nez Perces and Flatheads joined. As fast as horseman could arm and mount he galloped off; the valley was soon alive with white men and red men scouring at full speed.

Sublette ordered his men to keep to the camp, being recruits from St. Louis, and unused to Indian warfare. He and his friend Campbell prepared for action. Throwing off their coats, rolling up their sleeves, and arming themselves with pistols and rifles, they mounted their horses and dashed forward among the first. As they rode along, they made their wills in soldier-like style; each stating how his effects should be disposed of in case of his death, and appointing the other his executor.

The Blackfeet warriors had supposed the brigade of Milton Sublette all the foes they had to deal with, and were astonished to behold the whole valley suddenly swarming with horsemen, galloping to the field of action. They withdrew into their fort, which was completely hid from sight in the dark and tangled wood. Most of their women and children had retreated to the mountains. The trappers now sallied forth and approached the swamp, firing into the thickets at random; the Blackfeet had a better sight at their adversaries, who were in the open field, and a half-breed was wounded in the shoulder.

When Captain Sublette arrived, he urged to penetrate the swamp and storm the fort, but all hung back in awe of the dismal horrors of the place, and the danger of attacking such desperadoes in their savage den. The very Indian allies, though accustomed to bushfighting, regarded it as almost impenetrable, and full of frightful danger. Sublette was not to be turned from his purpose, but offered to lead the way into the swamp. Campbell stepped forward to accompany him. Before entering the perilous wood, Sublette took his brothers aside, and told them that in case he fell, Campbell, who knew his will, was to be his executor. This done, he grasped his rifle and pushed into the thickets, followed by Campbell. Sinclair, the partisan from Arkansas, was at the edge of the wood with his brother and a few of his men. Excited by the gallant example of the two friends, he pressed forward to share their dangers.

The swamp was produced by the labours of the beaver, which, by damming up a stream, had inundated a portion of the valley. The place was all overgrown with woods and thickets, so closely matted and entangled that it was impossible to see ten paces ahead, and the three associates in peril had to crawl along, one after another, making their way by putting the branches and vines aside; but doing it with caution, lest they should attract the eye of some lurking marksman. They took the lead by turns, each advancing about twenty yards at a time, and now and then hallooing to their men to follow. Some of the latter gradually entered the swamp, and followed a little distance in their rear.

They had now reached a more open part of the wood, and had glimpses of the rude fortress from between the trees. It was a mere breast-work, as we have said, of logs and branches, with blankets, buffalo robes, and the leathern covers of lodges, extended round the top as a screen. The movements of the leaders, as they groped their way, had been descried by the sharp-sighted enemy. As Sinclair, who was in the advance, was putting some branches aside, he was shot through the body. He fell on the spot. "Take me to my brother," said he to Campbell. The latter gave him in charge to some of the men, who conveyed him out of the swamp.

Sublette now took the advance. As he was reconnoitering the fort, he perceived an Indian peeping through an aperture. In an instant his rifle was levelled and discharged, and the ball struck the savage in the eye. While he was reloading, he called to Campbell, and pointed out to him the hole; "Watch that place," said he, "and you will soon have a fair chance for a shot." Scarce had he uttered the words, when a ball struck him in the shoulder, and almost wheeled him around. His first thought was to take hold of his arm with his other hand, and move it up and down. He ascertained, to his satisfaction, that the bone was not broken. The next moment he was so faint that he could not stand. Campbell took him in his arms and carried him out of the thicket. The same shot that struck Sublette wounded another man in the head.

A brisk fire was now opened by the mountaineers from the wood, answered occasionally from the fort. Unluckily, the trappers and their allies, in searching for the fort, had got scattered, so that Wyeth, and a number of Nez Perces, approached the fort on the northwest side, while others did the same on the opposite quarter. A cross-fire thus took place, which occasionally did mischief to friends as well as foes. An Indian was shot down, close to Wyeth, by a ball which, he was convinced, had been sped from the rifle of a trapper on the other side of the fort.

The number of whites and their Indian allies had by this time so much increased by arrivals from the rendezvous, that the Blackfeet were completely overmatched. They kept doggedly in their fort, however, making no offer of surrender. An occasional firing into the breastwork was kept up during the day. Now and then, one of the Indian allies, in bravado, would rush up to the fort, fire over the ramparts, tear off a buffalo robe or a scarlet blanket, and return with it in triumph to his comrades. Most of the savage garrison that fell, however, were killed in the first part of the attack.

At one time it was resolved to set fire to the fort; and the squaws belonging to the allies were employed to collect combustibles. This however, was abandoned; the Nez Perces being unwilling to destroy the robes and blankets, and other spoils of the enemy, which they felt sure would fall into their hands.

The Indians, when fighting, are prone to taunt and revile each other. During one of the pauses of the battle, the voice of the Blackfeet chief was heard.

"So long," said he, "as we had powder and ball, we fought you in the open field: when those were spent, we retreated here to die with our women and children. You may burn us in our fort; but, stay by our ashes, and you who are so hungry for fighting will soon have enough. There are four hundred lodges of our brethren at hand. They will soon be here— their arms are strong—their hearts are big—they will avenge us!"

This speech was translated two or three times by Nez Perce and creole interpreters. By the time it was rendered into English, the chief was made to say that four hundred lodges of his tribe were attacking the encampment at the other end of the valley. Every one now was for hurrying to the defence of the rendezvous. A party was left to keep watch upon the fort; the rest galloped off to the camp. As night came on, the trappers drew out of the swamp, and remained about the skirts of the wood. By morning, their companions returned from the rendezvous with the report that all was safe. As the day opened, they ventured within the swamp and approached the fort. All was silent. They advanced up to it without opposition. They entered: it had been abandoned in the night, and the Blackfeet had effected their retreat, carrying off their wounded on litters made of branches, leaving bloody traces on the herbage. The bodies of ten Indians were found within the fort; among them the one shot in the eye by Sublette. The Blackfeet afterward reported that they had lost twenty-six warriors in this battle. Thirty-two horses were likewise found killed; among them were some of those recently carried off from Sublette's party, in the night; which showed that these were the very savages that had attacked him. They proved to be an advance party of the main body of Blackfeet, which had been upon the trail of Sublette's party. Five white men and one halfbreed were killed, and several wounded.

Seven of the Nez Perces were also killed, and six wounded. They had an old chief, who was reputed as invulnerable. In the course of the action he was hit by a spent ball, and threw up blood; but his skin was unbroken. His people were now fully convinced that he was proof against powder and ball.

A striking circumstance is related as having occurred the morning after the battle. As some of the trappers and their Indian allies were approaching the fort through the woods, they beheld an Indian woman, of noble form and features, leaning against a tree. Their surprise at her lingering here alone, to fall into the hands of her enemies, was dispelled, when they saw the corpse of a warrior at her feet. Either she was so lost in grief as not to perceive their approach; or a proud spirit kept her silent and motionless. The Indians set up a yell, on discovering her, and before the trappers could interfere, her mangled body fell upon the corpse which she had refused to abandon. We have heard this anecdote discredited by one of the leaders who had been in the battle: but the fact may have taken place without his seeing it, and been concealed from him. It is an instance of female devotion, even to the death, which we are well disposed to believe and to record.

After the battle, the brigade of Milton Sublette, together with the free trappers, and Wyeth's New England band, remained some days at the rendezvous, to see if the main body of Blackfeet intended to make an attack; nothing of the kind occurring, they once more put themselves in motion, and proceeded on their route toward the southwest. Captain Sublette having distributed his supplies, had intended to set off on his return to St. Louis, taking with him the peltries collected from the trappers and Indians. His wound, however obliged him to postpone his departure. Several who were to have accompanied him became impatient of this delay. Among these was a young Bostonian, Mr. Joseph More, one of the followers of Mr. Wyeth, who had seen enough of mountain life and savage warfare, and was eager to return to the abodes of civilization. He and six others, among whom were a Mr. Foy, of Mississippi, Mr. Alfred K. Stephens, of St. Louis, and two grandsons of the celebrated Daniel Boon, set out together, in advance of Sublette's party, thinking they would make their way through the mountains.

It was just five days after the battle of the swamp that these seven companions were making their way through Jackson's Hole, a valley not far from the three Tetons, when, as they were descending a hill, a party of Blackfeet that lay in ambush started up with terrific yells. The horse of the young Bostonian, who was in front, wheeled round with affright, and threw his unskilled rider. The young man scrambled up the side of the hill, but, unaccustomed to such wild scenes, lost his presence of mind, and stood, as if paralyzed, on the edge of a bank, until the Blackfeet came up and slew him on the spot. His comrades had fled on the first alarm; but two of them, Foy and Stephens, seeing his danger, paused when they got half way up the hill, turned back, dismounted, and hastened to his assistance. Foy was instantly killed. Stephens was severely wounded, but escaped, to die five days afterward. The survivors returned to the camp of Captain Sublette, bringing tidings of this new disaster. That hardy leader, as soon as he could bear the journey, set out on his return to St. Louis, accompanied by Campbell. As they had a number of pack-horses richly laden with peltries to convoy, they chose a different route through the mountains, out of the way, as they hoped, of the lurking bands of Blackfeet. They succeeded in making the frontier in safety. We remember to have seen them with their band, about two or three months afterward, passing through a skirt of woodland in the upper part of Missouri. Their long cavalcade stretched in single file for nearly half a mile. Sublette still wore his arm in a sling. The mountaineers in their rude hunting dresses, armed with rifles and roughly mounted, and leading their pack-horses down a hill of the forest, looked like banditti returning with plunder. On the top of some of the packs were perched several half-breed children, perfect little imps, with wild black eyes glaring from among elf locks. These, I was told, were children of the trappers; pledges of love from their squaw spouses in the wilderness.

———

The Blackfeet warriors, when they effected their midnight retreat from their wild fastness in Pierre's Hole, fell back into the valley of the Seeds-ke-dee, or Green River where they joined the main body of their band. The whole force amounted to several hundred fighting men, gloomy and exasperated by their late disaster. They had with them their wives and children, which incapacitated them from any bold and extensive enterprise of a warlike nature; but when, in the course of their wanderings they came in sight of the encampment of Fontenelle, who had moved some distance up Green River valley in search of the free trappers, they put up tremendous war-cries, and advanced fiercely as if to attack it. Second thoughts caused them to moderate their fury. They recollected the severe lesson just received, and could not but remark the strength of Fontenelle's position; which had been chosen with great judgment.

A formal talk ensued. The Blackfeet said nothing of the late battle, of which Fontenelle had as yet received no accounts; the latter, however, knew the hostile and perfidious nature of these savages, and took care to inform them of the encampment of Captain Bonneville, that they might know there were more white men in the neighbourhood. The conference ended, Fontenelle sent a Delaware Indian of his party to conduct fifteen of the Blackfeet to the camp of Captain Bonneville. There was [sic] at that time two Crow Indians in the captain's camp, who had recently arrived there. They looked with dismay at this deputation from their implacable enemies, and gave the captain a terrible character of them, assuring him that the best thing he could possibly do, was to put those Blackfeet deputies to death on the spot. The captain, however, who had heard nothing of the conflict at Pierre's Hole, declined all compliance with this sage counsel. He treated the grim warriors with his usual urbanity. They passed some little time at the camp; saw, no doubt, that everything was conducted with military skill and vigilance; and that such an enemy was not to be easily surprised, nor to be molested with impunity, and then departed, to report all that they had seen to their comrades.

The two scouts which Captain Bonneville had sent out to seek for the band of free trappers, expected by Fontenelle, and to invite them to his camp, had been successful in their search, and on the 12th of August those worthies made their appearance.

To explain the meaning of the appellation, free trapper, it is necessary to state the terms on which the men enlist in the service of the fur companies. Some have regular wages, and are furnished with weapons, horses, traps, and other requisites. These are under command, and bound to do every duty required of them connected with the service; such as hunting, trapping, loading and unloading the horses, mounting guard; and, in short, all the drudgery of the camp. These are the hired trappers.

The free trappers are a more independent class; and in describing them, we shall do little more than transcribe the graphic description of them by Captain Bonneville. "They come and go," says he, "when and where they please; provide their own horses, arms, and other equipments; trap and trade on their own account, and dispose of their skins and peltries to the highest bidder. Sometimes, in a dangerous hunting ground, they attach themselves to the camp of some trader for protection. Here they come under some restrictions; they have to conform to the ordinary rules for trapping, and to submit to such restraints, and to take part in such general duties, as are established for the good order and safety of the camp. In return for this protection, and for their camp keeping, they are bound to dispose of all the beaver they take, to the trader who commands the camp, at a certain rate per skin; or, should they prefer seeking a market elsewhere, they are to make him an allowance, of from thirty to forty dollars for the whole hunt."

There is an inferior order, who, either from prudence or poverty, come to these dangerous hunting grounds without horses or accoutrements, and are furnished by the traders. These, like the hired trappers, are bound to exert themselves to the utmost in taking beaver, which, without skinning, they render in at the trader's lodge, where a stipulated price for each is placed to their credit. These though generally included in the generic name of free trappers, have the more specific title of skin trappers.

The wandering whites who mingle for any length of time with the savages have invariably a proneness to adopt savage habitudes; but none more so than the free trappers. It is a matter of vanity and ambition with them to discard everything that may bear the stamp of civilized life, and to adopt the manners, habits, dress, gesture, and even walk of the Indian. You cannot pay a free trapper a greater compliment, than to persuade him you have mistaken him for an Indian brave; and, in truth, the counterfeit is complete. His hair suffered to attain to a great length, is carefully combed out, and either left to fall carelessly over his shoulders, or plaited neatly and tied up in otter skins, or parti-colored ribands. A hunting-shirt of ruffled calico of bright dyes, or of ornamented leather, falls to his knee; below which, curiously fashioned legging, ornamented with strings, fringes, and a profusion of hawks' bells, reach to a costly pair of moccasons of the finest Indian fabric, richly embroidered with beads. A blanket of scarlet, or some other bright colour, hangs from his shoulders, and is girt around his waist with a red sash, in which he bestows his pistols, knife, and the stem of his Indian pipe; preparations either for peace or war. His gun is lavishly decorated with brass tacks and vermilion, and provided with a fringed cover, occasionally of buckskin, ornamented here and there with a feather. His horse, the noble minister to the pride, pleasure, and profit of the mountaineer, is selected for his speed and spirit, and prancing gait, and holds a place in his estimation second only to himself. He shares largely of his bounty, and of his pride and pomp of trapping. He is caparisoned in the most dashing and fantastic style; the bridles and crupper are weightily embossed with beads and cockades; and head, mane, and tail, are interwoven with abundance of eagles' plumes, which flutter in the wind. To complete this grotesque equipment, the proud animal is bestreaked and bespotted with vermilion, or with white clay, whichever presents the most glaring contrast to his real colour.

Such is the account given by Captain Bonneville of these rangers of the wilderness, and their appearance at the camp was strikingly characteristic. They came dashing forward at full speed, firing their fusees, and yelling in Indian style. Their dark sunburned faces, and long flowing hair, their legging, flaps, moccasons, and richly-dyed blankets, and their painted horses gaudily caparisoned, gave them so much the air and appearance of Indians, that it was difficult to persuade one's self that they were white men, and had been brought up in civilized life.

Captain Bonneville, who was delighted with the game look of these cavaliers of the mountains, welcomed them heartily to his camp, and ordered a free allowance of grog to regale them, which soon put them in the most braggart spirits. They pronounced the captain the finest fellow in the world, and his men all bons garcons, jovial lads, and swore they would pass the day with them. They did so; and a day it was, of boast, and swagger, and rodomontade. The prime bullies and braves among the free trappers had each his circle of novices, from among the captain's band;

mere greenhorns, men unused to Indian life; mangeurs de lard, or pork-eaters; as such new-comers are superciliously called by the veterans of the wilderness. These he would astonish and delight by the hour, with prodigious tales of his doings among the Indians; and of the wonders he had seen, and the wonders he had performed, in his adventurous peregrinations among the mountains.

In the evening, the free trappers drew off, and returned to the camp of Fontenelle, highly delighted with their visit and with their new acquaintances, and promising to return the following day. They kept their word: day after day their visits were repeated; they became "hail fellow well met" with Captain Bonneville's men; treat after treat succeeded, until both parties got most potently convinced, or rather confounded, by liquor. Now came on confusion and uproar. The free trappers were no longer suffered to have all the swagger to themselves. The camp bullies and prime trappers of the party began to ruffle up, and to brag, in turn, of their perils and achievements. Each now tried to out-boast and out-talk the other; a quarrel ensued as a matter of course, and a general fight, according to frontier usage. The two factions drew out their forces for a pitched battle. They fell to work and belabored each other with might and main; kicks and cuffs and dry blows were as well bestowed as they were well merited, until, having fought to their hearts' content, and been drubbed into a familiar acquaintance with each other's prowess and good qualities, they ended the fight by becoming firmer friends than they could have been rendered by a year's peaceable companionship.

While Captain Bonneville amused himself by observing the habits and characteristics of this singular class of men, and indulged them, for the time, in all their vagaries, he profited by the opportunity to collect from them information concerning the different parts of the country about which they had been accustomed to range; the characters of the tribes, and, in short, everything important to his enterprise. He also succeeded in securing the services of several to guide and aid him in his peregrinations among the mountains, and to trap for him during the ensuing season. Having strengthened his party with such valuable recruits, he felt in some measure consoled for the loss of the Delaware Indians, decoyed from him by Mr. Fontenelle.

CHAPTER 12

Journal of a Trapper

By Osborne Russell

Nothing quite captures the experiences of mountain men like their personal diaries, journals if you will. Although primitive in spelling, these works bring to us the felt life of being in the mountains with these trappers in the halcyon fur-trade years. We have several such stories in this book, and this excerpt from Osborne Russell's The Journal of a Trapper *is one of the best. Russell describes the challenges faced by these intrepid explorers in great clarity and detail. Russell was born in 1814 in Maine. He passed away in 1892 while living in California, far from the settings of adventures like those he describes here.*

ON THE 18TH OF MARCH THE WINTER COMMENCED BREAKING UP WITH a heavy rain, and four of us started up the river to commence the spring hunt, whilst the remainder of the party returned to the fort. After traveling through the canyon we found the ground bare in many places, whilst it still continued to rain. On the 30th of March we traveled to the mouth of Muddy. This we ascended and crossed the mountain with some difficulty, as the snow was very deep, on to the head waters of Gray's Creek. There two of our party (who were Canadians) left us and struck off for themselves. Our camp then consisted of myself and my old comrade, Elbridge. I say old comrade because we had been some time together, but he was a young man, from Beverly, Mass., and being bred a sailor, he was not much of a landsman, woodsman or hunter, but a great, easy, good-natured fellow, standing five feet ten inches and weighing 200 pounds.

On the 20th of April we crossed a high ridge in a north direction and encamped on a stream that sinks in the plain soon after leaving the mountain. Here we set our traps for beaver, but their dams were nearly all covered with ice, excepting some few holes which they had made for the purpose of obtaining fresh provisions.

We traveled in a southerly direction about twenty-five miles, crossing several of the head branches of Gray's Creek. On the 1st of May we traveled about ten miles east course and the next day went to the head of Gray's marsh, about twenty miles south course. There we deposited the furs we had taken, and the next day started for Salt River to get a supply of salt. We took an easterly direction about six miles and fell on to Gardner's Fork, which we descended to the valley, and on the 6th arrived at the Salt Springs on Scott's Fork of Salt River. Here we found twelve of our old comrades who had come, like ourselves, to gather salt. We staid two nights together at this place, when Elbridge and myself took leave of them and returned to Gray's marsh. From there we started toward Fort Hall, traveling one day and laying by five or six to fatten our horses, and arrived at the fort on the 5th of June.

This fort now belonged to the British Hudson Bay Company, who obtained it by purchase from Mr. Wyeth in the year 1837. We stopped at the fort until the 26th of June, then made up a party of four for the purpose of trapping in the Yellowstone and Wind Mountains, and arrived at Salt River valley on the 28th. 29th—We crossed the valley northeast, then left it, ascending Gray's River in an easterly direction about four miles, into a narrow, rugged pass, encamped and killed a sheep. 30th—We traveled up this stream thirty miles east and encamped in a small valley and killed a bull, and the next day we encamped in the south end of Jackson's Hole. July 2d—We traveled through the valley north until night, and the next day arrived at Jackson's Lake, where we concluded to spend the Fourth of July at the outlet.

July 4th—I caught about twenty very fine silver trout, which, together with fat mutton, buffalo beef and coffee, and the manner in which it was ground up, constituted a dinner that ought to be considered independent, even by Britons.

July 5th—We traveled north parallel with the lake, on the east side, and the next day arrived at the inlet or northern extremity. 7th—We left the lake and followed up Lewis Fork about eight miles in a northeasterly direction and encamped. On the day following we traveled about five miles, when we came to the junction of two equal forks. We took up the left hand on the west side, through the thick pines, and in many places so much fallen timber that we frequently had to make circles of a quarter of a mile to gain a few rods ahead, but our general course was north, and I suppose we traveled about sixteen miles in that direction. At night we encamped at a lake about fifteen miles in circumference, which formed the stream we had ascended. July 9th—We traveled round this lake to the inlet on the west side, and came to another lake about the same size. This had a small prairie on the west side, whilst the other was completely surrounded by thick pines. The next day we traveled along the border of the lake till we came to the northwest extremity, where we found about fifty springs of boiling hot water. We stopped here some hours, as one of my comrades had visited this spot the year previous and wished to show us some curiosities. The first spring we visited was about ten feet in diameter, which threw up mud with a noise similar to boiling soap. Close about this were numerous springs similar to it, throwing up mud and water five or six feet high. About thirty or forty paces from these, along the side of a small ridge, the hot steam rushed forth from holes in the ground, with a hissing noise which could be heard a mile distant. On a near approach we could hear the water bubbling underground, some distance from the surface. The sound of our footsteps over this place was like thumping over a hollow vessel of immense size. In many places were peaks from two to six feet high formed of limestone, which appeared of a snowy whiteness, deposited by the boiling water. The water, when cold, was perfectly sweet, except having a fresh limestone taste. After surveying these natural wonders for some time my comrade conducted me to what he called the "Hour Spring." At that spring the first thing which attracted the attention was a hole about fifteen inches in diameter in which the water was boiling slowly about four inches below the surface. At length it began to boil and bubble violently and the water commenced raising and shooting upwards until the column arose to the height of sixty feet, from whence it fell to the ground in drops in a circle about thirty feet in diameter, perfectly cold when it struck the ground. It continued shooting up in this manner five or six minutes and then sank back to its former state of slowly boiling for an hour and then it would shoot forth again as before. My comrade said he had watched the motions of this spring for one whole day and part of the night the year previous and found no irregularity whatever in its movements. After surveying these wonders for a few hours we left the place and traveled north about three miles over ascending ground, then descended a steep and rugged mountain four miles in the same direction and fell on to the head branch of the Jefferson branch of the Missouri. The whole country was still thickly covered with pines except here and there a small prairie. We encamped and set some traps for beaver and staid four days. At this place there was also a large number of hot springs, some of which had formed cones of limestone twenty feet high of a snowy whiteness, which makes a splendid appearance standing among the ever-green pines. Some of the lower peaks are very convenient for the hunter in preparing his dinner when hungry, for here his kettle is always ready and boiling. His meat being suspended in the water by a string is soon prepared for his meal without further trouble. Some of these spiral cones are twenty feet in diameter at the base and not more than twelve inches at the top, the whole being covered with small, irregular semicircular ridges about the size of a man's finger, having the appearance of carving in has relief, formed, I suppose, by the waters running over it for ages unknown. I should think this place to be 3,000 feet lower than the springs we left on the mountain. Vast numbers of black tailed deer are found in the vicinity of these springs and seem to be very familiar with hot water and steam, the noise of which seems not to disturb their slumbers, for a buck may be found carelessly sleeping where the noise will exceed that of three or four engines in operation. Standing upon an eminence and superficially viewing these natural monuments, one is half inclined to believe himself in the neighborhood of the ruins of some ancient city, whose temples had been constructed of the whitest marble.

July 15th—We traveled down the stream northwest about 12 miles, passing on our route large numbers of hot springs with their snow white monuments scattered among the groves of pines. At length we came to a boiling lake about 300 feet in diameter, forming nearly a complete circle as we approached on the south side. The steam which arose from it was of three distinct colors. From the West side for one-third of the diameter it was white, in the middle it was pale red, and the remaining third on the east, light sky blue. Whether it was something peculiar in the state of the atmosphere, the day being cloudy, or whether it was some chemical properties contained in the water which produced this phenomenon, I am unable to say, and shall leave the explanation to some scientific tourist who may have the curiosity to visit this place at some future period. The water was of deep indigo blue, boiling like an immense cauldron, running over the white rock which had formed around the edges to the height of four or five feet from the surface of the earth, sloping gradually for sixty or seventy feet. What a field of speculation this presented for chemist and geolcist.

The next morning we crossed the stream, traveled down the east side about five miles, then ascended another fork in an easterly direction about ten miles and encamped. From where we left the main fork it runs in a northwest direction about forty miles before reaching the Burnt Hole. July 17th—We traveled to the head of this branch, about twenty miles, east direction. 18th—After traveling in the same direction about seven miles over a low spur of the mountains, we came into a large plain on the Yellowstone River, about eight miles below the lake, and followed up the Yellowstone to the outlet of the lake and encamped and set our traps for beaver. We stopped here trapping until the 28th and from thence we traveled to the "Secluded Valley," where we staid one day. From there we traveled east to the head of Clark's Fork, where we stopped and hunted the small branches until the 4th of August, and then returned to the valley. On the 9th we left the valley and traveled two days over the mountain northwest and fell on to a stream running south into the Yellowstone, where we staid until the i6th, and then crossed the mountain, in a northwest direction, over the snow, and fell on to a stream running into the Yellowstone plains and entering that river about forty miles above the mouth of Twenty-five Yard River. 18th—We descended this stream within about a mile of the plain and set our traps.

The next day my comrades started for the plains to kill some buffalo cows. I remonstrated very hard against them going into the plains and disturbing the buffaloes in such a dangerous part of the country, when we had plenty of fat deer and mutton, but to no purpose. Off they started and returned at night with their animals loaded with cow meat. They told me they had seen where a village of 300 or 400 lodges of Blackfeet had left the Yellowstone in a north-westerly direction but three or four days previous. Aug. 22d—We left this stream and traveled along the foot of the mountains at the edge of the plain, about twenty miles west course, and encamped at a spring. The next day we crossed the Yellowstone River and traveled up the river on the west side to the mouth of Gardner's Fork, where we staid the next day. 25th—We traveled to "Gardner's Hole," then altered our course southeast, crossing the eastern point of the valley, and encamped on a small branch among the pines. 26th—We encamped on the Yellowstone in the big plain below the lake. The next day we went to the lake and set our traps on a branch running into it, near the outlet on the northeast side.

28th—After visiting my traps I returned to the camp, where, after stopping about an hour or two, I took my rifle and sauntered down the shore of the lake among the scattered groves of tall pines until tired of walking about (the day being very warm), I took a bath in the lake, probably half an hour, and returned to the camp about four o'clock p.m. Two of my comrades observed, "Let us take a walk among the pines and kill an elk," and started off, whilst the other was lying asleep. Some time after they were gone I went to a bale of dried meat which had been spread in the sun thirty or forty feet from the place where we slept. Here I pulled off my powder horn and bullet pouch, laid them on a log, drew my butcher knife and began to cut. We were encamped about a half mile from the lake on a stream running into it in a southwest direction through a prairie bottom about a quarter of a mile wide. On each side of this valley arose a bench of land about twenty feet high, running parallel with the stream and covered with pines. On this bench we were encamped on the south-east side of the stream. The pines immediately behind us were thickly intermingled with logs and fallen trees. After eating a few minutes I arose and kindled a fire, filled my tobacco pipe and sat down to smoke. My comrade, whose name was White, was still sleeping. Presently I cast my eyes toward the horses, which were feeding in the valley, and discovered the heads of some Indians who were gliding round under the bench within thirty steps of me. I jumped to my rifle and aroused White. Looking towards my powder horn and bullet pouch, it was already in the hands of an Indian, and we were completely surrounded. We cocked our rifles and started through their ranks into the woods, which seemed to be completely filled with Blackfeet, who rent the air with their horrid yells. On presenting our rifles, they opened a space about twenty feet wide, through which we plunged. About the fourth jump an arrow struck White on the right hip joint. I hastily told him to pull it out and as I spoke another arrow struck me in the same place, but this did not retard our progress. At length another arrow struck through my right leg beneath the flesh and above the knee, so that I fell with my breast across a log. The Indian who shot me was within eight feet of me and made a spring toward me with his uplifted battle ax. I made a leap and dodged the blow and kept hopping from log to log through a shower of arrows which flew around us like hail, lodging in the pines and logs. After we had passed them about ten paces we wheeled and took aim at them. They began to dodge behind the trees and shoot their guns. We then ran and hopped about fifty yards further in the logs and bushes and made a stand. I was very faint from the loss of blood and we sat down among the logs, determined to kill the two foremost when they came up and then die like men. We rested our rifles across a log. White aiming at the foremost and myself at the second. I whispered to him that when they turned their eyes toward us to pull trigger. About twenty of them passed by us within fifteen feet without casting a glance toward us. Another file came round on the opposite side within twenty or thirty paces, closing with the first few a few rods beyond us and all turning to the right, the next minute were out of sight among the bushes. They were well armed with fusees, bows and battle axes. We sat until the rustling among the bushes had died away, then arose, and after looking carefully around us, White asked in a whisper how far it was to the lake. I replied, pointing to the southeast, about a quarter of a mile. I was nearly fainting from the loss of blood and the want of water. We hobbled along forty or fifty rods and I was obliged to sit down a few minutes, then go a little further and rest again. We managed in this way until we reached the bank of the lake. Our next object was to obtain some of the water, as the bank was very steep and high. White had been perfectly calm and deliberate until now. His conversation became wild, hurried and despairing. He observed, "I cannot go down to that water, for I am wounded all over. I shall die." I told him to sit down while I crawled down and brought some in my hat. This I expected with a great deal of difficulty. We then hobbled along the border of the lake for a mile and a half, when it grew dark and we stopped. We could still hear the shouting of the savages over their booty. We stopped under a large pine tree near the lake, and I told White I could go no further. "Oh," said he, "let us go into the pines and find a spring." I replied there was no spring within a mile of us, which I knew to be a fact. "Well," said he, "if you stop here I shall make a fire." "Make as much as you please," I replied angrily. "This is a poor time now to undertake to frighten me." I then started to the water, crawling on my hands and one knee, and returned in about an hour with some in my hat. While I was at this he had kindled a small fire, and taking a draught of water from the hat he exclaimed, "Oh, dear, we shall die here; we shall never get out of these mountains." "Well," said I, "if you persist in thinking so you will die, but I can crawl from this place on my hands and one knee and kill two or three elk and make a shelter of the skins, dry the meat, until we get able to travel." In this manner I persuaded him that we were not in half so bad a situation as we might be, although he was not in half so bad a situation as I expected, for, on examining I found only a slight wound from an arrow on his hip bone. But he was not so much to blame, as he was a young man who had been brought up in Missouri, the pet of the family, and had never done or learned much of anything but horse racing and gambling whilst under the care of his parents (if care it could be called). I pulled off an old piece of a coat made of blanket (as he was entirely without clothing except his hat and shirt), set myself in a leaning position against a tree, ever and anon gathering such branches and rubbish as I could reach without altering the position of my body, to keep up a little fire, and in this manner miserably spent the night. The next morning,

August 29, I could not arise without assistance, when White procured a couple of sticks for crutches, by the help of which I hobbled to a small grove of pines about sixty yards distant. We had scarcely entered the grove when we heard a dog barking and Indians singing and talking. The sound seemed to be approaching us. They at length came near to where we were, to the number of sixty. Then they commenced shooting at a large band of elk that was swimming in the lake, killed four of them, dragged them to the shore and butchered them, which occupied about three hours. They then packed the meat in small bundles on their backs and traveled up along the rocky shore about a mile and encamped. We then left our hiding place and crept into the thick pines about fifty yards distant and started in the direction of our encampment in the hope of finding our comrades. My leg was very much swollen and painful, but I managed to get along slowly on my crutches by White carrying my rifle. When we were within about sixty rods of the encampment we discovered the Canadian hunting around among the trees as though he was looking for a trail. We approached him within thirty feet before he saw us, and he was so much agitated by fear that he knew not whether to run or stand still. On being asked where Elbridge was, he said they came to the camp the night before at sunset. The Indians pursued them into the woods, where they separated, and he saw him no more.

At the encampment I found a sack of salt. Everything else the Indians had carried away or cut to pieces. They had built seven large conical forts near the spot, from which we supposed their numbers to have been seventy or eighty, part of whom had returned to their village with the horses and plunder. We left the place, heaping curses on the head of the Blackfoot nation, which neither injured them nor alleviated our distress.

We followed down the shores of the lake and stopped for the night. My companions threw some logs and rubbish together, forming a kind of shelter from the night breeze, but in the night it took fire (the logs being of pitch pine) and the blaze ran to the tops of the trees. We removed a short distance, built another fire and laid by it until morning. We then made a raft of dry poles and crossed the outlet upon it. We then went to a small grove of pines near by and made a fire, where we stopped the remainder of the day in hopes that Elbridge would see our signals and come to us, for we left directions on a tree at the encampment which route we would take. In the meantime the Canadian went to hunt something to eat, but without success. I had bathed my wounds in salt water and made a salve of beaver's oil and castoriimi, which I applied to them. This had eased the pain and drawn out the swelling in a great measure. The next morning I felt very stiff and sore, but we were obliged to travel or starve, as we had eaten nothing since our defeat and game was very scarce on the west side of the lake. Moreover the Canadian had got such a fright we could not prevail on him to go out of our sight to hunt. So on we trudged slowly, and after getting warm I could bear half my weight on my lame leg, but it was bent considerably and swelled so much that my knee joint was stiff. About ten o'clock the Canadian killed a couple of small ducks, which served us for breakfast. After eating them we pursued our journey. At twelve o'clock it began to rain, but we still kept on until the sun was two hours high in the evening, when the weather clearing away, we encamped at some hot springs and killed a couple of geese. Whilst we were eating them a deer came swimming along in the lake within about loo yards of the shore. We fired several shots at him, but the water glancing the balls, he remained unhurt and apparently unalarmed, but still kept swimming to and fro in the lake in front of us for an hour and then started along up close to the shore. The hunter went to watch it in order to kill it when it should come ashore, but as he was lying in wait for the deer a doe elk came to the water to drink and he killed her, the deer being still out in the lake swimming to and fro until dark.

Now we had plenty to eat and drink but were almost destitute of clothing. I had on a pair of trousers and a cotton shirt which were completely drenched with the rain. We made a sort of shelter from the wind out of pine branches and built a large fire of pitch knots in front of it, so that we were burning on one side and freezing on the other, alternately, all night. The next morning we cut some of the elk meat in thin slices and cooked it slowly over a fire, then packed it in bundles, strung them on our backs and started. By this time I could carry my own rifle and limp along half as fast as a man could walk, but when my foot touched against the logs or brush the pain in my leg was very severe. We left the lake at the hot springs and traveled through the thick pines, over a low ridge of land, through the snow and rain together, but we traveled by the wind about eight miles in a southwest direction, when we came to a lake about twelve miles in circumference, which is the head spring of the right branch of Lewis Fork. Here we found a dry spot near a number of hot springs, under some thick pines. Our hunter had killed a deer on the way and I took the skin, wrapped it around me and felt prouder of my mantle than a monarch with his imperial robes. This night I slept more than four hours, which was more than I had slept at any one time since I was wounded, and arose the next morning much refreshed. These springs were similar to those on the Madison, and among these, as well as those, Sulpher is found in its purity in large quantities on the surface of the ground. We traveled along the shore on the south side about five miles in an easterly direction, fell in with a large band of elk, killed two fat does and took some of the meat. We then left the lake and traveled due south over a rough, broken country, covered with thick pines, for about twelve miles, when we came to the fork again, which ran through a narrow prairie bottom, followed down it about six miles and encamped at the forks. We had passed up the left hand fork on the 9th of July on horseback, in good health and spirits, and down on the right bank on the 31st of August on foot, with weary limbs and sorrowful countenances. We built a fire and laid down to rest, but I could not sleep more than fifteen or twenty minutes at a time, the night being so very cold. We had plenty of meat, however, and made moccasins of raw elk hide. The next day we crossed the stream and traveled down near to Jackson's Lake on the west side, then took up a small branch in a west direction to the head. We then had the Teton mountain to cross, which looked like a laborious undertaking, as it was steep and the top covered with snow. We arrived at the summit, however, with a great deal of difficulty, before sunset, and after resting a few moments, traveled down about a mile on the other side and stopped for the night.

After spending another cold and tedious night, we were descending the mountain through the pines at daylight and the next night we reached the forks of Henry's Fork of Snake River. This day was very warm, but the wind blew cold at night. We made a fire and gathered some dry grass to sleep on and then sat down and ate the remainder of our provisions. It was now ninety miles to Fort Hall and we expected to see little or no game on the route, but we determined to travel it in three days. We lay down and shivered with the cold till daylight, then arose and again pursued our journey toward the fork of Snake River, where we arrived sun about an hour high, forded the river, which was nearly swimming, and encamped. The weather being very cold and fording the river so late at night, caused me much suffering during the night. Sept. 4th—We were on our way at daybreak and traveled all day through the high sage and sand down Snake River. We stopped at dark, nearly worn out with fatigue, hunger and want of sleep, as we had now traveled sixty-five miles in two days without eating. We sat and hovered over a small fire until another day appeared, then set out as usual and traveled to within about ten miles of the fort, when I was seized with a cramp in my wounded leg, which compelled me to stop and sit down every thirty or forty rods. At length we discovered a half breed encamped in the valley, who furnished us with horses and went with us to the fort, where we arrived about sun an hour high, being naked, hungry, wounded, sleepy and fatigued. Here again I entered a trading post after being defeated by the Indians, but the treatment was quite different from that which I had received at Savonery's Fork in 1837, when I had been defeated by the Crows.

The fort was in charge of Mr. Courtney M. Walker, who had been lately employed by the Hudson Bay Company for that purpose. He invited us into a room and ordered supper to be prepared immediately. Likewise such articles of clothing and blankets as we called for. After dressing ourselves and giving a brief history of our defeat and sufferings, supper was brought in, consisting of tea, cakes, buttermilk, dried meat, etc. I ate very sparingly, as I had been three days fasting, but drank so much strong tea that it kept me awake till after midnight. I continued to bathe my leg in warm salt water and applied a salve, which healed it in a very short time, so that in ten days I was again setting traps for beaver. On the 13th of September Elbridge arrived safe at the fort. He had wandered about among the mountains several days without having any correct knowledge, but at length accidentally falling on to the trail which we had made in the summer, it enabled him to reach the plains and from there he traveled to the fort by his own knowledge. On the 20th of October we started to hunt buifalo and make meat for the winter. The party consisted of fifteen men. We traveled to the head of the JefFerson Fork of the Missouri, where we killed and dried our meat. From there we proceeded over the mountains through Camas prairie to the forks of the Snake River, where most of the party concluded to spend the winter. Four of us, however, who were the only Americans in the party, returned to Fort Hall on the loth of December. We encamped near the fort and turned our horses among the springs and timber to hunt their living during the winter, whilst ourselves were snugly arranged in our skin lodge, which was pitched among the large Cottonwood trees, and in it provisions to serve us till the month of April. There were four of us in the mess. One was from Missouri, one from Massachusetts, one from Vermont, and myself from Maine. We passed an agreeable winter. We had nothing to do but to eat, attend to the horses and procure firewood. We had some few books to read, such as Byron, Shakespeare and Scott's works, the Bible and Clark's Commentary on it, and other small works on geology, chemistry and philosophy. The winter was very mild and the ground was bare in the valley until the 15th of January, when the snow fell about eight inches deep, but disappeared again in a few days. This was the deepest snow and of the longest duration of any we had during the winter.

CHAPTER 13

The French Trapper: To Live Hard, Die Hard

By A. C. Laut

The opening of the fur trade in the west often had a French accent. From voyageurs in canoes to trappers on snowshoes in the mountains, the French trappers were trail-blazers in every sense. Here A. C. Laut tells us what they were like and what they experienced in this excerpt from his book The Story of the Trapper, *1902.*

To LIVE HARD AND DIE HARD, KING IN THE WILDERNESS AND PAUPER in the town, lavish to-day and penniless to-morrow—such was the life of the most picturesque figure in America's history.

Take a map of America. Put your finger on any point between the Gulf of Mexico and Hudson Bay, or the Great Lakes and the Rockies. Ask who was the first man to blaze a trail into this wilderness; and wherever you may point, the answer is the same—the French trapper.

Impoverished English noblemen of the seventeenth century took to freebooting, Spanish dons to piracy and search for gold; but for the young French noblesse the way to fortune was by the fur trade. Freedom from restraint, quick wealth, lavish spending, and adventurous living all appealed to a class that hated the menial and slow industry of the farm. The only capital required for the fur trade was dauntless courage. Merchants were keen to supply money enough to stock canoes with provisions for trade in the wilderness. What would be equivalent to $5,000 of modern money was sufficient to stock four trappers with trade enough for two years.

At the end of that time the sponsors looked for returns in furs to the value of eight hundred per cent on their capital. The original investment would be deducted, and the enormous profit divided among the trappers and their outfitters. In the heyday of the fur trade, when twenty beaver-skins were got for an axe, it was no unusual thing to see a trapper receive what would be equivalent to $3,000 of our money as his share of two years' trapping. But in the days when the French were only beginning to advance up the Missouri from Louisiana and across from Michilimackinac to the Mississippi vastly larger fortunes were made.

Two partners have brought out as much as $200,000 worth of furs from the great game preserve between Lake Superior and the head waters of the Missouri after eighteen months' absence from St. Louis or from Montreal. The fur country was to the young French nobility what a treasure-ship was to a pirate. In vain France tried to keep her colonists on the land by forbidding trade without a license. Fines, the galleys for life, even death for repeated offence, were the punishments held over the head of the illicit trader. The French trapper evaded all these by staying in the wilds till he amassed fortune enough to buy off punishment, or till he had lost taste for civilized life and remained in the wilderness, coureur des bois, voyageur, or leader of a band of half-wild retainers whom he ruled like a feudal baron, becoming a curious connecting link between the savagery of the New World and the noblesse of the Old.

Duluth, of the Lakes region; La Salle, of the Mississippi; Le Moyne d'Iberville, ranging from Louisiana to Hudson Bay; La Mothe Cadillac in Michilimackinac, Detroit, and Louisiana; La Vérendrye exploring from Lake Superior to the Rockies; Radisson on Hudson Bay—all won their fame as explorers and discoverers in pursuit of the fur trade. A hundred years before any English mind knew of the Missouri, French voyageurs had gone beyond the Yellowstone. Before the regions now called Minnesota, Dakota, and Wisconsin were known to New Englanders, the French were trapping about the head waters of the Mississippi; and two centuries ago a company of daring French hunters went to New Mexico to spy on Spanish trade.

East of the Mississippi were two neighbours whom the French trapper shunned—the English colonists and the Iroquois. North of the

St. Lawrence was a power that he shunned still more—the French governor, who had legal right to plunder the peltries of all who traded and trapped without license. But between St. Louis and MacKenzie River was a great unclaimed wilderness, whence came the best furs.

Naturally, this became the hunting-ground of the French trapper.

There were four ways by which he entered his hunting-ground: (1) Sailing from Quebec to the mouth of the Mississippi, he ascended the river in pirogue or dugout, but this route was only possible for a man with means to pay for the ocean voyage. (2) From Detroit overland to the Illinois, or Ohio, which he rafted down to the Mississippi, and then taking to canoe turned north. (3) From Michilimackinac, which was always a grand rendezvous for the French and Indian hunters, to Green Bay on Lake Michigan, thence up-stream to Fox River, overland to the Wisconsin, and down-stream to the Mississippi. (4) Up the Ottawa through "the Soo" to Lake Superior and westward to the hunting-ground. Whichever way he went his course was mainly up-stream and north: hence the name Pays d'en Haut vaguely designated the vast hunting-ground that lay between the Missouri and the MacKenzie River.

The French trapper was and is to-day as different from the English as the gamester is from the merchant. Of all the fortunes brought from the Missouri to St. Louis, or from the Pays d'en Haut to Montreal, few escaped the gaming-table and dram-shop. Where the English trader saves his returns, Pierre lives high and plays high, and lords it about the fur post till he must pawn the gay clothing he has bought for means to exist to the opening of the next hunting season.

It is now that he goes back to some birch tree marked by him during the preceding winter's hunt, peels the bark off in a great seamless rind, whittles out ribs for a canoe from cedar, ash, or pine, and shapes the green bark to the curve of a canoe by means of stakes and stones down each side. Lying on his back in the sun spinning yarns of the great things he has done and will do, he lets the birch harden and dry to the proper form, when he fits the gunwales to the ragged edge, lines the inside of the keel with thin pine boards, and tars the seams where the bark has crinkled and split at the junction with the gunwale.

It is in the idle summer season that he and his squaw—for the Pierre adapts, or rather adopts, himself to the native tribes by taking an Indian wife—design the wonderfully bizarre costumes in which the French trapper appears: the beaded toque for festive occasions, the gay moccasins, the buckskin suit fringed with horse-hair and leather in lieu of the Indian scalp-locks, the white caribou capote with horned head-gear to deceive game on the hunter's approach, the powder-case made of a buffalo-horn, the bullet bag of a young otter-skin, the musk-rat or musquash cap, and great gantlets coming to the elbow.

None of these things does the English trader do. If he falls a victim tothe temptations awaiting the man from the wilderness in the dram-shop of the trading-post, he takes good care not to spend his all on the spree. He does not affect the hunter's decoy dress, for the simple reason that he prefers to let the Indians do the hunting of the difficult game, while he attends to the trapping that is gain rather than game. For clothes, he is satisfied with cheap material from the shops. And if, like Pierre, the Englishman marries an Indian wife, he either promptly deserts her when he leaves the fur country for the trading-post or sends her to a convent to be educated up to his own level. With Pierre the marriage means that he has cast off the last vestige of civilization and henceforth identifies himself with the life of the savage.

After the British conquest of Canada and the American Declaration of Independence came a change in the status of the French trapper. Before, he had been lord of the wilderness without a rival. Now, powerful English companies poured their agents into his hunting-grounds. Before, he had been a partner in the fur trade. Now, he must either be pushed out or enlist as servant to the newcomer. He who had once come to Montreal and St. Louis with a fortune of peltries on his rafts and canoes, now signed with the great English companies for a paltry one, two, and three hundred dollars a year.

It was but natural in the new state of things that the French trapper, with all his knowledge of forest and stream, should become coureur des bois and voyageur , while the Englishman remained the barterer. In the Mississippi basin the French trappers mainly enlisted with four compa-nies: the Mackinaw Company, radiating from Michilimackinac to the

Mississippi; the American Company, up the Missouri; the Missouri Company, officered by St. Louis merchants, westward to the Rockies; and the South-West Company, which was John Jacob Astor's amalgamation of the American and Mackinaw. In Canada the French sided with the Nor' Westers and X. Y.'s, who had sprung up in opposition to the great English Hudson's Bay Company.

Though he had become a burden-carrier for his quondam enemies, the French trapper still saw life through the glamour of la gloire and noblesse, still lived hard and died game, still feasted to-day and starved to-morrow, gambled the clothes off his back and laughed at hardship; courted danger and trolled off one of his chansons brought over to America by ancestors of Normandy, uttered an oath in one breath at the whirlpool ahead and in the next crossed himself reverently with a prayer to Sainte Anne, the voyageurs' saint, just before his canoe took the plunge.

Your Spanish grandee of the Missouri Company, like Manuel Lisa of St. Louis, might sit in a counting-house or fur post adding up rows of figures, and your Scotch merchant chaffer with Indians over the value of a beaver-skin. As for Pierre, give him a canoe sliding past wooded banks with a throb of the keel to the current and the whistle of wild-fowl overhead; clear sky above with a feathering of wind clouds, clear sky below with a feathering of wind clouds, and the canoe between like a bird at poise. Sometimes a fair wind livens the pace; for the voyageurs hoist a blanket sail, and the canoe skims before the breeze like a seagull.

Where the stream gathers force and whirls forward in sharp eddies and racing leaps each voyageur knows what to expect. No man asks questions. The bowman stands up with his eyes to the fore and steel-shod pole ready. Every eye is on that pole. Presently comes a roar, and the green banks begin to race. The canoe no longer glides. It vaults—springs—bounds, with a shiver of live waters under the keel and a buoyant rise to her prow that mounts the crest of each wave fast as wave pursues wave. A fanged rock thrusts up in mid-stream. One deft push of the pole. Each paddler takes the cue; and the canoe shoots past the danger straight as an arrow, righting herself to a new course by another lightning sweep of the pole and paddles.

But the waters gather as if to throw themselves forward. The roar becomes a crash. As if moved by one mind the paddlers brace back. The lightened bow lifts. A white dash of spray. She mounts as she plunges; and the voyageurs are whirling down-stream below a small waterfall. Not a word is spoken to indicate that it is anything unusual to sauter les rapides, as the voyageurs say. The men are soaked. Now, perhaps, some one laughs; for Jean, or Ba'tiste, or the dandy of the crew, got his moccasins wet when the canoe took water. They all settle forward. One paddler pauses to bail out water with his hat.

Thus the lowest waterfalls are run without a portage. Coming back this way with canoes loaded to the water-line, there must be a disembarking. If the rapids be short, with water enough to carry the loaded canoe high above rocks that might graze the bark, all hands spring out in the water, but one man who remains to steady the craft; and the canoe is "tracked" up-stream, hauled along by ropes. If the rapids be at all dangerous, each voyageur lands, with pack on his back and pack-straps across his forehead, and runs along the shore. A long portage is measured by the number of pipes the voyageur smokes, each lighting up meaning a brief rest; and a portage of many "pipes" will be taken at a running gait on the hottest days without one word of complaint. Nine miles is the length of one famous portage opposite the Chaudière Falls on the Ottawa.

In winter the voyageur becomes coureur des bois to his new masters. Then for six months endless reaches, white, snow-padded, silent; forests wreathed and bossed with snow; nights in camp on a couch of pines or rolled in robes with a roaring fire to keep the wolves off, melting snow steaming to the heat, meat sputtering at the end of a skewered stick; sometimes to the marche donc! Marche donc! Of the driver, with crisp tinkling of dog-bells in frosty air, a long journey overland by dog-sled to the trading-post; sometimes that blinding fury which sweeps over the northland, turning earth and air to a white darkness; sometimes a belated traveller cowering under a snow-drift for warmth and wrapping his blanket about him to cross life's Last Divide.

These things were the every-day life of the French trapper.

At present there is only one of the great fur companies remaining— the Hudson's Bay of Canada. In the United States there are only two important centres of trade in furs which are not imported—St. Paul and

St. Louis. For both the Hudson's Bay Company and the fur traders of the Upper Missouri the French trapper still works as his ancestors did for the great companies a hundred years ago.

The roadside tramp of to-day is a poor representative of Robin Hoods and Rob Roys; and the French trapper of shambling gait and baggy clothes seen at the fur posts of the north to-day is a poor type of the class who used to stalk through the baronial halls of Montreal's governor like a lord and set the rafters of Fort William's council chamber ringing, and make the wine and the money and the brawls of St. Louis a by-word.

And yet, with all his degeneracy, the French trapper retains a something of his old traditions. A few years ago I was on a northern river steamer going to one of the Hudson's Bay trading-posts. A brawl seemed to sound from the steerage passengers. What was the matter? "Oh," said the captain, "the French trappers going out north for the winter, drunk as usual!"

As he spoke, a voice struck up one of those chansons populaires, which have been sung by every generation of voyageurs since Frenchmen came to America, A La Claire Fontaine, a song which the French trappers' ancestors brought from Normandy hundreds of years ago, about the fickle lady and the faded roses and the vain regrets. Then—was it possible?—these grizzled fellows, dressed in tinkers' tatters, were singing—what? A song of the Grand Monarque which has led armies to battle, but not a song which one would expect to hear in northern wilds—

"Malbrouck s'on va-t-en guerre
Mais quand reviendra a-t-il?"

Three foes assailed the trapper alone in the wilds. The first danger was from the wolf-pack. The second was the Indian hostile egged on by rival traders. This danger the French trapper minimized by identifying himself more completely with the savage than any other fur trader succeeded in doing. The third foe was the most perverse and persevering thief known outside the range of human criminals.

Perhaps the day after the trapper had shot his first deer he discovered fine footprints like a child's hand on the snow around the carcass.

He recognizes the trail of otter or pekan or mink. It would be useless to bait a deadfall with meat when an unpolluted feast lies on the snow. The man takes one of his small traps and places it across the line of approach. This trap is buried beneath snow or brush. Every trace of man-smell is obliterated. The fresh hide of a deer may be dragged across the snow. Pomatum or castoreum may be daubed on everything touched. He may even handle the trap with deer-hide. Pekan travel in pairs. Besides, the dead deer will be likely to attract more than one forager; so the man sets a circle of traps round the carcass.

The next morning he comes back with high hope. Very little of the deer remains. All the flesh-eaters of the forest, big and little, have been there. Why, then, is there no capture? One trap has been pulled up, sprung, and partly broken. Another carried a little distance off and dumped into a hollow. A third had caught a pekan; but the prisoner had been worried and torn to atoms. Another was tampered with from behind and exposed for very deviltry. Some have disappeared altogether.

Among forest creatures few are mean enough to kill when they have full stomachs, or to eat a trapped brother with untrapped meat a nose-length away.

The French trapper rumbles out some maledictions on le sacré carcajou. Taking a piece of steel like a cheese-tester's instrument, he pokes grains of strychnine into the remaining meat. He might have saved himself the trouble. The next day he finds the poisoned meat mauled and spoiled so that no animal will touch it. There is nothing of the deer but picked bones. So the trapper tries a deadfall for the thief. Again he might have spared himself the trouble. His next visit shows the deadfall torn from behind and robbed without danger to the thief.

Several signs tell the trapper that the marauder is the carcajou or wolverine. All the stealing was done at night; and the wolverine is nocturnal. All the traps had been approached from behind. The wolverine will not cross man's track. The poison in the meat had been scented. Whether the wolverine knows poison, he is too wary to experiment on doubtful diet. The exposing of the traps tells of the curiosity which characterizes the wolverine. Other creatures would have had too much fear. The tracks run back to cover, and not across country like the badger's or the fox's.

Fearless, curious, gluttonous, wary, and suspicious, the mischief-maker and the freebooter and the criminal of the animal world, a scavenger to save the northland from pollution of carrion, and a scourge to destroy wounded, weaklings, and laggards—the wolverine has the nose of a fox, with long, uneven, tusk-like teeth that seem to be expressly made for tearing. The eyes are well set back, greenish, alert with almost human intelligence of the type that preys. Out of the fulness of his wrath one trapper gave a perfect description of the wolverine. He didn't object, he said, to being outrun by a wolf, or beaten by a respectable Indian, but to be outwitted by a little beast the size of a pig with the snout of a fox, the claws of a bear, and the fur of a porcupine's quills, was more than he could stand.

In the economy of nature the wolverine seems to have but one design—destruction. Beaver-dams two feet thick and frozen like rock yield to the ripping onslaught of its claws. He robs everything: the musk-rats' haycock houses; the gopher burrows; the cached elk and buffalo calves under hiding of some shrub while the mothers go off to the watering-place; the traps of his greatest foe, man; the cached provisions of the forest ranger; the graves of the dead; the very tepees and lodges and houses of Indian, half-breed, and white man. While the wolverine is averse to crossing man's track, he will follow it for days, like a shark behind a ship; for he knows as well as the man knows there will be food in the traps when the man is in his lodge, and food in the lodge when the man is at the traps.

But the wolverine has two characteristics by which he may be snared—gluttony and curiosity.

After the deer has disappeared the trapper finds that the wolverine has been making as regular rounds of the traps as he has himself. It is then a question whether the man or the wolverine is to hold the hunting-ground. A case is on record at Moose Factory, on James Bay, of an Indian hunter and his wife who were literally brought to the verge of starvation by a wolverine that nightly destroyed their traps. The contest ended by the starving Indians travelling a hundred miles from the haunts of that "bad devil—oh—he—bad devil—carcajou!" Remembering the curiosity and gluttony of his enemy, the man sets out his strongest steel-traps.

He takes some strong-smelling meat, bacon or fish, and places it where the wolverine tracks run. Around this he sets a circle of his traps, tying them securely to poles and saplings and stakes. In all likelihood he has waited his chance for a snowfall which will cover traces of the man-smell.

Night passes. In the morning the man comes to his traps. The meat has been taken. All else is as before. Not a track marks the snow; but in mid-winter meat does not walk off by itself. The man warily feels for the hidden traps. Then he notices that one of the stakes has been pulled up and carried off. That is a sign. He prods the ground expectantly. It is as he thought. One trap is gone. It had caught the wolverine; but the cunning beast had pulled with all his strength, snapped the attached sapling, and escaped. A fox or beaver would have gnawed the imprisoned limb off. The wolverine picks the trap up in his teeth and hobbles as hard as three legs will carry him to the hiding of a bush, or better still, to the frozen surface of a river, hidden by high banks, with glare ice which will not reveal a trail. But on the river the man finds only a trap wrenched out of all semblance to its proper shape, with the spring opened to release the imprisoned leg.

The wolverine had been caught, and had gone to the river to study out the problem of unclinching the spring.

One more device remains to the man. It is a gun trick. The loaded weapon is hidden full-cock under leaves or brush. Directly opposite the barrel is the bait, attached by a concealed string to the trigger. The first pull will blow the thief's head off.

The trap experience would have frightened any other animals a week's run from man's tracks; but the wolverine grows bolder, and the trapper knows he will find his snares robbed until carcajou has been killed.

Perhaps he has tried the gun trick before, to have the cord gnawed through and the bait stolen. A wolverine is not to be easily tricked; but its gluttony and curiosity bring it within man's reach.

The man watches until he knows the part of the woods where the wolverine nightly gallops. He then procures a savoury piece of meat heavy enough to balance a cocked trigger, not heavy enough to send it off. The gun is suspended from some dense evergreen, which will hide the weapon. The bait hangs from the trigger above the wolverine's reach.

Then a curious game begins.

One morning the trapper sees the wolverine tracks round and round the tree as if determined to ferret out the mystery of the meat in mid-air.

The next morning the tracks have come to a stand below the meat. If the wolverine could only get up to the bait, one whiff would tell him whether the man-smell was there. He sits studying the puzzle till his mark is deep printed in the snow.

The trapper smiles. He has only to wait.

The rascal may become so bold in his predatory visits that the man may be tempted to chance a shot without waiting.

But if the man waits Nemesis hangs at the end of the cord. There comes a night when the wolverine's curiosity is as rampant as his gluttony. A quick clutch of the ripping claws and a blare of fire-smoke blows the robber's head into space.

The trapper will hold those hunting-grounds.

He has got rid of the most unwelcome visitor a solitary man ever had; but for the consolation of those whose sympathies are keener for the animal than the man, it may be said that in the majority of such contests it is the wolverine and not the man that wins.

CHAPTER 14

The Personal Narrative
of James O. Pattie of Kentucky

By James O. Pattie

Pattie was only 26 when he submitted his manuscript to the editor of the Western Monthly Review *in Cincinnati in 1830. He looked older and talked earnestly about his journey into the west with his father to hunt furs. The trip had ended in failure after the pair reached California when arguments with authorities there left them penniless, "robbed" Pattie said. Pattie's account of the journey through the mountains, down to Santa Fe, interested the editor, and the book was eventually published in 1831. Much of Pattie's book seems so far-fetched and self-aggrandizing that doubts about its veracity cannot be avoided. For instance, in one sentence he says he spotted 220 "white bears" in one day. We assume he means grizzlies, and there is no way he spotted that many in one day. Still, he packs a life of life in these pages, and if you can believe him, you'll feel what it was like for the true mountain men.*

I PASS BY, AS UNIMPORTANT IN THIS JOURNAL, ALL THE CIRCUMSTANCES of our arrangements for setting out on our expedition; together with my father's sorrow and mine, at leaving the spot where his wife and my mother was buried, the place, which had once been so cheerful, and was now so gloomy to us. We made our purchases at St. Louis. Our company consisted of five persons. We had ten horses packed with traps, trapping utensils, guns, ammunition, knives, tomahawks, provisions, blankets, and some surplus arms, as we anticipated that we should be able to gain some additions to our number by way of recruits, as we proceeded onward. But when the trial came, so formidable seemed the danger, fatigue, distance, and uncertainty of the expedition, that not an individual could be persuaded to share our enterprize.

June 20, 1824, we crossed the Missouri at a small town called Newport, and meandered the river as far as Pilcher's fort, without any incident worthy of record, except that one of our associates, who had become too unwell to travel, was left at Charaton, the remotest village on this frontier of any size. We arrived at Pilcher's fort, on the 13th day of July. There we remained, until the 28th, waiting the arrival of a keel boat from below, that was partly freighted with merchandize for us, with which we intended to trade with the Indians.

On the 28th, our number diminished to four, we set off for a trading establishment eight miles above us on the Missouri, belonging to Pratte, Choteau and Company. In this place centres most of the trade with the Indians on the upper Missouri. Here we met with Sylvester, son of Gen. Pratte, who was on his way to New Mexico, with purposes similar to ours. His company had preceded him, and was on the river Platte waiting for him.

We left this trading establishment for the Council Bluffs, six miles above. When we arrived there, the commanding officer demanded to see our license for trading with the Indians. We informed him, that we neither had any, nor were aware that any was necessary. We were informed, that we could be allowed to ascend the river no higher without one. This dilemma brought our onward progress to a dead stand.

We were prompt, however, in making new arrangements. We concluded to sell our surplus arms in exchange for merchandize, and change our direction from the upper Missouri, to New Mexico. One of our number was so much discouraged with our apparent ill success, and so little satisfied with this new project, that he came to the determination to leave our ranks. The remainder, though dispirited by the reduction of our number, determined not to abandon the undertaking. Our invalid having rejoined us, we still numbered four. We remained some time at this beautiful position, the Council Bluffs. I have seen much that is beautiful, interesting and commanding in the wild scenery of nature, but no prospect above, around, and below more so than from this spot. Our object and destination being the same as Mr. Pratte's, we concluded to join his company on the Platte.

The night after we left this village, we encamped on the banks of a small creek called the Mad Buffaloe. Here we could find no wood for cooking, and made our first experiment of the common resort in these wide prairies; that is, we were obliged to collect the dung of the buffaloe for that purpose.

It may be imagined, that such a caravan made no mean figure, or inconsiderable dust, in moving along the prairies. We started on the morning of the 6th of August, travelling up the main Platte, which at this point is more than a hundred yards wide, very shallow, with a clean sand bottom, and very high banks. It is skirted with a thin belt of cotton-wood and willow trees, from which beautiful prairie plains stretch out indefinitely on either side. We arrived in the evening at a village of the Pawnee Loups. It is larger than the village of the Republican Pawnees, which we had left behind us. The head chief of this village received us in the most affectionate and hospitable manner, supplying us with such provisions as we wanted. He had been all the way from these remote prairies, on a visit to the city of Washington. He informed us, that before he had taken the journey, he had supposed that the white people were a small tribe, like his own, and that he had found them as numberless as the spires of grass on his prairies. The spectacle, however, that had struck him with most astonishment, was bullets as large as his head, and guns of the size of a log of wood.

His people cultivate corn, beans, pumpkins and watermelons. Here we remained five days, during which time Mr. Pratte purchased six hundred Buffalo skins, and some horses. A Pawnee war party came in from an expedition against a hostile tribe of whom they had killed and scalped four, and taken twenty horses.

This evening we arrived on one of the forks of the Osage, and encamped. Here we caught a beaver, the first I had ever seen. On the 20th, we started late, and made a short day's travel, encamping by water. Next morning we discovered vast numbers of buffaloes, all running in one direction, as though they were flying from some sort of pursuit.

We immediately detached men to reconnoitre and ascertain, whether they were not flying from the Indians. They soon discovered a large body of them in full chase of these animals, and shooting at them with arrows. As their course was directly towards our camp, they were soon distinctly in sight. At this moment one of our men rode towards them, and discharged his gun. This immediately turned their attention from the pursuit of the game, to us. The Indians halted a moment, as if in deliberation, and rode off in another direction with great speed. We regretted that we had taken no measures to ascertain, whether they were friendly or not. In the latter case we had sufficient ground to apprehend, that they would pursue us at a distance, and attack us in the night. We made our arrangements, and resumed our march in haste, travelling with great caution, and posting a strong guard at night.

About ten at night it commenced raining; the rain probably caused us to intermit our caution; for shortly after it began, the Indians attacked our encampment, firing a shower of arrows upon us. We returned their fire at random, as they retreated: they killed two of our horses, and slightly wounded one of our men; we found four Indians killed by our fire, and one wounded. The wounded Indian informed our interpreter, that the Indians, who attacked us, were Arrickarees. We remained encamped here four days, attending our wounded man, and the wounded Indian, who died, however, the second day, and here we buried him.

We left this encampment on the 26th, and through the day met with continued herds of buffaloes and wild horses, which, however, we did not disturb. In the evening we reached a fork of the Platte, called Hyde Park. This stream, formerly noted for beavers, still sustains a few. Here we encamped, set our traps, and caught four beavers. In the morning we began to ascend this stream, and during our progress, we were obliged to keep men in advance, to affrighten the buffaloes and wild horses from our path. They are here in such prodigious numbers, as literally to have eaten down the grass of the prairies.

Here we saw multitudes of prairie dogs. They have large village establishments of burrows, where they live in society. They are sprightly, bold and self important animals, of the size of a Norwegian rat. On the morning of the 28th, our wounded companion was again unable to travel, in consequence of which we were detained at our encampment three days. Not wholly to lose the time, we killed during these three days no buffaloes, of which we saved only the tongues and hump ribs.

On the morning of the 31st, our wounded associate being somewhat recovered, we resumed our march. Ascending the stream, in the course of the day we came upon the dead bodies of two men, so much mangled, and disfigured by the wild beasts, that we could only discover that they were white men. They had been shot by the Indians with arrows, the ground near them being stuck full of arrows. They had been scalped. Our feelings may be imagined, at seeing the mangled bodies of people of our own race in these remote and unpeopled prairies. We consoled ourselves with believing that they died like brave men. We had soon afterwards clear evidence of this fact, for, on surveying the vicinity at the distance of a few hundred yards, we found the bodies of five dead Indians. The ground all around was torn and trampled by horse and footmen. We collected the remains of the two white men, and buried them. We then ascended the stream a few miles, and encamped. Finding signs of Indians, who could have left the spot but a few hours before, we made no fire for fear of being discovered, and attacked in the night. Sometime after dark, ten of us started up the creek in search of their fires. About four miles from our encampment, we saw them a few hundred yards in advance. Twenty fires were distinctly visible. We counselled with each other, whether to fire on them or not. Our conclusion was, that the most prudent plan was to return, and apprize our companions of what we had seen. In consequence of our information, on our return, sixty men were chosen, headed by my father, who set off in order to surround their camp before daylight. I was one of the number, as I should have little liked to have my father go into battle without me, when it was in my power to accompany him. The remainder were left in charge of our camp, horses, and mules. We had examined our arms and found them in good order. About midnight we came in sight of their fires, and before three o'clock were posted all around them, without having betrayed ourselves. We were commanded not to fire a gun, until the word was given. As it was still sometime before daylight, we became almost impatient for the command. As an Indian occasionally arose and stood for a moment before the fire,

I involuntarily took aim at him with the thought, how easily I could destroy him, but my orders withheld me. Twilight at length came, and the Indians began to arise. They soon discovered two of our men, and instantly raising the war shout, came upon us with great fury. Our men stood firm, until they received the order which was soon given. A well directed and destructive fire now opened on them, which they received, and returned with some firmness. But when we closed in upon them they fled in confusion and dismay. The action lasted fifteen minutes. Thirty of their dead were left on the field, and we took ten prisoners, whom we compelled to bury the dead. One of our men was wounded, and died the next day. We took our prisoners to our encampment, where we questioned them with regard to the two white men, we had found, and buried the preceding day. They acknowledged, that their party killed them, and assigned as a reason for so doing, that when the white men were asked by the chief to divide their powder and balls with him, they refused. It was then determined by the chief, that they should be killed, and the whole taken. In carrying this purpose into effect, the Indians lost four of their best young men, and obtained but little powder and lead, as a compensation.

We then asked them to what nation they belonged? They answered the Crow. This nation is distinguished for bravery and skill in war. Their bows and arrows were then given them, and they were told, that we never killed defenceless prisoners, but that they must tell their brothers of us, and that we should not have killed any of their nation, had not they killed our white brothers; and if they did so in future, we should kill all we found of them, as we did not fear any number, they could bring against us. They were then allowed to go free, which delighted them, as they probably expected that we should kill them, it being their custom to put all their prisoners to death by the most shocking and cruel tortures. That they may not lose this diabolical pleasure by the escape of their prisoners, they guard them closely day and night. One of them, upon being released, gave my father an eagle's feather, saying, you are a good and brave man, I will never kill another white man.

We pursued our journey on the 1st of September. Our advance was made with great caution, as buffaloes were now seen in immense herds, and the danger from Indians was constant. Wandering tribes of these people subsist on the buffaloes, which traverse the interior of these plains, keeping them constantly in sight.

On the morning of the 2d, we started early. About ten o'clock we saw a large herd of buffaloes approaching us with great speed. We endeavoured to prevent their running among our pack mules, but it was in vain. They scattered them in every direction over the plain; and although we rode in among the herd, firing on them, we were obliged to follow them an hour, before we could separate them sufficiently to regain our mules. After much labor we collected all, with the exception of one packed with dry goods, which the crowd drove before them. The remainder of the day, half our company were employed as a guard, to prevent a similar occurrence. When we encamped for the night, some time was spent in driving the buffaloes a considerable distance from our camp. But for this precaution, we should have been in danger of losing our horses and mules entirely.

The following morning, we took a S. S. W. course, which led us from the stream, during this day's journey. Nothing occurred worthy of mention, except that we saw a great number of wolves, which had surrounded a small herd of buffaloe cows and calves, and killed and eaten several. We dispersed them by firing on them. We judged, that there were at least a thousand. They were large and as white as sheep. Near this point we found water, and encamped for the night.

On the morning of the 4th, a party was sent out to kill some buffaloe bulls, and get their skins to make moccasins for our horses, which detained us until ten o'clock. We then packed up and travelled six miles. Finding a lake, we encamped for the night. From this spot, we saw one of the most beautiful landscapes, that ever spread out to the eye. As far as the plain was visible in all directions, innumerable herds of wild horses, buffaloes, antelopes, deer, elk, and wolves, fed in their wild and fierce freedom. Here the sun rose, and set, as unobscured from the sight, as on the wastes of ocean. Here we used the last of our salt, and as for bread, we had seen none, since we had left the Pawnee village. I hardly need observe, that these are no small deprivations.

The next day we travelled until evening, nothing occurring, that deserves record. Our encampment was near a beautiful spring, called Bellefontaine, which is visited by the Indians, at some seasons of the year. Near it were some pumpkins, planted by the Indians. I cooked one, but did not find it very palateable: The next day we encamped without water. Late in the evening of the following day we reached a stream, and encamped. As we made our arrangements for the night, we came upon a small party of Indians. They ran off immediately, but we pursued them, caught four, and took them to the camp they had left, a little distant from ours. It contained between twenty and thirty women and children, beside three men. The women were frightened at our approach, and attempted to run. The Indians in our possession said something to them in their own language, that induced them to stop; but it was some time, before they were satisfied, that we intended them no harm. We returned to our camp, and were attending to our mules and horses. Our little Indian boy was playing about the camp, as usual. Suddenly our attention was arrested by loud screams or cries; and looking up, we saw our little boy in the arms of an Indian, whose neck he was closely clasping, as the Indian pressed him to his bosom, kissing him, and crying at the same time. As we moved towards the spot, the Indian approached us, still holding the child in his arms; and falling on his knees, made us a long speech, which we understood only through his signs. During his speech, he would push the child from him, and then draw it back to him, and point to us. He was the father of this boy, whom we saved from being burnt by the Pawnees. He gave us to understand by his signs, that his child was carried off by his enemies. When the paroxysm of his joy was past, we explained, as well as we could, how we obtained the child. Upon hearing the name Pawnee, he sprang upon his feet, and rushed into his tent. He soon came out, bringing with him two Indian scalps, and his bow and arrows, and insisted, that we should look at the scalps, making signs to tell us, that they were Pawnee scalps, which he took at the time he lost his child. After he finished this explanation, he would lay the scalps a short distance from him, and shoot his arrows through them, to prove his great enmity to this nation. He then presented my father a pair of leggings and a pipe, both neatly decorated with porcupine quills; and accompanied by his child, withdrew to his tent, for the night. Just as the morning star became visible, we were aroused from our slumbers, by the crying and shouting of the Indians in their tent. We arose, and approached it, to ascertain the cause of the noise. Looking in, we saw the Indians all laying prostrate with their faces to the ground. We remained observing them, until the full light of day came upon them.—They then arose, and placed themselves around the fire. The next movement was to light a pipe, and begin to smoke. Seeing them blow the smoke first towards the point where the sun arose, and then towards heaven, our curiosity was aroused, to know the meaning of what we had seen. The old chief told us by signs, that they had been thanking the Great Spirit for allowing them to see another day. We then purchased a few beaver skins of them, and left them. Our encampment for the evening of this day, was near a small spring, at the head of which we found a great natural curiosity. A rock sixteen yards in circumference, rises from eighty to ninety feet in height, according to our best judgment, from a surface upon which, in all directions, not the smallest particle of rock, not even a pebble can be found. We were unable to reach the top of it, although it was full of holes, in which the hawks and ravens built their nests. We gave the spring the name of Rock Castle spring. On the morning of the 9th, we left this spot, and at night reached the foot of a large dividing ridge, which separates the waters of the Platte from those of the Arkansas. After completing our arrangements for the night, some of us ascended to the top of the ridge, to look out for Indians; but we saw none.

The succeeding morning we crossed the ridge, and came to water in the evening, where we encamped. Here we killed a white bear, which occupied several of us at least an hour. It was constantly in chase of one or another of us, thus withholding us from shooting at it, through fear of wounding each other. This was the first, I had ever seen. His claws were four inches long, and very sharp. He had killed a buffaloe bull, eaten a part of it, and buried the remainder. When we came upon him, he was watching the spot, where he had buried it, to keep off the wolves, which literally surrounded him.

On the 11th, we travelled over some hilly ground. In the course of the day, we killed three white bears, the claws of which I saved, they being of considerable value among the Indians, who wear them around the neck, as the distinguishing mark of a brave. Those Indians, who wear this ornament, view those, who do not, as their inferiors. We came to water, and encamped early. I was one of the guard for the night, which was rather cloudy. About the middle of my guard, our horses became uneasy, and in a few moments more, a bear had gotten in among them, and sprung upon one of them. The others were so much alarmed, that they burst their fastenings, and darted off at full speed. Our camp was soon aroused, and in arms, for defence, although much confused, from not knowing what the enemy was, nor from what direction to expect the attack. Some, however, immediately set off in pursuit of our horses. I still stood at my post, in no little alarm, as I did not know with the rest, if the Indians were around us or not. All around was again stillness, the noise of those in pursuit of the horses being lost in the distance. Suddenly my attention was arrested, as I gazed in the direction, from which the alarm came, by a noise like that of a struggle at no great distance from me. I espied a hulk, at which I immediately fired. It was the bear devouring a horse, still alive. My shot wounded him. The report of my gun, together with the noise made by the enraged bear, brought our men from the camp, where they awaited a second attack from the unknown enemy in perfect stillness. Determined to avenge themselves, they now sallied forth, although it was so dark, that an object ten steps in advance could not be seen. The growls of the bear, as he tore up the ground around him with his claws, attracted all in his direction. Some of the men came so near, that the animal saw them, and made towards them. They all fired at him, but did not touch him. All now fled from the furious animal, as he seemed intent on destroying them. In this general flight one of the men was caught. As he screamed out in his agony, I, happening to have reloaded my gun, ran up to relieve him. Reaching the spot in an instant, I placed the muzzle of my gun against the bear, and discharging it, killed him. Our companion was literally torn in pieces. The flesh on his hip was torn off, leaving the sinews bare, by the teeth of the bear. His side was so wounded in three places, that his breath came through the openings; his head was dreadfully bruised, and his jaw broken. His breath came out from both sides of his windpipe, the animal in his fury having placed his teeth and claws in every part of his body. No one could have supposed, that there was the slightest possibility of his recovery, through any human means. We remained in our encampment three days, attending upon him, without seeing any change for the worse or better in his situation. He had desired us from the first to leave him, as he considered his case as hopeless as ourselves did. We then concluded to move from our encampment, leaving two men with him, to each of whom we gave one dollar a day, for remaining to take care of him, until he should die, and to bury him decently.

On the 14th we set off, taking, as we believed, a final leave of our poor companion. Our feelings may be imagined, as we left this suffering man to die in this savage region, unfriended and unpitied. We travelled but a few miles before we came to a fine stream and some timber. Concluding that this would be a better place for our unfortunate companion, than the one where he was, we encamped with the intention of sending back for him. We despatched men for him, and began to prepare a shelter for him, should he arrive. This is a fork of Smoke Hill river, which empties into the Platte. We set traps, and caught eight beavers, during the night. Our companions with the wounded man on a litter, reached us about eight o'clock at night.

In the morning we had our painful task of leave taking to go through again. We promised to wait for the two we left behind at the Arkansas river. We travelled all day up this stream.—I counted, in the course of the day, two hundred and twenty white bears. We killed eight, that made an attack upon us; the claws of which I saved. Leaving the stream in the evening we encamped on the plain. A guard of twenty was relieved through the night, to prevent the bears from coming in upon us. Two tried to do it and were killed.

In the morning we began our march as usual: returning to the stream, we travelled until we came to its head. The fountain, which is its source, boils up from the plain, forming a basin two hundred yards in circumference, as clear as crystal, about five feet in depth. Here we killed some wild geese and ducks. After advancing some distance farther we encamped for the night. Buffaloes were not so numerous, during this day's journey, as they had been some time previous, owing, we judged, to the great numbers of white bears.

On the 17th we travelled until sunset, and encamped near water. On the 18th we found no water, but saw great numbers of wild horses and elk. The succeeding morning we set off before light, and encamped at 4 o'clock in the afternoon by a pond, the water of which was too brackish to drink. On the 20th we found water to encamp by. In the course of the day I killed two fat buffaloe cows. One of them had a calf, which I thought I would try to catch alive. In order to do so, I concluded it would be well to be free from any unnecessary incumbrances, and accordingly laid aside my shot-pouch, gun and pistols. I expected it would run, but instead of that, when I came within six or eight feet of it, it turned around, and ran upon me, butting me like a ram, until I was knocked flat upon my back. Every time I attempted to rise, it laid me down again. At last I caught by one of its legs, and stabbed it with my butcher knife, or I believe it would have butted me to death. I made up my mind, that I would never attempt to catch another buffaloe calf alive, and also, that I would not tell my companions what a capsizing I had had, although my side did not feel any better for the butting it had received.

On the 5th of November we again set off in company with a party of Iotans. The Arkansas is here wide and shallow, like the Platte; and has wide but thinly timbered bottoms on both sides. Extending from the bottom ten or twelve miles on the south side, are low hills composed principally of sand. We found travelling upon them very fatiguing, particularly as we met with no water. Late in the evening we reached water, and encamped.

The next morning we resumed our journey. We were exceedingly diverted, during the day, to see the Iotan Indians in company with us, chase the buffaloes on horseback. They killed them with their arrows. The force, with which they shoot these arrows, is astonishing. I saw one of them shoot an arrow through a buffaloe bull, that had been driven close to our camp. We were again upon level plains, stretching off in all directions beyond the reach of the eye. The few high mounds scattered over them could not but powerfully arrest the curiosity. From the summit of one I again looked down upon innumerable droves of wild animals, dotting the surface, as they seemed to forget their savage natures, and fed, or reposed in peace. I indulged the thoughts natural to such a position and scene. The remembrance of home, with its duties and pleasures, came upon my mind in strong contrast with my actual circumstances. I was interrupted by the discharge of guns, and the screams and yells of Indians. The Iotans had found six Nabahoes a half a mile from us, and were killing them. Three were killed. The others, being well mounted, made their escape. The Iotans came to our camp with their scalps, leaving their bodies to be eaten by wild animals. My father sent men to bury them. The Iotans danced around these scalps all night, and in the morning took up the bodies, we had buried, and cut them in pieces. They then covered themselves with the skins of bears and panthers, and, taking the hearts of the dead men, cut them into pieces of the size of a mouthful, and laid them upon the ground, and kneeling put their hands on the ground, and crawled around the pieces of hearts, growling as though they were enraged bears, or panthers, ready to spring upon them, and eat them. This is their mode of showing hatred to their enemies. Not relishing such detestable conduct, we so manifested our feelings, that these Indians went to their own camps.

We encamped the evening of the next day near water. Nothing worthy of record occurred during the journey of the four succeeding days, except that we came to a small creek called Simaronee. Here we encamped, and killed some buffaloes, and shod our horses. We travelled up this stream some distance, and left it on the 15th.

On the 16th we encamped on a creek, where we found four gentle mules, which we caught. I could not account for their being there. Nothing of importance occurred in the two last days.

From the 17th to the 20th, we journied without interruption. The latter day we came in view of a mountain covered with snow, called Taos mountain. This object awakened in our minds singular but pleasant feelings. On the 23d we reached its foot. Here Mr. Pratte concealed a part of his goods by burying them in the ground. We were three days crossing this mountain.

On the evening of the 26th, we arrived at a small town in Taos, called St. Ferdinando, situated just at the foot of the mountain on the west side. The alcalde asked us for the invoice of our goods, which we showed him, and paid the customary duties on them. This was a man of a swarthy complexion having the appearance of pride and haughtiness. The doorway of the room, we were in, was crowded with men, women and children, who stared at us, as though they had never seen white men before, there being in fact, much to my surprize and disappointment, not one white person among them. I had expected to find no difference between these people and our own, but their language. I was never so mistaken. The men and women were not clothed in our fashion, the former having short pantaloons fastened below the waist with a red belt and buck skin leggings put on three or four times double. A Spanish knife is stuck in by the side of the leg, and a small sword worn by the side. A long jacket or blanket is thrown over, and worn upon the shoulders. They have few fire arms, generally using upon occasions which require them, a bow and spear, and never wear a hat, except when they ride. When on horse back, they face towards the right side of the animal. The saddle, which they use, looks as ours would, with something like an arm chair fastened upon it.

The women wear upon the upper part of the person a garment resembling a shirt, and a short petticoat fastened around the waist with a red or blue belt, and something of the scarf kind wound around their shoulders. Although appearing as poorly, as I have described, they are not destitute of hospitality; for they brought us food, and invited us into their houses to eat, as we walked through the streets.

The first time my father and myself walked through the town together, we were accosted by a woman standing in her own door-way. She made signs for us to come in. When we had entered, she conducted us up a flight of steps into a room neatly whitewashed, and adorned with images of saints, and a crucifix of brass nailed to a wooden cross. She gave us wine, and set before us a dish composed of red pepper, ground and mixed with corn meal, stewed in fat and water. We could not eat it. She then brought forward some tortillas and milk. Tortillas are a thin cake made of corn and wheat ground between two flat stones by the women. This cake is called in Spanish, metate. We remained with her until late in the evening, when the bells began to ring. She and her children knelt down to pray. We left her, and returned. On our way we met a bier with a man upon it, who had been stabbed to death, as he was drinking whiskey.

This town stands on a beautiful plain, surrounded on one side by the Rio del Norte, and on the other by the mountain, of which I have spoken, the summit being covered with perpetual snow.

We set off for Santa Fe on the 1st of November.

CHAPTER 15

40 Years a Fur Trader
on the Upper Missouri

By Charles Larpenteur

In this excerpt from his book, Larpenteur takes us with his group of trappers heading into winter quarters. Ahead are adventures with trapping, furs, Indians and snowstorms. All were part of the lives of the mountain men.

ABOUT THE 1ˢᵀ OF DECEMBER, 1842, I MADE MY ENTRANCE AGAIN IN Fort Union. It was at night; a large trading party were at the highest pitch of drunkenness; boss and clerks not far behind them in this respect. But I did not find it strange or surprising. Mr. Culbertson, on seeing me, remarked, "Well, Larpenteur, I am mighty glad to see you. We are having a hot time, and I'm tired of it. I suppose you are tired, too, and want to go to sleep." I supposed that he, having drunk so much, did not think about eating, for I had not got that invitation as yet, so I replied, "I'm not so tired as I am hungry." "Well," said he, "there's plenty to eat." I ran to the kitchen, and the cook got me up a rousing supper. I ate too much, and next morning found myself foundered; but I had received orders to resume the grog department, and, notwithstanding my stiffness, went on to set things in order. They needed it very much.

In the course of time I was informed of the cause of this appointment. A certain individual by the name of Ebbitt had, a year previous, brought up a small equipment and made his way as far as the Sioux district. He had a small Mackinaw with 12 men, which was considered by the American Fur Company too slight an affair to oppose; in consequence of which he made a very profitable return of 500 packs of robes. Elated with his success he went to New York with his returns, and there formed an acquaintance with the great firm of Fox, Livingston and Co., telling them how cheaply he had traded, and also remarking that the American Fur Company so abused the Indians and clerks that everything was working against them—in fact, if a large company, such as would inspire confidence among whites and Indians, should be organized, the American Fur Company would soon leave the country. This story took well; such a company was formed, and started in charge of a gentleman by the name of Kelsey, one of the members of the new firm. Mr. Kelsey had not ascended the Missouri very far before he began to regret what he had done, which was that he had put $20,000 into the concern. The farther he came up river the more he regretted it; and when he arrived at the mouth of the Yellowstone and saw Fort Union in its full splendor, he could not refrain from remarking to Mr. Culbertson, "Had I known how the American Fur Company were situated, I would have kept clear of investing in this opposition"; and concluded by saying, "I hope you will not be too hard on us." The old gentleman went off, leaving a man named Cotton in charge. Mr. Kelsey, who, according to agreement, was to remain in the Indian country and make his headquarters among the Sioux, chose a point 20 miles below Fort Pierre, opposite a beautiful island. Upon this there were four men living in a small cabin, which he considered his. He ordered them several times to leave; but they paid no attention to him, and remained in possession. One morning the old gentleman armed himself and determined to make the men leave. On entering the cabin he fired at one of them, who was in the act of taking a kettle off the fire, and who fell dead in the fire. Another one, who ran out, was also shot, and fell dead over the fence. By that time a third man, who was trying to escape in double-quick time, was shot through the shoulder, of which wound he came near losing his life. During the following night the old gentleman made his escape. I was informed that he went to Mexico. This was the last of Mr. Kelsey.

Mr. Cotton, the person left in charge at Fort William, which he now called Fort Mortimer, had not yet got dry—he was still green cotton, full of Mr. Ebbitt's stories about the general discontentment of Indians and

whites. He soon commenced to try his hand on one of the most important chiefs of the tribe, Crazy Bear, who, like many others, on learning
that a big Opposition had arrived, came in with his band to pay them
a visit. Mr. Cotton invited him into his room, made him a great speech,
dressed him up in a splendid military suit, such as had never been brought
into the country before, and then laid a two-gallon keg of whiskey at his
feet. Crazy Bear's band was at Union, waiting for his return; but, instead
of going directly to them, he went into Mr. Culbertson's private room, not
very drunk, took a seat, and remained some time without saying a word.
Mr. Culbertson, surprised to see him so splendidly dressed, and thinking
that he had lost his chief, was also silent. Finally Crazy Bear broke the
ice by saying, "I suppose you think I have left our big house. No; I am not
a child. I went below to see the chief, who treated me well. I did not ask
him for anything. I did not refuse his presents. But these cannot make me
abandon this house, where are buried the remains of our fathers, whose
tracks are yet fresh in all the paths leading to this place. No, I will not
abandon this house!" After which he rose from his seat and took off his
fine fur hat and feathers, which he threw on the floor with all his might;
then unbuckled his beautiful sword, with which he did the same; and kept
on till he had stripped himself of all his fine clothes, without speaking a
word. When this performance was over he said to Mr. Culbertson, who
stood in great astonishment, "Take away all these things and give me
such as you see fit, and don't think I am a child who can be seduced with
trinkets." This Crazy Bear, who was not at all crazy, proved afterward to
be the greatest chief of the Assiniboines.

Mr. Cotton, on hearing of this, was so surprised he could scarcely
believe it; but when Mr. Culbertson showed him the suit which had been
badly torn, he was convinced, and began to think that Mr. Ebbitt's stories
had been somewhat exaggerated. That was the way the green cotton
commenced to dry. Still, his trade was pushed to the extreme. He had
plenty of goods and was very liberal with them. Both sides then began to
send out men to the Indian camps; but as all the most important camps
were soon supplied, I began to think that I might escape that disagreeable
trade. Being always an unlucky man, I was still disappointed in this.

One evening toward the last of January [1844], while I was thinking of anything but that which was forthcoming, Mr. Culbertson sent for me to come to his room. It was extremely cold and a great deal of snow was on the ground. This, I believe, was the reason he did not broach the subject at once, but finally said, "Larpenteur, I want you to go to Woody Mountain to a camp of Crees and Chippewas, who have plenty of robes, and have sent for traders from both companies. The Assiniboines have also sent for traders at the meat-pen, which is on the same road that you are going. I want you and Mr. Denig to go into the store, get up your equipment to-night, and start in the morning." Such were my orders, at short notice, after thinking I was going to remain at the fort. I had to make a trip of at least 100 miles, northward into the British possessions, and this was not calculated to make me feel very good. But Mr. Denig and I went to work, and at midnight the equipments were ready. Next morning with one sled apiece, two mules and one driver to each sled, we started on our journey, accompanied by several Indians, among whom was one called Wounded Leg, chief of the band of the Rocks, whose camp was at the sand hills, about 60 miles on our road from the fort to Woody Mountain.

At our first camp my interpreter, a half-breed named Andrew, was taken sick; he complained of headache, and in the morning he was so ill that I had to let him go back to the fort. I understood some little Cree, and, as many of them spoke Assiniboine, I thought I could do without him. Next day we reached Wounded Leg's camp, and took a night's lodging with him. My friend Denig had been for the past few days in such a state that it was impossible for him to freeze—he was too full of alcohol. He had not walked one step; this disgusted the chief, who proved an enemy afterward. The morning was so stormy that we would not have left camp had we not learned that the Opposition had gone by with dogsleds. Not wishing to be outdone by them, I awoke Mr. Denig, who was still under the influence of liquor, and told him that we must be off—that the Opposition had gone by, and that if they could travel I did not see why we should not. When the chief saw that I was determined to leave, he remarked that it would be well for us to go; that a certain Indian was expected from the fort with a large keg of whiskey, and that it would not be well for us to remain in camp while they were drunk;

for, as he knew, we had to leave Mr. Denig behind. The mules were soon harnessed up, and into the hard storm we started, with but one Indian, who was my guide. It was an awful day; we could see no distance in any direction, floundered in deep snowdrifts, and knew not where to go for timber. But our guide was a good one, who brought us to a small cluster of scrubby elms. The snow had drifted so deep that we could find no dry wood and had to go to bed without a fire. We made ourselves as comfortable as we could by digging holes in the snow for shelter. We were then only a little distance from the meat-pen, where Mr. Denig was to stop, and reached it early next day. Mr. Denig wanted me to remain with him over night, but as he had to make a liquor trade, and I did not wish to be serenaded, I declined his kind offer. Having packed the contents of my sled on my two mules, and left the sled, which I found to be a nuisance, I proceeded on my journey to Woody Mountain. After this snowstorm the wind changed to a strong, extremely cold northwester. There were only three of us—myself; my guide, a young Chippewa; and my driver, a young Canadian named Piché, which means pitcher. As my poor Pitcher contained more water than whiskey, I was much afraid he would freeze and crack; but he was made of good metal, that could stand heat or cold. Early this evening we came to a good camping place, with plenty of dry firewood; but it was so intensely cold, and we had to dig so deep in the snow to make a fireplace, that it was with the greatest difficulty we could start a fire. But we succeeded at last in making a comfortable camp—the best one we had had since we left the fort. A little while after this we were sitting at a good supper of dried buffalo meat, a few hard-tacks we had saved, and a strong cup of coffee. After supper arrangements were made for sleeping, as a bedroom had yet to be cleared out, in a deep snowdrift, where my friend Pitcher was to be my bedfellow. We proceeded to excavate, and soon had ourselves buried alive in the snow. I believe this was the coldest night I ever felt. The guide got up first, to make a fire, to the delight of Pitcher and myself. A breakfast much like our supper was soon ready, the mules were packed, and we were off again. We had not traveled more than an hour when the wind rose, and the snow began to drift, so blinding us that we could scarcely see. We had over 10 miles to travel to timber; but, fortunately, we were on the main road, which the Indians had made so hard, in going from one camp to another, that the drifting snow could not lodge on it; so the tracks remained visible, which enabled us to reach camp in good time. At sunset the wind fell, and we had an easy time in making preparations for our last night out. There being no road between this place and the Indian camp, which was 20 miles off, over level prairie, and wishing to reach the camp in good time, we made an early start next morning.

The day was clear, cold, and calm. In my small outfit I had about five gallons of alcohol, in two kegs of three and two gallons, neatly packed in the bales of goods. I thought this quantity would be too much to bring in camp at once and concluded to cache one of the kegs on the road, for I knew it would be impossible to keep it concealed in the Indian lodge. In order to do this my guide must be dispatched ahead, for I did not think he could be trusted. So, when we got within about five miles of the camp, I remarked to him that I wished him to go on into camp and tell Broken Arm, the chief of the Crees, that I wished him to prepare me a large lodge and make ready for a big spree to-night. To this proposition the guide readily consented, and, having pointed out the direction of the camp, he left on a dogtrot. As soon as he was out of sight and we had reached a place that my friend Pitcher would be sure to find again, we cached the smaller keg in a snowbank and resumed our journey.

We had made but a few miles when we came in sight of Indians; but, as we could see no lodges, we presumed they were Indians returning from a hunt. We soon discovered men, women, and children; still no camp, and the prairie looking level as far as the eye could reach. We could not imagine what this meant, and were not relieved of our uneasiness till some of the bucks came running up and told us that there was the camp, pointing to a deep valley. Having gone about half a mile we came to a precipice, on the north of which the Indians were camped, near the bottom. It was an awful place; I could not imagine how they could stand such a place without freezing, for the sun did not reach them more than two hours out of the twenty-four. "Now," said I, to my friend Pitcher, "we are north of north here." "Yes, sir," said he, "and we'll freeze. I can't see what made them d -d Indians camp here." For the first time my good Pitcher was overflowing with bad humor, and indeed I did not blame him, for the prospect of staying in such a hole was anything but encouraging. But there was no alternative; we had to enter the lodge—a large double one—which we found already prepared for our reception. After our mules were unpacked and our baggage was arranged, a kettle of boiled buffalo tongues was brought in; a strong cup of coffee was made from our own stores, and we took supper alongside a good fire, after which symptoms of good humor returned.

Being now ready for operations, I sent for water, telling the Indians it was to make fire-water, and it was not long in forthcoming; the news circulated through the camp, and before I was prepared to trade the lodge was full of Indians, loaded with robes, ready for the spree. The liquor trade commenced with a rush, and it was not long before the whole camp was in a fearful uproar; but they were good Indians, and there was no more trouble than is usual on such occasions.

This was the first time that I ever felt snowblind; during the spree, which lasted the whole night, I complained considerably of sore eyes, attributing it to the smoky lodge. They told me the lodge did not smoke, except at the place where it ought to, and said I must be getting snow-blind. This I found to be the case, and, though I was soon over it, it was bad enough to be extremely painful. By morning I had traded 150 fine robes, about all there were dressed in the camp, and during the day I traded 30 more for goods. I then feared no opposition, as their robes were nearly all traded—that is, the dressed ones. We had plenty of leisure after that, but tremendously cold weather. It frequently happens in that part of the country, that, after a clear, calm morning, a cloud rises in the northwest about ten o'clock, and in a very short time a tremendous snowdrift comes on, which lasts all day; but the weather generally becomes calm at sunset, turning very clear and cold. Such weather we were blessed with most of the time we remained there, which was about six weeks. Imagine the pleasant time we spent in camp under that steep hill, where I am certain the sun did not shine more than 24 hours altogether during those six weeks.

The third day after we arrived I sent my Pitcher to see how the mules were getting along; the Indians had them in their charge, but I wanted to know their actual condition from a surer source during such intensely cold weather: The Pitcher was so benumbed that he was unable to tell the news on his return until he had warmed his mouth, which appeared so stiff with cold that he could not move his jaws; but I could see in his countenance that something was wrong. Being anxious to learn what the matter was, and giving him scarcely time to thaw out, I said, "Well, Pitcher, how are the mules?" "Ha! The mules both froze dead—one standing up, the other down. My good fat white mule standing up—thought she alive, but she standing stiff dead." By this time his jaws had got limber, and he made them move at a great rate, with some mighty rude expressions in regard to the place where we were. When well warmed up he began to crack a smile again, and all went well until a couple of days afterward, when I found him so much out of humor one morning that I thought surely my poor Pitcher must be broken, or at least badly cracked. When breakfast was served by the wife of Mr. Broken Arm, the great chief of the Crees, who had been to Washington, Pitcher would not partake. "What is the matter, Pitcher," said I, "are you sick? Why not have some of this good fat buffalo meat?" "Not much the matter," he replied; "I will tell after a while"—fearing perhaps that the story he had to tell would not agree with my digestive organs. Some time after that, when the things were removed, dishes washed up, and the cook had gone out, my Pitcher poured out his story. "Mr. Larpenteur," he said, "if you please, after this I will do our cooking." "Why so," said I. "Why, sir, because that enfant de garce—that old squaw is too dirty. Sacré! She scrape the cloths of that baby of hers with her knife, give it a wipe, cut up the meat with it, and throw into the kettle. This morning I see same old crust on the knife—that what the matter—too much for me." After this explanation I was no longer surprised at poor Pitcher's looking so broken; and if my digestive powers had not been strong, as they have always proven to be, I am afraid my own breakfast would have returned the way it went; but with me, whenever the meat-trap was once shut down it was not easily opened again, and things had to take their natural course.

Shortly after the death of our two mules, I traded a pony of an Indian, and Pitcher would now and then go to see how the animal stood this latitude. Then the time came when I thought the Indians might have robes enough dressed to raise a frolic; so one morning I sent for the keg of alcohol I had cached on the road. Not wishing the Indians to know what we were about, on their asking where my man was going, I told them he was going to look after my pony. He delayed longer than they thought necessary, and they remarked it; but finally he appeared in the lodge with the keg on his back—that being the kind of a pony he had gone to take care of. I was soon prepared for operations, and another glorious drunk took place; but the robe trade was light, only 50 in number. This ended the business, there being no liquor and hardly any robes left in camp.

I then sent the Indian to Fort Union with a letter for Mr. Culbertson, requesting from him the means to bring back the robes I had traded. Notwithstanding continued severely cold weather, ten days afterward a party of eight men and 20 horses arrived in camp, in charge of the hunter of the fort, Antoine Le Brun. Those men had suffered so much with the cold that it was almost impossible to recognize them—noses, cheeks, and eyes all scabby from frost-bite, and so dark from exposure that they looked more like Indians than white men. Mr. Culbertson's letter was anything but satisfactory, its contents being about as follows: "Larpenteur, I send you 20 horses, thinking them sufficient to bring in your trade; if not, try to get some good Indians to help you; tell them I will pay them well. From what I can learn some Indians, who are moving north on your route, have said they will steal all your horses; therefore I advise you to take a different route."

Now, what to do? The snow was drifted so deep in all the hollows that I could not possibly take any road but the old beaten one. To go any other way would be at the risk of freezing to death—or at least of losing all my animals in the snow; I preferred to take the chances of being robbed and perhaps beaten on the old road.

Next morning by ten o'clock we were under way, with all my trade. I had some few goods remaining, which I carefully concealed between the packs of robes, so that they could not be seen by the Indians whom we expected to meet; and I kept a few trinkets in sight, to make some small presents, should it be necessary. With much difficulty we made out to extricate ourselves from the awful abyss into which we had plunged when we came to this camp. The morning was clear, but extremely cold, and as we reached the level prairie we perceived the usual cloud, indicating a snowdrift. Not long afterward it came on, so bad that we had great trouble to keep our horses in the track. As the old saying is, "There is no bad wind but what will bring some good." This wind was one of them. We should have reached our camping place in good time, had it not been for this heavy snowdrift. A little before dark, when we came to camp, we were surprised by the barking of Indian dogs, which appeared to be not far off. The country was here very broken, and wooded with small oaks. We concluded that this was the camp of the very Indians who intended to rob us. Owing to the heavy snowdrift, which had lasted all day, they had not discovered us, and we arrived unknown to them. Finding ourselves undiscovered, I told the men to make no noise, build no fires, and early in the morning to go for the horses, as I wanted to be off by the peep of day. Some were reluctant to obey orders, but consented to do so on my telling them they did not know what might happen. Sleeping without any fire, in such cold weather, was certainly a hardship, but I thought it necessary for our safety. Supper was made on a little dried buffalo meat—about all we had. After a long, sleepless night, at break of day the horses were all brought up to pack, and at clear day we were under march. On the first hill we ascended we perceived an Indian with his hand on his mouth, which is a sign of surprise. He called out, "Ho! Ho! Have you traveled all night?" I answered, "No, we camped at the spring." "Why," said he, "did you not come to our camp? You would have been well off with us—we have meat, sugar, and coffee." I told him that if I had known the camp was so near, I certainly would have gone there. All this time my men were filing by, and as each one passed me I told him to hurry up; that I would remain behind with my packhorse, and get out of the scrape the best I could. The news soon reached the Indian camp, and in a little while I was surrounded. Their main object was to trade horses, and they wanted me to stop my men. I told them the men would not stop; they were cold, and had gone too far off. "Well," said they, "we have got a few robes we would like to trade." I found from their actions, after my poor excuse for declining the horse trade, that they were not so badly disposed as Mr. Culbertson had represented them to be; yet, if they had got the chance at night, I believe they would have relieved me of some of the horses, if not the whole band. They brought a few robes, which I traded; and not wishing my men to get too far off, I made the Indians a present of what little stuff I had left. When they found I was so generous they let me go in peace, with my good Pitcher, whom I had kept by me.

With much relieved hearts we started double-quick, and soon overtook the party. We found them delighted at our good success, and glad they had followed my advice, saying, "If we had been discovered, we should not have one horse left, and God knows what would become of us." One said, "Did you see that big painted rascal, how he look? Bet you he'd have mounted one of them"; and, after several such expressions, it was agreed among them that I was a first-rate leader.

The day became pleasant, we traveled well, and came to camp at the meat-pen, where we fell in with two Indian lodges. One of these was that of He Who Fears his War Club, a respectable and brave man, who I knew could be relied on. After we had gotten everything righted in camp, the old fellow told me to come to his lodge, that he had something to tell me. As we had little to eat in camp I was in hopes that I would get a supper out of him, and perhaps something for my men to eat; but I was disappointed in that, for he was as bad off as we were. On entering he bade me sit down; and having smoked a few whiffs, he asked me if I had heard the latest news from the fort. I told him I had learned none since the news brought to me by my men. "Well," said he, "something very bad has taken place since, and, if I were in your place, I would not go to Wounded Leg's camp; for he has had a quarrel with Long Knife (meaning Mr. Denig) and your chief (meaning Mr. Culbertson). They took him by the arms and legs and threw him out of the fort, and he has sworn vengeance against the whites. It will not be good for you to go to his camp, or even in sight of it, for I tell you he is very mad."

This news struck me pretty hard. I had got out of one scrape, but was already in another; this was something else for me to cipher on that night, and if my stomach was empty my head was full. On my return to camp I was asked what the old fellow had said; the men suspected that all was not quite right, so I told them the whole story. "Now we are in a pretty fix again," said one. "Yes," said another, "they get drunk with the Indians and fight, but don't think much of us poor fellows on the prairie," and all such expressions. One said, "Don't go that way"; and another replied,

"You d -d old fool, what other way can we go in this deep snow?" Finding them disconcerted, I said, "Don't be uneasy, boys; I'll figure out a plan to get through."

Meanwhile two strapping big bucks made their appearance in camp, and, of course, they were supposed to be horse thieves; but their story was that they were going to the fort, expecting to join a war party. Notwithstanding this, a guard was placed over them and I took care that they should have a good bed in camp, where they could be easily watched. Early in the morning all hands were roused up; our thieves were all right, but one of the old chief's little boys, about fourteen, had got up still earlier and mounted one of our best horses. He was seen in the act, but could not be overtaken. His father, a good man, was very sorry, and said that the horse would not be lost to the Company. The theft, at this time, was of great importance, as all our horses were getting very poor and weak.

From this place to Wounded Leg's camp was a good level road, about 25 miles, which we expected to make early. Now that all was ready for the move, the boys expressed a desire to know what plan I had to get them through safe. I said to them, "This is my plan: I am going on this road right straight to Wounded Leg's lodge. I know him well; he is a good friend of mine, and I am sure I can fetch him all right. When we come in sight of the camp I will go ahead alone. You can come on slowly; if anything happens to me, do the best you can for yourselves; but if things are all right, I will make you signs to come in." They were apparently satisfied, placing confidence in me and so we started; but, moving at too fast a gait, we were obliged to leave two horses, which had given out. This made three loads which had been divided on the others; it was very hard on them, and we commenced to think we should be forced to leave some of our robes on the way also.

About three in the afternoon the dreaded camp was in sight. I caused all hands to halt, and told them, Now, boys, I am going to the camp. When you get within 400 or 500 yards of it, stop. If you see Indians coming, not out of a walk, remain until they reach you; but if they come rushing, make up your minds that Larpenteur is gone up, and defend yourselves the best you can." Off I started. When I came into camp I inquired for

Wounded Leg's lodge, which was immediately shown to me. On entering I found his old woman alone. She felt somewhat surprised, but looked cheerful, and we shook hands. She had always been a good friend of mine, and I thought myself pretty safe as far as she was concerned. I asked her where her old man was. She said he had gone to the lodge of such a one. I then requested her to send for him, which she did, and a few minutes afterward he made his appearance. His countenance was not calculated to inspire confidence. Having shaken hands, he sat down and prepared to smoke, as is customary before conversing. I had to hold my tongue, but my eyes were wide open, watching the face of my enemy while he was making ready for the smoke. To my great satisfaction I thought I could perceive a change in my favour. The pipe being ready a few whiffs were exchanged, and time to break silence came. Upon which I commenced, saying, "Comrade, I have heard some very bad talk about you. I was told not to come to your lodge, or to your camp; that you intended to harm me and my men. Knowing you to be a good friend of mine, I would not mind that talk, and you see I have come straight to your lodge." His first remark was, "Who told you all this?" On my naming the individual, he said, "He told you the truth. I did say all that. I was very angry at the way in which I had been treated at the big house. But I have thought the matter over, and given up the idea of putting my threat into execution; though I am not pleased yet." I soon found that I was in a pretty fair way of success; yet something farther on my part was to be said. So, knowing the Indian character, and, for one thing, that praise of their children goes a long way with them, I commenced thus: "Now, my comrade, you know that the difficulty you had with those men at the big house was when you were all in liquor. You know very well that you are liked by the whites. You are a chief; you have a son—your only child you love him. He is a fine boy. Although but a boy, you know that the chief of the big house has already armed him like a chief.

Would you do anything to deprive your only child, as well as yourself, of chiefhood? No! certainly not. I know you too well for that." At this speech I heard the old woman groan; and, during the pause which ensued, I observed that I had them both about melted down into my affections. The idea of his boy's being so much liked and respected by the whites took the old man's fancy, and a pleasanter or more cheerful chap could scarcely have been raked up.

"Now," said I, "this is not all. I want my men to come in camp and stay with you to-night, and I want you to go to the fort with me. I assure you they will be glad to see you, and I will see that you are well paid for your trouble." Turning to the old lady, I added, "I will send you a nice cotillion." "How!" said she, which meant "Thank you!" Then Wounded Leg said, "That is all right, but you must not come into this camp; it would not be good for you. We are starving, our dogs also; they would eat up your saddles and the cords of your packs. You had better go to camp in the cherry bushes," which he then showed me about a mile off.

Taking his advice, I started back to the boys, and when near them made signs for them to come on. Meeting me and learning the result of my mission, they could not help laughing at the way I had "buttered the old fool," as they said. We steered our course for the cherry bushes, which we reached at sunset. The wind had changed to the north; it became again very cold, and to save our lives we could not get a fire out of those green bushes. There was not a stick of dry wood to be found, and a tremendous hard night we had. Sleep was out of the question, and it was too cold to stand a good guard; the result was that the two bucks, who had followed us thus far, disappeared with two of our best horses, one of which we called Father De Smet, because he had been brought from the Flatheads on that missionary's return from the Columbia. We were then nearly 50 miles from the fort, which distance would have taken us two days; but now, being short of horses, it would take us double that time. I found an Indian, whom I knew to be a good traveler, and asked him if he could go to the fort by sunset; he said he could, for he had already done it. I dispatched him with a letter to Mr. Culbertson to send me more horses, and also some dried meat, as we were starving. Dividing the loads as best we could, we got under way again, making but slow progress, with Wounded Leg, several other men, and some squaws in company. We again camped, as we all hoped for the last time; but where was supper to come from? We had not a thing to eat and were mighty hungry. I thought of trying rawhide cords, of which we had a few bundles left. I got a squaw to cut them up fine and boil them; besides which, as a great favor, I got an Indian dog killed and boiled. That

I knew would be good; and as I could not obtain more than one dog, the cords, if the cooking proved successful, would help to fill up. I am sorry to say that I was defeated there, for the longer they boiled the harder they got, and they could not be brought into condition to swallow. So there was only the dog for supper. I had sent it to a squaw to cook for us, and when she gave it to us some of the boys cried, "Mad dog! Mad dog!" Sure enough, he did look like a mad dog; for there was his head sticking partly out of the kettle, with a fine set of ivories, growling as it were, and the scum was frothing about his teeth. After the mirth had abated, and no one offered to dish out the "mad dog," I appointed Pitcher master of ceremonies, thinking a pitcher could pour out soup and hold some of it too. He commenced with great dignity, but some of the boys refused to partake, saying they would rather be excused, and could stand it until they got to the fort. This made the portions so much the larger for the balance of us; the biggest part of the thigh fell to my share, which I soon demolished, and I must say it sat very well on my stomach. But some of the boys began to say the "mad dog" was trying to run out the same way he went in; and some noises heard outside might have been taken to signify that the animal was escaping.

It was no trouble to get all hands up next morning, but some of our worn-out horses had to be whipped up. When once loaded and warmed up by means of the whip, they could only be made to keep on their feet by the same cruel means, which we were obliged to use pretty lively all the morning. Between the hours of eleven and twelve o'clock we perceived the re-enforcement from the fort, at which a great cry of joy was heard throughout the company. The loads were soon rearranged; each man took a piece of dried buffalo meat in his hands to eat on the way; the march was resumed, all eating and whipping, as there was no time to spare to reach the fort that day. Owing to those double exertions, by sunset we were on the ridge, in sight of Union and of its fine large American flag. This had been hoisted on our return from an expedition which had caused much uneasiness, from the many reports which had made it doubtful whether we could ever get back. We were also in sight of the Opposition, and I afterward heard that Mr. Cotton, on seeing us, said, "Well, Larpenteur was not badly robbed—see what a fine lot of robes he has!" In ten minutes after reaching the ridge we were safe in the fort.

Chief Wounded Leg, like the rest of us, met with a cordial welcome; and as a large trading party had just arrived, a keg of liquor was presented him, to drink with his friends. Among them was a certain Indian named The Hand, the greatest rascal in the tribe, it was believed, who had retaken two horses from some Assiniboines who had stolen them from the fort, and he had come to return them, in company with us. In some drunken spree he had killed an individual whose relations were in the trading party above mentioned. Fearing that he might be killed, I remarked to Mr. Culbertson that it would not be advisable to let him go out and drink with the other Indians—better let him have a little liquor in the fort, and if he got too troublesome we could tie him. This plan was adopted; and as I was much fatigued, I retired, telling Mr. Culbertson to awaken me in case they could not manage him without me. He got so drunk they could do nothing with him, and insisted on leaving; so the door was opened and the gentleman turned out. Early in the morning, I was again on duty. The doors were still shut; but, being tired of hearing a constant knocking, I went to see who was there. By the sound of the voice I knew who he was, and that he was all right; so I opened the small door. "Here," said the Indian, "I killed a dog last night. Take him in and shut the door." This dog was Mr. Hand, whose corpse had been wrapped up in his robe and bundled on a dog-travaille. So much for him, and we were not sorry, as he was a devil.

Shortly afterward we learned that another individual had killed his own father. I shall have occasion to mention him again. Some time before our return I learned that my interpreter had died about eight days after he reached the fort, complaining of headache. The vulgar said he died of the hollow horn; and others, of the hollow head. My good friend Pitcher, I was informed long afterward, struck for Virginia City, where I hope he became a pitcher full of gold.

CHAPTER 16

The Young Trapper

By George Bird Grinnell

In this story excerpt from his book Beyond the Old Frontier: Adventurers of Indian-Fighters, Hunters, and Fur-Traders, Grinnell uses a time-honored format of story-telling. You have the old veteran teaching the kid. In this case the veteran is a mountain man in his later years, and although he's not fighting Indians now, he's still using trapping skills he learned back in the day. The focus here is on trapping the beaver, as taught by a real mountain man to a kid eager to listen.

FOR SEVERAL MILES THE BOTTOM WAS WIDE AND USUALLY THICKLY fringed with willows. Several times they dismounted, tied their horses, and went in as far as they could toward the main stream, but twice they were stopped by water, or mud, or by beaver sloughs that were too wide for them to cross. Hugh said little, but shook his head from time to time as he looked over the valley. It was evident that he was dissatisfied. Jack forebore to ask questions, for he could see that Hugh was occupied in observing, and was thinking hard. They had gone five or six miles up the valley, and it was now about noon, when, on rounding a point of willows, they could see before them quite a large pond.

Hugh drew up his horse and for ten or fifteen minutes sat there watching, and then drawing back, he rode up behind the willows, dismounted, and tied his horse. Jack did the same.

"This looks better, son," said Hugh. "We'll go in here afoot as far as we can and watch this pond and see what we can see. I think there are beaver here, and probably this is the place we want to camp by."

As quietly as possible they made their way toward the edge of the water, passing on the way several trails where the beaver had been dragging brush to the water. The signs showed that this had been done no longer ago than last night, for on the ground were scattered fresh, green willow and cottonwood leaves, and in two or three places the bark had been knocked off willow stems by whatever had been dragged along, and these wounds were absolutely fresh. Presently they came to the edge of the willows, and still keeping themselves concealed, crept up to a little knoll, where they sat down and peered through the tangle of stems out over the pond. There before them was a long dam which Jack, with his experience of the day before fresh in his mind, could see had been recently worked on. Out in the water were a number of the hay-stack-shaped houses of the beaver, and even while they were looking, to Jack's astonishment and delight a beaver appeared on one of them, carrying in his mouth a long, white, peeled stick which he placed among others on the roof. Jack looked at Hugh, wondering if he had seen the beaver, too, and Hugh gave a little motion of his head. At two or three points on the dam animals were at work, beaver, of course, but too far off to be certainly recognized. Jack wished with all his heart that he had brought his glasses.

For nearly an hour they sat there, and then crept away as noiselessly as they had come, apparently unobserved by the animals.

"Well, son," said Hugh, as he was cooking breakfast next morning, "we've got a full day's work cut out for us, and we'd better make it as light as possible. You may as well go and catch up the saddle horses and bring them in. We have a load of traps to carry, but we can put them on our saddles. Down in this country, and at this time, we can set our traps without danger, and yet, just as a matter of habit, we'd better take our guns along. Those and the ax and our traps and my bottle of 'medicine' will be all that we'll need."

"All right," said Jack; "I'll go now, and bring the horses in and saddle up"; which he did.

By the time the horses were saddled, breakfast was ready, and soon after they had finished, the sack of traps was emptied on the ground, and Hugh tied four behind his saddle, and Jack four behind his.

"My, but these traps are heavy," observed Jack; "and strong, too. I should think that they would hold any animal except, perhaps, a bear."

"Yes," said Hugh, "they're strong enough, and they've got to be to hold a beaver, for he pulls pretty hard when he gets his foot in a trap. However, if they are properly set he doesn't have a chance to struggle long, for he plunges right for deep water and the trap holds him down, so that he drowns."

Just as they were about to start, Hugh disappeared into the tent, and rummaging around among the packages there, presently emerged with a good-sized stick of wood in his hand, to one end of which was tied a long buckskin thong forming a loop, which he hung over his head so that the stick rested on his breast.

Jack looked at it in some astonishment, and then saw that the stick was apparently a big wooden bottle formed of a birch stick three inches or more in diameter, in which a hole had been bored. This hole was stopped by a wooden plug driven into the hole, thus corking the bottle tightly. Evidently the stick had been used a long time, for it was worn and polished by much handling.

"Well, Hugh," said Jack, "I suppose that is your beaver medicine, but I never had any idea that you carried it in a bottle like that."

"Yes, son, that's the bottle, and I have used it for a good many years. You know that in old times when I first came out into this country glass bottles and tin cans weren't very plenty here, and glass doesn't last long anyhow. This is the sort of a bottle that everybody used in early days, and I've had this for a long time and had considerable luck with it."

"I never dared ask you what the medicine was made of, Hugh," said Jack, "but I suppose when you get to using it you'll let me have a smell of it, won't you?"

"Sure," said Hugh. "That's what it's made for, to be smelled of. But before you know what beaver medicine is made of, you'll have to be a real trapper."

The two swung themselves into the saddles and started off up the stream. Jack carried the ax, the head of which was protected by a leather case which covered its cutting edge, in his rifle scabbard under his leg.

"Now, son," said Hugh, "judging from what you said yesterday about the creek above here, I believe it's worth our while to ride quite a way up and see whether it gets narrow. If it does, we can perhaps set our traps first up there, because they will be easier to handle. I don't want to set around these big ponds if I can help it. There is too much danger of our losing some of our traps, and then if a beaver gets out into deep water it's barely possible that we might lose the float-stick, or else that it might get hidden, and even if we should find it out in deep water there's no way to get at it except to swim for it. You and I don't want to do that if we can help it. This water is pretty cold, for it comes right down from the snow."

"That is one of the things I was wondering about, Hugh; how you were going to find your traps or your beaver in case they got out into the water in these ponds a long way from shore."

"I'll show you how we fix that sort of thing, son; but as I say, we haven't traps enough to take very much risk."

As they went on up the stream Jack pointed out to Hugh where he had killed the panther the day before, and showed him the pond where he had seen the birds.

Not very far above this they came to a place where a few willows grew, and where a beaver dam, holding back the water, had made a long, narrow, and rather deep pond running through the meadow.

"There," said Hugh, pointing to it, "that looks like a good place to set, but we'll go on further and see what we find."

Above this pond the stream for some distance rippled noisily over a rocky bottom, but soon they came to another dam, above which was found another long and narrow pond with two or three houses near its lower end. At two places toward the upper end there were grassy points which projected into the pond, and one of which ran nearly across it.

"That looks like a good place for us to set a couple of traps, son," said Hugh. "Now, I wish that you would go into that pine timber just at the edge of the meadow and get me a couple of dead pines if you can find them, six or eight feet long and three inches through at the butt. Then sharpen the butt end so that I can drive it good and deep into the mud, so that it will hold. When you get the sticks, come around by the outer edge of the meadow and then ride in as near the edge of the pond as you can, coming well below me. I am going over now to the edge of the water to sort o' prospect."

Jack rode up into the timber and soon found a couple of young, dead trees which he chopped down, and from which he cut the required lengths. Then trimming the branches from the sticks, he sharpened the butt of each, and hanging one of them on either side of the horse, rode slowly back.

Hugh's black horse was grazing at the edge of the meadow, and Hugh himself could be seen down close to the water's edge.

Jack left Pawnee by Hugh's horse, and taking the sticks on his shoulder walked over to the water's edge, making a circle so as to come toward Hugh from the down-stream side. Before he had reached the water, Hugh signed to him to stop, and then came back toward him and said, "There's a good place here for two traps, and I'll set them, and you may as well come with me and watch what I do." Jack noticed that Hugh had stuck in his belt half a dozen straight willow twigs from a foot and a half to three feet long and about as large around as a lead pencil.

"Now, the first thing you want to remember, son, is that you mustn't leave any sign or any scent for the beaver to notice. They're smart animals, and if they see anything unusual, or if they smell anything strange, it puts them on their guard and you're not likely to have them go to your traps. Of course, here it's a little different because these beaver seem so tame, but you may as well try to begin right."

"Now I'm going to set two traps, one on each of these little points that you see running out into the pond. We've got to start in here and walk in the water up to where we're going to set, and I think that right close under the bank here we'll find the bottom hard enough for us to travel on. Just away from the bank it drops off sharply, and that is the best kind of water to set in for beaver. Now I will go ahead with these traps and you follow after me, carrying those sticks. You've cut them just about right, and I'll show you pretty soon what they're for. They are what we call float-sticks."

Hugh took two of the heavy traps in his hand and entering the water began to wade up the stream. Jack noticed that he kept far enough from the banks so that his clothing did not touch any of the overhanging grass or weeds. The water was not so deep as Jack had supposed, and did not come up within several inches of the tops of his rubber boots. He stepped into the water after Hugh, and tried to imitate all his motions, dragging after him the two float-sticks, but keeping also away from the bank. Presently Hugh stopped at the lower of the two points and waded out a step or two, but the water deepened so rapidly that he at once drew back. He now turned to Jack, and reaching toward him.

Jack passed Hugh one of the float-sticks. Hugh made a large loop of the long chain which was attached to the trap and passing it over the small end of the pole let it down to within a foot or two of the butt, and then drew the loop close between the stubs of the branches which Jack had cut off in trimming the little tree. Hugh took some pains with this, working on the chain until it tightly encircled the stick and could not be pulled up or down. Then taking the stick by its smaller end, he felt with it for the bottom some six or eight feet out from the bank, and when he had found a place that was satisfactory to him, thrust the sharpened end of the stick into the mud at the bottom. By repeated efforts he drove the stick so deep that the end which he held in his hand was almost submerged. Meantime, the trap, which was fast to the other end of the chain, lay on the bottom close to his foot. He now took the trap, and rolling up his sleeves, stood with one foot on either spring of the trap and by his weight bent these springs down so that he could set the trap. Then holding it by the chain he lifted the trap out of the water and brought it within ten or twelve inches of the grassy margin of the pond. Then he said to Jack, who stood silently near him, "We can't do much talking here, son, but after we get these traps set I'll explain to you what I've been doing, and why. Take notice, though, that I'm putting this trap in pretty shallow water, but that there's deep water just outside."

Hugh worked a little while on the bottom until he had scraped out a flat, firm bed in which the trap was placed, then from the up-stream side of the trap he scraped up one or two handfuls of soft mud and scattered it above the trap so that two or three minutes later, when the water had cleared, Jack could barely see the outline of the jaws showing in the mud which covered trap and chain. Then Hugh drew from his belt one of the shorter of the willow twigs, submerged it, and with his knife, also held under water, split the twig in half a dozen places for an inch or two from the end. Then he returned his knife to its sheath, and still holding the twig under water with his other hand, drew the cork from the bottle of beaver medicine, lifted the twig from the water and thrust the split end into the bottle and drew it out dripping with a brownish fluid, the odour of which, as it came to Jack's nostrils, seemed exactly that of a rotten apple. Then Hugh thrust the other end of the willow twig into the bottom on the shoreward side of the trap, so that the split end stood about ten inches above the trap. "There," said Hugh, "that's done. Now let's go on, but be very careful when you come to the trap to keep out from the shore as far as you can, and to step well over the chair."

A little further on, when they came to the second point, this operation was repeated almost in the same way, except that here Hugh took eight willow twigs and thrust them into the bottom, running out toward the deep water, four on the up-stream side of the trap and four on the down-stream side, the twigs being so arranged as to form a wide V which might guide the beaver toward the bait-stick which formed the apex of the V. In arranging these guiding wings, Hugh was careful not to touch any part of the twigs which projected above the water with his hand, but when he thrust the twigs into the bottom he held his hand under water, and the portion of the twig that he had touched was also under water.

Hugh and Jack now retraced their steps, going down the stream until they reached the point where they had entered it. Then Hugh motioned Jack to go ashore, and after he had done so, Hugh splashed the bank where Jack had stepped, plentifully with water, and passing on a few yards further down the stream left it by a little bay, the shore of which he plentifully wetted with water before he stepped out on the grass. Then the two went over to their horses, mounted, and rode up the stream.

Jack had watched closely what Hugh had done and understood why most of the operations that he had gone through with had been performed, yet there were many questions that he felt like asking.

"Now, son," said Hugh, after they had reached the upper end of the meadow, "let us go into this little piece of pine timber of yours and cut some more float-sticks; it is worth our while to carry some of them along with us. I don't know whether in trimming those sticks you intended to leave those branches sticking out as long as you did, but whether you meant to do it or not, it was just the right thing."

"Yes, Hugh," said Jack, "I understood from what you had told me what you wanted those sticks for, and of course I could see that you wanted them fixed so that the chain in the trap would not slip either way."

"That's it, exactly," said Hugh; "and I'm glad you listened so carefully and understood so well. Now, of course, if we couldn't find sticks with the branches just right, as those two sticks had, we might have to cut a notch in the float-stick, or we might have to try to bind the chain to it in some way or another. But there's work enough about beaver trapping at best, and if you can find the right kind of sticks, always better use them."

In the pine timber there were plenty of dead young trees, from which they selected four which made good float-sticks.

"I don't know, Hugh," said Jack, as they were hanging the sticks on their saddles, "just why you take a dry stick."

"Well," said Hugh, "there are two or more reasons for that. In the first place the beaver, if they happen to find the dry float-stick, are less likely to try their teeth on it than they would be if the stick were green. If you used a green cottonwood or willow or birch stick for your float-stick, very likely the beaver might carry it and your trap off into deep water before they got near the trap. Besides that, if a trapped beaver dives for deep water and manages to pull up your float-stick and it floats away, a dry one will float higher than a green stick and will be more easily seen and recovered."

"Yes, I see," said Jack. "That's plain enough. I suppose that you kept your hands under water so much in order to wash away the human scent."

"Yes," said Hugh, "that is so. There are lots of men who will never hold the trap or the bait-stick or anything connected with the trap, so that the wind will blow from them to it. They believe that the human scent will stick to anything, and that the beaver can smell it. I don't go quite as far as that, but I do know that if there were a hard breeze blowing I'd always get to the leeward of the trap and of all the things I left near the trapping ground."

"Well," said Jack, "I wondered as I saw you setting those traps to see how awful careful you were about everything you did."

"Well," said Hugh, "I suppose that's habit, but it's necessary. You take a man that is careless, and that leaves sign about everywhere, and you'll find that he never catches any fur. I have been out with men of that kind, and they were always poor trappers."

As the two started on Jack looked at the sun and asked, "Do you know what time it is, Hugh?"

"About noon, I guess," said Hugh.

"I guess so, too," said Jack, "and just think, it's taken us a whole morning to set two traps."

"Yes," replied Hugh; "it has taken a long time, and we'll be lucky if we get two or three more set before it's time for us to turn back to camp, but in two or three days you'll find that things will run along a good deal smoother and we won't have to take quite so much time as we have to-day."

They went on up the stream, keeping well back from it, but occasionally, where there was an opening in the brush, riding out to the bank. A mile or two further on another dam was found with a pond smaller than the one below, and immediately above this the rise of the valley was sharper so that the stream was swift and shallow.

After they had left the horses and were prospecting along the bank for a place to set, Hugh pointed out to Jack a slide from the grassy bank down into the water, which he said had been made, not by the beaver, but by an otter. "Sometime," he said, "we may try to catch that fellow. We're not rigged for it to-day, and I guess we'd better stick to beaver." At a little point near the head of the pond on the east side Hugh set another trap just as he had set the two previous ones, and then going to the head of the pond they crossed over and set another on the west side. Here the main current ran close under the bank, and Hugh was obliged to build up a little bed of stones and gravel on which to rest his trap.

"You see, son," he said, "you must have your trap so near to the top of the water that when the beaver makes a kind of a dive with his foot to raise his head up close to the medicine on the bait-stick, he will strike the pan of the trap with a foot and so spring it. Sometimes, if the water is a little deeper over the trap than a man thinks is just right, and he hasn't any way of building up a firm bed for the trap to rest on, he will take a stick and thrust it into the bank, pointing out level into the water about two inches below the surface. The beaver, swimming along toward the medicine, will hit this stick and it will stop him, and then when he makes a strong effort with his foot to get over it he will sink his foot so deep under water as to hit the pan of the trap.

"There," he said, as he backed away from the last trap set. "Now let us walk up the stream for a little way, and then go out of it and around to the horses. I have always thought that if a man takes reasonable care in setting his traps, there is more danger that the beaver will notice where he's gone in and out of the stream than there is of their suspecting something about the trap. Of course, you've got to be careful always in setting, but I've always had an idea that when a beaver gets the scent of the medicine in his nose he becomes so intent on that that he doesn't notice other signs right about the trap."

They kept on up the stream for quite a little way, and then leaving it, went around to their horses again. Hugh looked at the sun as they mounted, and said, "We have lots of time to get back to camp, and I think it might be worth while for us, on our way back, to go down to the two traps we set below. We might easily have something in one of them, seeing how tame these beaver are, and how they seem to be out all day long."

On the way back, they stopped as suggested, but only went near enough to the bank of the stream to see that neither trap had been disturbed, and then returned to camp. Half an hour was spent in stretching the lion's skin that Jack had killed the day before, and while they were at work at this Hugh said, "There seem to be quite a lot of lions in this country, son, and it's worth while to kill one every chance we get. We might run across a camp of Utes down here, and the Utes, like all other Indians that I know anything about, think a great deal of lion's skins. The chances are that you could trade this skin for three or four good beaver, and of course those would be worth a great deal more than a lion's skin, which is good for nothing except to look at. The Indians, you know, like lions' skins to make bow cases and quivers. I have often thought that maybe they have the same idea about the lion's skin that they do about the feathers of hawks or owls."

"How do you mean, Hugh?" asked Jack.

"Why," said Hugh, "you know that the Indians think a great deal of all the birds that catch their prey; that is, the eagles, hawks, and owls; they value them and their feathers in war, and they think that wearing those things helps them to be successful in war. I suppose the idea is that as the hawk or the eagle is fierce and strong and successful in attacking his enemies, so they, if they wear his feathers, will be fierce and strong and successful. In other words, they think that the qualities of the bird will be given to them if they have about them something that belongs to the bird.

"Well, now, here's a mountain lion; he is cunning and cautious, creeping about and scarcely ever being seen, able to catch his prey and hold and kill it with his sharp claws and his strong teeth, and maybe the Indians think that if they have about them something that belongs to him they will also have some of his qualities."

"Jerusalem, Hugh," said Jack, "I like to hear you tell about what the Indians believe, and why they believe it. I wonder if most men who have seen much of Indians understand as well as you do how they think about things. Of course, it's fun to hear you tell about their habits and what they do, but it's better fun yet to hear you tell about how they think about the different matters of their living."

"Well, son," said Hugh, "I've talked a heap with Indians about all these matters, and I do like to hear how they feel about them. I guess maybe there are lots of other people feel the way you and I do; but most of the old-time hunters and mountain men didn't think about much of anything except gathering a lot of fur and then going in and selling it, and getting their money and spending it as quick as they could, and then starting out to get more fur.

"I mind that once your uncle, when I was telling him some story about Indians, said to me, 'The proper study of mankind is man,' and when I told him I thought so, too, he said that that was something that some poet said a couple of hundred years ago."

"Well, I guess it's so, Hugh," said Jack, "no matter who it was said it."

When the panther skin had been stretched, Hugh told Jack to put around it the same protection that they had stretched about the grizzly bear skin, and soon after this had been done supper was ready. The dishes were washed before the sun had set, and building up the fire, the two companions lounged about it with the comfortable feeling which follows a day of hard work. For setting traps, although it does not sound like very hard work, had really required a good deal of effort.

"Now, son," remarked Hugh, "we want to get started to-morrow morning in good season, and we ought to be on our way before it's plain daylight. Of course, I hope that we'll find a beaver in every trap, but it may be that we won't find anything but feet."

"How do you mean, Hugh? Is it so that the beaver will gnaw their feet off to get out of a trap?"

"Not so," said Hugh. "I don't reckon a beaver knows enough for that in the first place, or could do it in the second. A beaver's foot is made up of a whole lot of pretty strong bones, and I question whether even a beaver could cut through those bones, and then he wouldn't know enough to do it. All a beaver knows when he gets caught is to struggle, and pull, and twist, and turn, and try to get away. Very often, if the traps are not properly set, they do get away, leaving their feet in the trap, but they don't gnaw their feet off; they twist them off. That is something that can be done and often is done, and that's the reason, as maybe I've told you before, that we always try to set our traps so that a beaver as soon as he gets caught, will plunge into deep water, and will be held there by the trap until he drowns. Then he has no opportunity of fighting with the trap and trying to get free. Of course, it often happens that it isn't possible to set your traps so that your beaver will drown, and where that isn't possible, you are likely to lose a good many of the beaver that you catch. It used to be a common thing to catch beaver with only three feet, sometimes with only two, and I once caught one that had only one foot, a hind foot that he got into the trap."

"I should think, Hugh, that a beaver that had been caught once and had got away would be mighty hard to catch again."

"Yes," said Hugh, "that's so, of course. He's always on the lookout for a trap, and then, too, if a beaver has lost a foot, a quarter of the chance of getting him is gone. If he's lost two feet he's only got two feet that can get into the trap, instead of having four, like an ordinary beaver. Lots of queer things happen in beaver trapping. I reckon I never told you that story of old Jim Beckwourth's about the beaver and the trap that was stolen by a buffalo."

"No," answered Jack. "That sounds as if it ought to be a queer story or a pretty good lie."

"Well," replied Hugh, "Jim Beckwourth had the name of being the biggest liar that ever traveled these prairies, but I wouldn't be surprised if he told the truth that time, and, anyway, Jim Bridger was with him when he found the trap with the beaver in it out on the high prairie a couple miles from where it was set.

"It seems, according to the story—it happened long before my time—that Jim came to a place where he'd set a trap and found that it was gone. There was sign there that some buffalo had crossed the creek just at this point. Jim hunted up and down the stream and couldn't find hair nor hide of the trap. The next day he and Jim Bridger went back again and looked some more, and not being able to find anything, they started on to join their party that was moving, and followed the buffalo trail that led from the place where the trap had been set. They had gone a couple of miles out on the prairie when they saw something, and going up to it found it to be a beaver, still in the trap, with the chain and float-stick all attached. Jim always claimed that one of the buffalo when crossing the creek got his head tangled in the chain of the trap and carried beaver, trap, and float-stick away out to the prairie before dropping it. It's a good story, but I'd hate to swear to it or to anything else that Jim Beckwourth ever said."

"That is a good story, Hugh," said Jack. "Isn't it wonderful," he added after a pause, "what strange things happen out here on the prairie, but there are lots of them that people back East wouldn't believe at all."

"Well, of course," said Hugh, "we all of us measure things up by what we ourselves have seen and done, and when we hear about things that are outside of the range of our own experience, we think they're wonderful."

For an hour or two longer they sat about the fire chatting over various matters, and then on Hugh's repeating the suggestion that to-morrow morning they must be early afoot, they went to bed.

The crackling of the fire was the first thing to rouse Jack next morning, and when he sat up in bed he saw that it was still dark, and that Hugh was at work cooking breakfast.

"Time to be astir, son," said Hugh, who had heard Jack's movement, and in a very short time Jack was dressed and down by the spring dousing himself with the cold water. The air was sharp and Jack crowded close to the fire, but soon a cup of coffee and some hot antelope meat warmed him up. The horses were brought in and saddled, and carrying the four traps on their saddles, and the ax, the two started up the stream. Dawn was beginning to show in the east, and before they had reached the first of the beaver traps the sun was up.

As they rode along after it got light, Hugh kept close to the edge of the willows and seemed to be looking for something, which presently he found. This was a willow sapling which forked just above the ground, sending up two sprouts to a height of twelve or fifteen feet. He cut the sapling off below the fork, cut off one of the main branches close to the fork and then trimmed the other branch, having thus a limber pole ten or twelve feet long with a stout hook on its heavier end. This he carried with him. When they left the horses he gave it to Jack, saying: "Pack this for me, son, while I carry the ax and a couple of traps."

They approached the stream by the same route that they had followed the day before, and when they had come in sight of the place where the first trap had been, Hugh said, "Something has happened here"; and pointed to the stream just below where the trap had been set, where Jack saw one end of the float-stick projecting above the water.

"Well," said Hugh, "I reckon we've got to get back that trap of ours and see what there is in it."

When they had come opposite the float stick, Hugh put the ax in the water, and taking the long willow pole from Jack, reached out, caught the float-stick and pulled it in within reach of his hand, and he gave the willow back to Jack and began to drag the trap toward him. Almost at once he said to Jack, "Well, son, we've got a beaver, I reckon"; and a moment or two later, after hauling in the chain, he lifted the trap out of the water, and Jack saw the head and shoulders of a good-sized beaver.

"Now," said Hugh, "we'll go up and look at the other trap, and then set over again. These are pretty good places, and we might catch several beaver here."

As Jack passed the trap and the beaver, which here lay almost at the surface of the water, he looked down at it with the greatest interest, but there was no time to stop and examine it. Hugh was plowing along through the water toward the other point, and Jack could see the end of the float-stick of the trap there just sticking out of the water, and looking much as it had looked the day before, after the trap had been set. Hugh said nothing, but advanced to the point, and then motioned to Jack to give him the willow pole, with which he felt in the water near the base of the float-stick and after two or three efforts hauled in the trap, in which there was a beaver.

"Pretty good luck so far, son," said Hugh. "Now I am going to set this trap over again here, because that float-stick is firm and this is a rattling good place. Suppose you take this beaver and drag it down to the place where we leave the creek, and then maybe take the other beaver down there, too. By the time you've done that, I'll have set the two traps, and then we'll take the two beaver out."

Jack took the dead beaver by a fore-paw and walked back along the shore. When he had reached the other trap, he tried to take the other beaver from it, but the springs were too stiff, and so he left it and went on down to the point where they were to go out of the water. As he looked back, he saw Hugh coming down to the trap in which the beaver was, and leaving the animal that he had been dragging at the edge of the water, he went back to Hugh, who by this time had freed the other beaver and was at work resetting the trap. Jack dragged this beaver down to the first one, and in a few moments Hugh had overtaken him, and they started across the meadow, dragging the beaver over the grass.

When they reached the horses one of the animals was put on behind each saddle and they started up the creek to visit the other traps. Here their luck had been equally good, and two beaver were taken from these two traps and the traps reset.

"Well, son," said Hugh, "if this sort of thing keeps up we'll have to bring a pack horse along with us to carry the beaver into camp. Now let us take all four of these animals up into that pine timber over there and skin them and save ourselves the trouble of carrying them to camp. If we need any of the meat we can take that down, of course."

"It looks to me, Hugh," said Jack, "as if the skinning of these four beaver was going to be quite a job." "Well," said Hugh, "so it will. I didn't suppose that we'd get more than two to-day, and figured that we would take them down to camp, but after this I think it would be a good idea for us to carry our skinning knives and whetstones with us."

"Our skinning knives, Hugh?" questioned Jack. "Why, we've both got our skinning knives in our belts now."

"Yes," said Hugh, "that's so, but those are not the best kind of knives to skin beaver with. They're all right when you are skinning game where you make wide sweeps, and do a lot of stripping; but where you've got to naturally whittle a hide off, as you have to do with a beaver, and at the same time have to be mighty careful not to make any cuts, a smaller, shorter knife is better. It is easier to handle, and you can work more quickly with it. I'll show you the knives we'll use when we get back to camp to-night. Now, if you've got such a thing in your pocket as a jack-knife, and I'm pretty sure you have, you better get that out, and we will look for a couple of whetstones as we go along."

They loaded the two additional beaver on their horses, and walked, leading them.

After they got out away from the bottom, Hugh stopped three or four times and picked up several stones, most of which he threw away, but at last he seemed to find two that suited him.

They had gone some distance from the place where the last beaver were captured, when, at the edge of a little piece of pine timber, Hugh stopped and said, "Here is a good place, son, to tackle this job; throw down those beaver that are on your horse and drop your rope, and we'll let the horses feed while we work."

The beaver were drawn off to one side, and then Hugh gave Jack one of the stones that he had picked up and explained to him how to whet the blade of his jack-knife so as to get a keen edge on it. Then the toil of beaver skinning began. It seemed to Jack pretty slow, and he had no more than half finished his first beaver when Hugh threw the hide from his to one side and pushed the carcass away.

Jack, however, finished his beaver before Hugh had finished the second one, and the two worked together on Jack's second beaver, and when they started back they had a couple hours' daylight yet before them.

"Now," said Hugh, "we'll stop and get some willows on our way back to camp and stretch these hides to-night. Then we'll be able to start in fresh in the morning. If you ever let this work pile up on you, your troubles begin sure. I'd rather skin all night than leave one beaver over till next morning."

After they got into camp that night, Hugh gave Jack a lesson in making the hoops on which to stretch the pelts; and the fur that they had taken during the day was hung up in one of the trees to dry. Jack looked at the stretched beaver skins, and thought that they seemed like great furry shields, only that they were about four times as big as any shield that he had ever seen.

Jack was tired that night as he sprawled on the ground by the fire, and it did seem to him as if everything in camp smelled of beaver. He said to Hugh: "I wish there was some way of getting rid of this smell of the beaver and the beaver grease."

"Oh," laughed Hugh, "you haven't got used to it yet. If you don't like the smell of beaver grease you'll never be a real trapper. That's what the trapper lives in, and after a while he gets so he likes it. If you are going to handle beaver and skin beaver, you can't help but smell of them."

"Well," said Jack sleepily, "I think it's a pretty high price to pay for the fur."

"Well," replied Hugh, "try it a few days, and if you don't like it better, why, we can quit trapping and turn to something else. I noticed to-day along the creek, son," he went on, "a lot of mink tracks. Now, of course, mink isn't worth much of anything. Not much more than muskrat, but it's fur all the same, and if you feel like it we can make a few dead-falls and get some mink. They ought to be pretty good here, close to the mountains."

"You catch them with dead-falls, do you, Hugh?" asked Jack.

"Yes, the mink is a pretty simple-minded animal, and he'll go into 'most any kind of a trap. We ought to have some fish or bird for bait, though. I suppose maybe we could get some suckers out of this creek, but I guess the easiest way would be to kill one of those birds that you showed me the other day."

"Oh, no, Hugh," said Jack, waking up, "don't let's do that; they're all breeding now, and it would be a pity to break up a family. Wouldn't mink go into a trap baited with beaver meat?"

253

"Maybe," answered Hugh; "I never heard of anybody using that for bait. We'll get something, though, and catch a few if you like, but if the beaver are going to act as they did to-day, why, they'll keep us busy for a little while. To-morrow, if we get time, I want to go round on the other side of that pond and set a couple of traps there, and then come down below and set two traps there. We've got eight traps, and they might as well all be in use."

"Well," said Jack, "I can imagine beaver getting too thick. I am surely going to buck if this trip comes down to just plain beaver trapping."

"Well, don't make up your mind in too much of a hurry, son," said Hugh. "You'll be able to use your hands a little better after two or three days' practice, and I am sure you'd like to take a nice pack of beaver back East to show to your friends."

CHAPTER 17

Oregon Trail Explorers

By Francis Parkman

Later perhaps, when settlers were streaming west in convoys of covered wagons, bound for Oregon, they no longer could be called "Mountain Men." In the beginning of the fledgling trail, when Francis Parkman was part of the pioneering group and wrote about it in his classic The Oregon Trail, completing the journey qualifies with mountain man experiences. As this excerpt from the original book reveals, the route, the Indians, the game available for hunting—they all posed questions on which survival was hanging.

FOUR DAYS ON THE PLATTE, AND YET NO BUFFALO! LAST YEAR'S SIGNS OF them were provokingly abundant; and wood being extremely scarce, we found an admirable substitute in bois de vache, which burns exactly like peat, producing no unpleasant effects. The wagons one morning had left the camp; Shaw and I were already on horseback, but Henry Chatillon still sat cross-legged by the dead embers of the fire, playing pensively with the lock of his rifle, while his sturdy Wyandotte pony stood quietly behind him, looking over his head. At last he got up, patted the neck of the pony (whom, from an exaggerated appreciation of his merits, he had christened "Five Hundred Dollar"), and then mounted with a melancholy air.

"What is it, Henry?"

"Ah, I feel lonesome; I never been here before; but I see away yonder over the buttes, and down there on the prairie, black—all black with buffalo!"

In the afternoon he and I left the party in search of an antelope; until at the distance of a mile or two on the right, the tall white wagons and the little black specks of horsemen were just visible, so slowly advancing that they seemed motionless; and far on the left rose the broken line of scorched, desolate sand-hills. The vast plain waved with tall rank grass that swept our horses' bellies; it swayed to and fro in billows with the light breeze, and far and near antelope and wolves were moving through it, the hairy backs of the latter alternately appearing and disappearing as they bounded awkwardly along; while the antelope, with the simple curiosity peculiar to them, would often approach as closely, their little horns and white throats just visible above the grass tops, as they gazed eagerly at us with their round black eyes.

I dismounted, and amused myself with firing at the wolves. Henry attentively scrutinized the surrounding landscape; at length he gave a shout, and called on me to mount again, pointing in the direction of the sand-hills. A mile and a half from us, two minute black specks slowly traversed the face of one of the bare glaring declivities, and disappeared behind the summit. "Let us go!" cried Henry, belaboring the sides of Five Hundred Dollar; and I following in his wake, we galloped rapidly through the rank grass toward the base of the hills.

From one of their openings descended a deep ravine, widening as it issued on the prairie. We entered it, and galloping up, in a moment were surrounded by the bleak sand-hills. Half of their steep sides were bare; the rest were scantily clothed with clumps of grass, and various uncouth plants, conspicuous among which appeared the reptile-like prickly-pear. They were gashed with numberless ravines; and as the sky had suddenly darkened, and a cold gusty wind arisen, the strange shrubs and the dreary hills looked doubly wild and desolate. But Henry's face was all eagerness. He tore off a little hair from the piece of buffalo robe under his saddle, and threw it up, to show the course of the wind. It blew directly before us. The game were therefore to windward, and it was necessary to make our best speed to get around them.

We scrambled from this ravine, and galloping away through the hollows, soon found another, winding like a snake among the hills, and so deep that it completely concealed us. We rode up the bottom of it, glancing through the shrubbery at its edge, till Henry abruptly jerked his rein, and slid out of his saddle. Full a quarter of a mile distant, on the outline of the farthest hill, a long procession of buffalo were walking, in Indian file, with the utmost gravity and deliberation; then more appeared, clambering from a hollow not far off, and ascending, one behind the other, the grassy slope of another hill; then a shaggy head and a pair of short broken horns appeared issuing out of a ravine close at hand, and with a slow, stately step, one by one, the enormous brutes came into view, taking their way across the valley, wholly unconscious of an enemy. In a moment Henry was worming his way, lying flat on the ground, through grass and prickly-pears, toward his unsuspecting victims. He had with him both my rifle and his own. He was soon out of sight, and still the buffalo kept issuing into the valley. For a long time all was silent. I sat holding his horse, and wondering what he was about, when suddenly, in rapid succession, came the sharp reports of the two rifles, and the whole line of buffalo, quickening their pace into a clumsy trot, gradually disappeared over the ridge of the hill. Henry rose to his feet, and stood looking after them.

"You have missed them," said I.

"Yes," said Henry; "let us go." He descended into the ravine, loaded the rifles, and mounted his horse.

We rode up the hill after the buffalo. The herd was out of sight when we reached the top, but lying on the grass not far off, was one quite lifeless, and another violently struggling in the death agony.

"You see I miss him!" remarked Henry. He had fired from a distance of more than a hundred and fifty yards, and both balls had passed through the lungs—the true mark in shooting buffalo.

The darkness increased, and a driving storm came on. Tying our horses to the horns of the victims, Henry began the bloody work of dissection, slashing away with the science of a connoisseur, while I vainly endeavoured to imitate him. Old Hendrick recoiled with horror and indignation when I endeavored to tie the meat to the strings of raw hide, always carried for this purpose, dangling at the back of the saddle. After some difficulty we overcame his scruples; and heavily burdened with the more eligible portions of the buffalo, we set out on our return. Scarcely had we emerged from the labyrinth of gorges and ravines, and issued upon the open prairie, when the pricking sleet came driving, gust upon gust, directly in our faces. It was strangely dark, though wanting still an hour of sunset. The freezing storm soon penetrated to the skin, but the uneasy trot of our heavy-gaited horses kept us warm enough, as we forced them unwillingly in the teeth of the sleet and rain, by the powerful suasion of our Indian whips. The prairie in this place was hard and level. A flourishing colony of prairie dogs had burrowed into it in every direction, and the little mounds of fresh earth around their holes were about as numerous as the hills in a cornfield; but not a yelp was to be heard; not the nose of a single citizen was visible; all had retired to the depths of their burrows, and we envied them their dry and comfortable habitations. An hour's hard riding showed us our tent dimly looming through the storm, one side puffed out by the force of the wind, and the other collapsed in proportion, while the disconsolate horses stood shivering close around, and the wind kept up a dismal whistling in the boughs of three old half-dead trees above. Shaw, like a patriarch, sat on his saddle in the entrance, with a pipe in his mouth, and his arms folded, contemplating, with cool satisfaction, the piles of meat that we flung on the ground before him. A dark and dreary night succeeded; but the sun rose with heat so sultry and languid that the captain excused himself on that account from way-laying an old buffalo bull, who with stupid gravity was walking over the prairie to drink at the river. So much for the climate of the Platte!

But it was not the weather alone that had produced this sudden abatement of the sportsmanlike zeal which the captain had always professed. He had been out on the afternoon before, together with several members of his party; but their hunting was attended with no other result than the loss of one of their best horses, severely injured by Sorel, in vainly chasing a wounded bull. The captain, whose ideas of hard riding were all derived from transatlantic sources, expressed the utmost amazement at the feats of Sorel, who went leaping ravines, and dashing at full speed up and down the sides of precipitous hills, lashing his horse with the reck-lessness of a Rocky Mountain rider. Unfortunately for the poor animal he was the property of R., against whom Sorel entertained an unbounded aversion. The captain himself, it seemed, had also attempted to "run" a buffalo, but though a good and practiced horseman, he had soon given over the attempt, being astonished and utterly disgusted at the nature of the ground he was required to ride over.

Nothing unusual occurred on that day; but on the following morning Henry Chatillon, looking over the oceanlike expanse, saw near the foot of the distant hills something that looked like a band of buffalo. He was not sure, he said, but at all events, if they were buffalo, there was a fine chance for a race. Shaw and I at once determined to try the speed of our horses.

"Come, captain; we'll see which can ride hardest, a Yankee or an Irishman."

But the captain maintained a grave and austere countenance. He mounted his led horse, however, though very slowly; and we set out at a trot. The game appeared about three miles distant. As we proceeded the captain made various remarks of doubt and indecision; and at length declared he would have nothing to do with such a breakneck business; protesting that he had ridden plenty of steeple-chases in his day, but he never knew what riding was till he found himself behind a band of buffalo day before yesterday. "I am convinced," said the captain, "that, 'running' is out of the question. Take my advice now and don't attempt it. It's dangerous, and of no use at all." [The method of hunting called "running" consists in attacking the buffalo on horseback and shooting him with bullets or arrows when at full-speed. In "approaching," the hunter conceals himself and crawls on the ground toward the game, or lies in wait to kill them.]

"Then why did you come out with us? What do you mean to do?"

"I shall 'approach,'" replied the captain.

"You don't mean to 'approach' with your pistols, do you? We have all of us left our rifles in the wagons."

The captain seemed staggered at the suggestion. In his characteristic indecision, at setting out, pistols, rifles, "running" and "approaching" were mingled in an inextricable medley in his brain. He trotted on in silence between us for a while; but at length he dropped behind and slowly walked his horse back to rejoin the party. Shaw and I kept on; when lo! As we advanced, the band of buffalo were transformed into certain clumps of tall bushes, dotting the prairie for a considerable distance. At this ludicrous termination of our chase, we followed the example of our late ally, and turned back toward the party. We were skirting the brink of a deep ravine, when we saw Henry and the broad-chested pony coming toward us at a gallop.

"Here's old Papin and Frederic, down from Fort Laramie!" shouted Henry, long before he came up. We had for some days expected this encounter. Papin was the bourgeois of Fort Laramie. He had come down the river with the buffalo robes and the beaver, the produce of the last winter's trading. I had among our baggage a letter which I wished to commit to their hands; so requesting Henry to detain the boats if he could until my return, I set out after the wagons. They were about four miles in advance. In half an hour I overtook them, got the letter, trotted back upon the trail, and looking carefully, as I rode, saw a patch of broken, storm-blasted trees, and moving near them some little black specks like men and horses. Arriving at the place, I found a strange assembly. The boats, eleven in number, deep-laden with the skins, hugged close to the shore, to escape being borne down by the swift current. The rowers, swarthy ignoble Mexicans, turned their brutish faces upward to look, as I reached the bank. Papin sat in the middle of one of the boats upon the canvas covering that protected the robes. He was a stout, robust fellow, with a little gray eye, that had a peculiarly sly twinkle. "Frederic" also stretched his tall rawboned proportions close by the bourgeois, and "mountain-men" completed the group; some lounging in the boats, some strolling on shore; some attired in gayly painted buffalo robes, like Indian dandies; some with hair saturated with red paint, and beplastered with glue to their temples; and one bedaubed with vermilion upon his forehead and each cheek. They were a mongrel race; yet the French blood seemed to predominate; in a few, indeed, might be seen the black snaky eye of the Indian half-breed, and one and all, they seemed to aim at assimilating themselves to their savage associates.

I shook hands with the bourgeois, and delivered the letter; then the boats swung round into the stream and floated away. They had reason for haste, for already the voyage from Fort Laramie had occupied a full month, and the river was growing daily more shallow. Fifty times a day the boats had been aground, indeed; those who navigate the Platte invariably spend half their time upon sand-bars. Two of these boats, the property of private traders, afterward separating from the rest, got hopelessly involved in the shallows, not very far from the Pawnee villages, and were soon surrounded by a swarm of the inhabitants. They carried off everything that they considered valuable, including most of the robes; and amused themselves by tying up the men left on guard and soundly whipping them with sticks.

We encamped that night upon the bank of the river. Among the emigrants there was an overgrown boy, some eighteen years old, with a head as round and about as large as a pumpkin, and fever-and-ague fits had dyed his face of a corresponding colour. He wore an old white hat, tied under his chin with a handkerchief; his body was short and stout, but his legs of disproportioned and appalling length. I observed him at sunset, breasting the hill with gigantic strides, and standing against the sky on the summit, like a colossal pair of tongs. In a moment after we heard him screaming frantically behind the ridge, and nothing doubting that he was in the clutches of Indians or grizzly bears, some of the party caught up their rifles and ran to the rescue. His outcries, however, proved but an ebullition of joyous excitement; he had chased two little wolf pups to their burrow, and he was on his knees, grubbing away like a dog at the mouth of the hole, to get at them.

Before morning he caused more serious disquiet in the camp. It was his turn to hold the middle guard; but no sooner was he called up, than he coolly arranged a pair of saddle-bags under a wagon, laid his head upon them, closed his eyes, opened his mouth and fell asleep. The guard on our side of the camp, thinking it no part of his duty to look after the cattle of the emigrants, contented himself with watching our own horses and mules; the wolves, he said, were unusually noisy; but still no mischief was anticipated until the sun rose, and not a hoof or horn was in sight! The cattle were gone! While Tom was quietly slumbering, the wolves had driven them away.

Then we reaped the fruits of R.'s precious plan of traveling in company with emigrants. To leave them in their distress was not to be thought of, and we felt bound to wait until the cattle could be searched for, and, if possible, recovered. But the reader may be curious to know what punishment awaited the faithless Tom. By the wholesome law of the prairie, he who falls asleep on guard is condemned to walk all day leading his horse by the bridle, and we found much fault with our companions for not enforcing such a sentence on the offender. Nevertheless had he been of our party, I have no doubt he would in like manner have escaped scot-free. But the emigrants went farther than mere forebearance; they decreed that since Tom couldn't stand guard without falling asleep, he shouldn't stand guard at all, and henceforward his slumbers were unbroken. Establishing such a premium on drowsiness could have no very beneficial effect upon the vigilance of our sentinels; for it is far from agreeable, after riding from sunrise to sunset, to feel your slumbers interrupted by the butt of a rifle nudging your side, and a sleepy voice growling in your ear that you must get up, to shiver and freeze for three weary hours at midnight.

"Buffalo! Buffalo!" It was but a grim old bull, roaming the prairie by himself in misanthropic seclusion; but there might be more behind the hills. Dreading the monotony and languor of the camp, Shaw and I saddled our horses, buckled our holsters in their places, and set out with Henry Chatillon in search of the game. Henry, not intending to take part in the chase, but merely conducting us, carried his rifle with him, while we left ours behind as incumbrances. We rode for some five or six miles, and saw no living thing but wolves, snakes, and prairie dogs.

"This won't do at all," said Shaw.

"What won't do?"

"There's no wood about here to make a litter for the wounded man; I have an idea that one of us will need something of the sort before the day is over."

There was some foundation for such an apprehension, for the ground was none of the best for a race, and grew worse continually as we proceeded; indeed it soon became desperately bad, consisting of abrupt hills and deep hollows, cut by frequent ravines not easy to pass. At length, a mile in advance, we saw a band of bulls. Some were scattered grazing over a green declivity, while the rest were crowded more densely together in the wide hollow below. Making a circuit to keep out of sight, we rode toward them until we ascended a hill within a furlong of them, beyond which nothing intervened that could possibly screen us from their view. We dismounted behind the ridge just out of sight, drew our saddle-girths, examined our pistols, and mounting again rode over the hill, and descended at a canter toward them, bending close to our horses' necks. Instantly they took the alarm; those on the hill descended; those below gathered into a mass, and the whole got in motion, shouldering each other along at a clumsy gallop. We followed, spurring our horses to full speed; and as the herd rushed, crowding and trampling in terror through an opening in the hills, we were close at their heels, half suffocated by the clouds of dust. But as we drew near, their alarm and speed increased; our horses showed signs of the utmost fear, bounding violently aside as we approached, and refusing to enter among the herd. The buffalo now broke into several small bodies, scampering over the hills in different directions, and I lost sight of Shaw; neither of us knew where the other had gone. Old Pontiac ran like a frantic elephant up hill and down hill, his ponderous hoofs striking the prairie like sledge-hammers. He showed a curious mixture of eagerness and terror, straining to overtake the panic-stricken herd, but constantly recoiling in dismay as we drew near. The fugitives, indeed, offered no very attractive spectacle, with their enormous size and weight, their shaggy manes and the tattered remnants of their last winter's hair covering their backs in irregular shreds and patches, and flying off in the wind as they ran. At length I urged my horse close behind a bull, and after trying in vain, by blows and spurring, to bring him alongside, I shot a bullet into the buffalo from this disadvantageous position. At the report, Pontiac swerved so much that I was again thrown a little behind the game. The bullet, entering too much in the rear, failed to disable the bull, for a buffalo requires to be shot at particular points, or he will certainly escape. The herd ran up a hill, and I followed in pursuit. As Pontiac rushed headlong down on the other side, I saw Shaw and Henry descending the hollow on the right, at a leisurely gallop; and in front, the buffalo were just disappearing behind the crest of the next hill, their short tails erect, and their hoofs twinkling through a cloud of dust.

At that moment, I heard Shaw and Henry shouting to me; but the muscles of a stronger arm than mine could not have checked at once the furious course of Pontiac, whose mouth was as insensible as leather. Added to this, I rode him that morning with a common snaffle, having the day before, for the benefit of my other horse, unbuckled from my bridle the curb which I ordinarily used. A stronger and hardier brute never trod the prairie; but the novel sight of the buffalo filled him with terror, and when at full speed he was almost incontrollable. Gaining the top of the ridge, I saw nothing of the buffalo; they had all vanished amid the intricacies of the hills and hollows. Reloading my pistols, in the best way I could, I galloped on until I saw them again scuttling along at the base of the hill, their panic somewhat abated. Down went old Pontiac among them, scattering them to the right and left, and then we had another long chase. About a dozen bulls were before us, scouring over the hills, rushing down the declivities with tremendous weight and impetuosity, and then labouring with a weary gallop upward. Still Pontiac, in spite of spurring and beating, would not close with them. One bull at length fell a little behind the rest, and by dint of much effort I urged my horse within six or eight yards of his side. His back was darkened with sweat; he was panting heavily, while his tongue lolled out a foot from his jaws. Gradually I came up abreast of him, urging Pontiac with leg and rein nearer to his side, then suddenly he did what buffalo in such circumstances will always do; he slackened his gallop, and turning toward us, with an aspect of mingled rage and distress, lowered his huge shaggy head for a charge. Pontiac with a snort, leaped aside in terror, nearly throwing me to the ground, as I was wholly unprepared for such an evolution. I raised my pistol in a passion to strike him on the head, but thinking better of it fired the bullet after the bull, who had resumed his flight, then drew rein and determined to rejoin my companions. It was high time. The breath blew hard from Pontiac's nostrils, and the sweat rolled in big drops down his sides; I myself felt as if drenched in warm water. Pledging myself (and I redeemed the pledge) to take my revenge at a future opportunity, I looked round for some indications to show me where I was, and what course I ought to pursue; I might as well have looked for landmarks in the midst of the ocean. How many miles I had run or in what direction, I had no idea; and around me the prairie was rolling in steep swells and pitches, without a single distinctive feature to guide me. I had a little compass hung at my neck; and ignorant that the Platte at this point diverged considerably from its easterly course, I thought that by keeping to the northward I should certainly reach it. So I turned and rode about two hours in that direction. The prairie changed as I advanced, softening away into easier undulations, but nothing like the Platte appeared, nor any sign of a human being; the same wild endless expanse lay around me still; and to all appearance I was as far from my object as ever. I began now to consider myself in danger of being lost; and therefore, reining in my horse, summoned the scanty share of woodcraft that I possessed (if that term he applicable upon the prairie) to extricate me. Looking round, it occurred to me that the buffalo might prove my best guides. I soon found one of the paths made by them in their passage to the river; it ran nearly at right angles to my course; but turning my horse's head in the direction it indicated, his freer gait and erected ears assured me that I was right.

But in the meantime my ride had been by no means a solitary one. The whole face of the country was dotted far and wide with countless hundreds of buffalo. They trooped along in files and columns, bulls cows, and calves, on the green faces of the declivities in front. They scrambled away over the hills to the right and left; and far off, the pale blue swells in the extreme distance were dotted with innumerable specks. Sometimes I surprised shaggy old bulls grazing alone, or sleeping behind the ridges I ascended. They would leap up at my approach, stare stupidly at me through their tangled manes, and then gallop heavily away. The antelope were very numerous; and as they are always bold when in the neighborhood of buffalo, they would approach quite near to look at me, gazing intently with their great round eyes, then suddenly leap aside, and stretch lightly away over the prairie, as swiftly as a racehorse. Squalid, ruffianlike wolves sneaked through the hollows and sandy ravines. Several times I passed through villages of prairie dogs, who sat, each at the mouth of his burrow, holding his paws before him in a supplicating attitude, and yelping away most vehemently, energetically whisking his little tail with every squeaking cry he uttered. Prairie dogs are not fastidious in their choice of companions; various long, checkered snakes were sunning themselves in the midst of the village, and demure little gray owls, with a large white ring around each eye, were perched side by side with the rightful inhabitants. The prairie teemed with life. Again and again I looked toward the crowded hillsides, and was sure I saw horsemen; and riding near, with a mixture of hope and dread, for Indians were abroad, I found them transformed into a group of buffalo. There was nothing in human shape amid all this vast congregation of brute forms.

When I turned down the buffalo path, the prairie seemed changed; only a wolf or two glided past at intervals, like conscious felons, never looking to the right or left. Being now free from anxiety, I was at leisure to observe minutely the objects around me; and here, for the first time, I noticed insects wholly different from any of the varieties found farther to the eastward. Gaudy butterflies fluttered about my horse's head; strangely formed beetles, glittering with metallic luster, were crawling upon plants that I had never seen before; multitudes of lizards, too, were darting like lightning over the sand.

I had run to a great distance from the river. It cost me a long ride on the buffalo path before I saw from the ridge of a sand-hill the pale surface of the Platte glistening in the midst of its desert valleys, and the faint outline of the hills beyond waving along the sky. From where I stood, not a tree nor a bush nor a living thing was visible throughout the whole extent of the sun-scorched landscape. In half an hour I came upon the trail, not far from the river; and seeing that the party had not yet passed, I turned eastward to meet them, old Pontiac's long swinging trot again assuring me that I was right in doing so. Having been slightly ill on leaving camp in the morning six or seven hours of rough riding had fatigued me extremely. I soon stopped, therefore; flung my saddle on the ground, and with my head resting on it, and my horse's trail-rope tied loosely to my arm, lay waiting the arrival of the party, speculating meanwhile on the extent of the injuries Pontiac had received. At length the white wagon coverings rose from the verge of the plain. By a singular coincidence, almost at the same moment two horsemen appeared coming down from the hills. They were Shaw and Henry, who had searched for me a while in the morning, but well knowing the futility of the attempt in such a broken country, had placed themselves on the top of the highest hill they could find, and picketing their horses near them, as a signal to me, had laid down and fallen asleep. The stray cattle had been recovered, as the emigrants told us, about noon. Before sunset, we pushed forward eight miles farther.

June 7, 1846.—Four men are missing; R., Sorel and two emigrants. They set out this morning after buffalo, and have not yet made their appearance; whether killed or lost, we cannot tell.

I find the above in my notebook, and well remember the council held on the occasion. Our fire was the scene of it; or the palpable superiority of Henry Chatillon's experience and skill made him the resort of the whole camp upon every question of difficulty. He was moulding bullets at the fire, when the captain drew near, with a perturbed and care-worn expression of countenance, faithfully reflected on the heavy features of Jack, who followed close behind. Then emigrants came straggling from their wagons toward the common center; various suggestions were made to account for the absence of the four men, and one or two of the emigrants declared that when out after the cattle they had seen Indians dogging them, and crawling like wolves along the ridges of the hills. At this time the captain slowly shook his head with double gravity, and solemnly remarked:

"It's a serious thing to be traveling through this cursed wilderness"; an opinion in which Jack immediately expressed a thorough coincidence. Henry would not commit himself by declaring any positive opinion.

"Maybe he only follow the buffalo too far; maybe Indian kill him; maybe he got lost; I cannot tell!"

With this the auditors were obliged to rest content; the emigrants, not in the least alarmed, though curious to know what had become of their comrades, walked back to their wagons and the captain betook himself pensively to his tent. Shaw and I followed his example.

"It will be a bad thing for our plans," said he as we entered, "if these fellows don't get back safe. The captain is as helpless on the prairie as a child. We shall have to take him and his brother in tow; they will hang on us like lead."

"The prairie is a strange place," said I. "A month ago I should have thought it rather a startling affair to have an acquaintance ride out in the morning and lose his scalp before night, but here it seems the most natural thing in the world; not that I believe that R. has lost his yet."

If a man is constitutionally liable to nervous apprehensions, a tour on the distant prairies would prove the best prescription; for though when in the neighborhood of the Rocky Mountains he may at times find himself placed in circumstances of some danger, I believe that few ever breathe that reckless atmosphere without becoming almost indifferent to any evil chance that may befall themselves or their friends.

Shaw had a propensity for luxurious indulgence. He spread his blanket with the utmost accuracy on the ground, picked up the sticks and stones that he thought might interfere with his comfort, adjusted his saddle to serve as a pillow, and composed himself for his night's rest. I had the first guard that evening; so, taking my rifle, I went out of the tent. It was perfectly dark. A brisk wind blew down from the hills, and the sparks from the fire were streaming over the prairie. One of the emigrants, named Morton, was my companion; and laying our rifles on the grass, we sat down together by the fire. Morton was a Kentuckian, an athletic fellow, with a fine intelligent face, and in his manners and conversation he showed the essential characteristics of a gentleman. Our conversation turned on the pioneers of his gallant native State. The three hours of our watch dragged away at last, and we went to call up the relief.

R.'s guard succeeded mine. He was absent; but the captain, anxious lest the camp should be left defenceless, had volunteered to stand in his place; so I went to wake him up. There was no occasion for it, for the captain had been awake since nightfall. A fire was blazing outside of the tent, and by the light which struck through the canvas, I saw him and Jack lying on their backs, with their eyes wide open. The captain responded instantly to my call; he jumped up, seized the double-barrelled rifle, and came out of the tent with an air of solemn determination, as if about to devote himself to the safety of the party. I went and lay down, not doubting that for the next three hours our slumbers would be guarded with sufficient vigilance.

CHAPTER 18

The Frontiersman

By Charles Haven Ladd Johnston

This tribute to The Frontiersman, *which most emphatically includes mountain men, is actually a story told in verse. Excerpted from Johnston's book* Famous Frontiersmen and Heroes of the Border *(1913), a veteran frontiersman looks back on his years in the mountains with vivid and immense memories. In the last sentence, he hints that he knows the years of* The Frontiersman *are finished: The settlers are coming.*

He stood 'neath the whispering pines, by his cabin,
Lanky and gaunt, his face seamed and scarred,
Knotted his hands and blackened with toiling,
Bronzed well his face; his palms rough and hard.
Strangely he gazed in the dim, filmy distance,
Gazed, as the smoke from the fire curled and swayed,
Rapt was his look, for a voice from the forest
Spoke—and in accents disquieting—said:

Come! Freeman! Come! To the swirl of the river,
Come! Where the wild bison ranges and roams,
Come! Where the coyote and timber wolves whimper,
Come! Where the prairie dogs build their rough homes.
Come to the hills where the blossoms are swaying,
Come to the glades where the elk shrills his cry,

Come—for the wild canyon echoes are saying,
Come—only come—climb my peaks to the sky.

A thrill shook the frame of the woodsman and trapper,
A strange light of yearning came to his eye,
Restless and roving by nature,—this wanderer,
Shuddered and paled at the wild, hidden cry;
Trembling he turned towards the hut in the shadow,
Shaking he strode to the low, darkened door,
Then stopped,—as sounded the voice from the meadow,
Mutt'ring the challenge—o'er and o'er.

Come, will you come, where the brown ouzel nestles,
Come, where the waterfall dashes and plays,
Come, where the spike-horn rollicks and wrestles,
On a carpet of moss, in the warm Autumn haze;
The cloud banks are blowing o'er Leidy and Glenrock,
On Wessex and Cassa the sun hides its head,
Come, will you come, where the trout leaps in splendor,
Come, only come, let the veldt be your bed.

By the rough, oaken chair lay the grim, shining rifle,
On a nail o'er the fire swung the curled powder-horn,
With a smiling grimace he seized on these weapons,
Wild emblems of conquest,—storm-battered and worn.
"Stay," whirred the loom, as it stood in the shadow,
"Stay," purred the cat, as it lay near the stove,
"Stay where the woodbine and iris are trailing,
Stay, only stay, calm this spirit to rove."

But, "come" shrilled the voice on the dim, distant prairie,
"Come, where the Cheyennes are roving and free,
Where the beavers are damming the wild, rushing ice stream,
Where the lean puma snarls in the shaggy, pine tree.
Come—for the call of the wild is resounding,

THE FRONTIERSMAN

From Laramie's peaks rolls the smoke of the fire.
Lighted by scouts, where the herds are abounding,
Fattened and sleek, for the red man's desire."

❧

Thus came the call, and thus trekked the plainsman,
Westward, yet westward his grim step led on,
By the wide, sedgy steppes, where the Platte curled and whispered,
By the brackish salt lake, stretching gray 'neath the sun,
Where the purple, red flowers in clusters lay glist'ning,
Where the wild kestrel whirled o'er the precipice sheer,
He conquered the wild, while the grizzly stood list'ning,
And growled, as the white canvased wagons drew near.

Sources

"Introduction" Excerpt: From *The Story of the Trapper*, by A. C. Laut, 1902.

"Bold Men, Shining Mountains," from *The Last Buffalo Hunt and Other Stories*, 2012, by Jim Merritt. Reprinted by permission of the author.

"The Explorer," by Rudyard Kipling, from *Collected Verse of Rudyard Kipling*, 1915.

"For Love of the Wild Places," by George Laycock, from his book *The Mountain Men*, Lyons Press, 1988. Reprinted by permission.

"The Free Trapper, Life at Its Most Dangerous," by A. C. Laut, from *The Story of the Trapper*, 1902.

"The Happy Mountain Man," by George Laycock, from his book *The Mountain Men*, Lyons Press, 1988. Reprinted by permission.

"The Snow Tramp," by Lewis H. Garrard, from his book *Wah-To-Yah and the Taos Trail*, 1850.

"Beaver Country: Skills and Lore of the Mountain Men," by A. C. Laut, from his book *The Story of the Trapper*, 1902.

"The Way West: Lewis and Clark Reach the Pacific," from *The Journals of Lewis and Clark*. Many editions have been published.

"Trails, Camps and Fights for Life in the High Country," by George Frederick Ruxton, from his book *Life in the Far West*, 1848.

"Captain Bonneville Among the Blackfeet," by Washington Irving, from his book *The Adventures of Captain Bonneville U.S.A. in the Rocky Mountains of the Far West*, 1837.

"Journal of a Trapper," by Osborne Russell, is from his book of the same title, 1914.

"The French Trapper: To Live Hard, Die Hard," by A. C. Laut, from his book *The Story of the Trapper*, 1902.

"The Personal Narrative Of James O. Pattie of Kentucky," by James O. Pattie from his book of the same title, 1831.

"40 Years a Fur Trader on the Upper Missouri," by Charles Larpenteur, from his book of the same title, 1898.

"The Young Trapper," by George Bird Grinnell, from his book *Beyond the Old Frontier: Adventures of Indian-Fighters, Hunters, and Fur-Traders*, 1913.

"Oregon Trail Explorers," by Francis Parkman, from his book *The Oregon Trail*, 1849.

"The Frontiersman," by Charles Haven Ladd Johnston, from his book *Famous Frontiersmen and Heroes of the Border*, 1913.

GLOSSARY OF MOUNTAIN MEN WORDS AND EXPRESSIONS

Bells—Hawking bells, prized as trading goods, along with beads, blankets, powder and ball, and knives.

Boudins—Buffalo intestines, a favorite delicacy of mountain men.

Bourgeois—The leader, the boss, of a brigade or band of trappers; man in charge of a fort, or in charge of a French voyageur group.

Brigade—A large band of trappers, organized out of necessity to work and travel in dangerous Indian country, especially deep in the lands of the dreaded Blackfeet.

Bull boat—A primitively built craft made of buffalo skins, barely manageable afloat, but able to ferry large loads of furs downriver.

Cache—A place to hide or store goods until they were needed. Mountain men usually dug a deep hole and wrapped the supplies in furs for protection, carefully concealing the hiding place.

"The Company"—Usually a scowling reference to the much-despised American Fur Company, formed by New Yorker John Jacob Astor. Ruthless in its attempts to break the backs of other companies, the AFC fought off the Hudson Bay Company, the North West Company, and the Rocky Mountain Fur Company, set up by Jim Bridger, Tom Fitzpatrick, Milton Sublette, Jean Gervais and Henry Fraeh.

"Coon"—Common mountain men self-reference. "This coon . . .," along with, "This child . . ." "This hoss . . ." "This nigger . . ."

Diggers—Lowest order of the Ute Indian nation, living miserably in the desert regions of what today are Utah and Nevada.

Divide—The Continental Divide, the backbone of the Rocky Mountains.

Doings—Any form of happenings or events: "poor doings . . ." or "fat doings . . ."

Fat—The best, like "fat meat" or "fat doings."

Fleece—Highly prized buffalo meat, the flesh between the spine and the ribs.

Fort Up—To build a mini-fortress out of whatever materials the forest provided, usually to make a winter encampment.

Free Trapper—A trapper on his own, not associated with a company or brigade. A very dangerous occupation.

Gone Under—Killed by Indians or wilderness hardships. (It is interesting how the expressions has been embraced today to describe businesses failing.)

Green River Knife—Really just a generic butcher knife, long wide blade, capable of many tasks.

Hawken—The prize firearm of the mountain man's time. The creation of Jake and Samuel Hawken of St. Louis.

Hobble—To tie up horses by linking their two front feet with a short piece of leather so the animals could not wander far from a campsite at night.

"Hump It!"—Expletive to hurry up, to carry the load, get it done.

Hump-rib or Hump Meat—Prime meat of the buffalo, like tenderloin.

Jackson's Hole—Famed location below the Teton Mountains, at the Snake River.

Jerky—Smoked meat, dried and preserved. Much favoured as quick food for the trail.

Lodge—An Indian hut or encampment.

Lodge Pole—The lodge pole pine, very straight and common throughout the west. Useful in building shelters and travois (which see).

Medicine—Substance made from beaver glands to make the trap lure irresistible to the animals. Also used as an expression by Indians of spiritual powers. For instance, to the Blackfeet the area around what is today Yellowstone Park, with its mysterious geysers, was "Bad Medicine!"

Painter—Panther, cougar, or mountain lion.

Parfleche—Leather carrying pouch, capable of holding many possessions. Often made by squaws.

Pemmican—A higher, tastier form of smoked dried meat like jerky. With fat and bristle removed, pressed into a more cake-like form.

Pierre's Hole—Now Teton Basin, near the three Tetons and the Snake River.

Plews—Prime beaver skins.

Possibles—Belongings. The bag carrying such items was often called a "Possibles Bag."

Rendezvous—the place where trappers exchanged their skins for money to buy the goods they needed to continue another year in the mountains. There was plenty of whiskey, Indian women, and even games of contest. Sometimes the drunkenness led to fights.

Rubbed Out—Killed, usually by Indians.

Seeds-Kee-Dee—The Green River today.

Shine—To stand out; to achieve.

Sign—Clues for tracking and locating game, or the presence of Indians: tracks, broken branches, etc.

Stick—Attached by a line to a beaver trap, then anchored in the bank or mud to keep the trap from being pulled away. If pulled loose from the ground, the stick would float, showing the trapper the beaver's location.

Three Forks—Where the Gibbon, Madison, and Gallatin Rivers meet to form the Missouri.

To Winter—To stay in an encampment of lodges, or a fort, for the winter, when the mountain passes were closed by snow and serious travel difficult.

Topknot—Hair and skin of the head. "Watch your topknot!" means "Don't get scalped!"

Travois—Indian contraption built by laying a platform over two long, parallel lodge poles for carrying supplies or even useful for hauling the injured. The poles were pulled by dragging them over the ground. Wheels had never been thought of or invented.

"Wagh"—The mountain men's favorite expletive, meaning, "Why . . ." Not the question Why? but as in, "Why . . . it's all obvious." A typical way to lead off a strong comment, like, "Wagh! This child knows where the beaver's so thick . . ."

About the Editor

Lamar Underwood's long-time editing and writing career includes fifteen anthologies he has edited for Lyons Press. With titles ranging through such diverse subjects as survival, military history, aviation, and adventure, Lamar's anthologies also include his first mountain man book, *Tales of the Mountain Men*, published by Lyons in 2004. Books he has written include *The Quotable Soldier*, *The Quotable Warrior*, and *The Quotable Writer*—all Lyons Press—and the novel *On Dangerous Ground*, 1989. He is former editor-in-chief of both *Sports Afield* and *Outdoor Life* magazines and has written numerous articles published in a wide list of magazines.